# Ronald Harwood

# ADAPTATIONS

## FROM OTHER WORKS INTO FILMS

Oscar winner Ronald Harwood is currently one of the most successful, prolific and in-demand adaptors of screenplays in the world. Born and raised in South Africa, he has lived and worked in London for all of his adult life. He is also an award-winning playwright and novelist.

*Adaptation* © Izhar Cohen at Artworks

# Ronald Harwood's
# ADAPTATIONS
## FROM OTHER WORKS INTO FILMS

**Edited by**
**David Nicholas Wilkinson**
**and Emlyn Price**

First published 2007
guerilla books limited
www.guerilla-books.com

Printed in Great Britain by Cromwell Press Ltd, Trowbridge, Wiltshire
Typeset by Bookcraft Limited, Stroud, Gloucestershire
Cover design: FINKFILM
Cover photographs: Carole Latimer

ISBN 978-0-9554943-0-7

# Contents

# Introduction

When I was a schoolboy, I stumbled across the George Bernard Shaw quote *'Those who can, do; those who can't, teach'*. I have frequently been reminded of this in my forty years in the entertainment business. Whenever I have been invited to attend a course or a lecture or to review a book on the film business by someone who has only made one single film, or more alarmingly and in a great many cases, none at all, I have politely declined.

Whilst doubtless risking the possibility of being deprived of considerable pearls of wisdom on the art and craft of filmmaking's diverse elements, I cannot shake the notion that being taught the theory of operating a car by someone who has barely passed his own driving test, if at all, is a questionable pursuit at best. How could one possibly know if such untried advice actually works?

This impression certainly applies to screenwriting. I am astonished by the huge number of books that are written by people whose actual hands-on experience ranges from being severely limited to non-existent. They may be great teachers with an interesting insight into the structure and construction of a screenplay; but, nonetheless, untested theories remain just that – theories.

In November 2003, when I was distributing the film of Ronald Harwood's *Taking Sides*, I had asked him if he would accompany me on a publicity tour around the UK. He would be my star, rather than Harvey Keitel or Stellan Skarsgård. Almost the minute we set off, the informal lesson in adapting screenplays began to roll off his tongue. It soon dawned on me that this enthralling journey was also going to be a uniquely privileged master class. I was spellbound at what I was learning.

Our last stop was at the UGC Birmingham. By the most extraordinary coincidence, in another screen, there were around 40 film students and industry professionals attending a one-week course on screenwriting. I discovered that this was to finish half an hour before Ronnie was due to start his Q&A. I found the organiser from Screen West Midlands. To my surprise, instead of jumping at the chance to take part, he declined my offer to join the *Taking Sides* audience. He could not see the value! That year, Ronnie had won an Oscar for *The Pianist*. An acquaintance of mine, David Griffith, who was on the course, sneaked away and joined us. After the Q&A, he said he had learnt as much in that one hour as he had on the entire week of the course, and that it was such a pity that the other aspiring screenwriters could not have been present.

Indeed it was. It was then that I decided that Ronald Harwood's tried, tested and very successful approach to screenplay adaptation should be recorded for posterity. Given that he is now amongst the very top echelon of screenwriters and, as such, is in constant demand, working with many of the world's leading directors and producers, he agreed to produce a book on the proviso that all he had to do was answer questions as he simply did not have the time to construct such a book himself.

Therefore, the format of this book is structured as an extended question and answer session. Emlyn Price and I worked out a series of questions which we put to him over a period of time. We have also sat with him whilst he watched and commented on *The Dresser, Taking Sides, The Pianist* and *Oliver Twist*. (Incidentally, in order to get the most out of the chapters that deal with these films, it would be helpful to watch each of them beforehand.) The final chapter is a series of questions and answers specifically aimed at Adapting Screenplays. This is followed by specific comparative illustrations from the original source material and the resulting screenplay from the stage plays *The Dresser* and *Taking Sides* as well as the novel *Oliver Twist*.

This is not a *How To Do It* manual; it is a *How I Have Done It* roadmap by one who has made a career of successfully and consistently finding his way to his intended destination.

David Nicholas Wilkinson

# Pre-Title Sequence

Extracts from ON WRITING SCREENPLAYS, a lecture given on behalf of Sources 2 at Bäckaskog Castle in Sweden on 22 June 2004

I want to begin with a prologue or, more appropriately for a screen-writer, a pre-title sequence.

At the beginning of 2000, I was alone in my study minding my own business, which is to say I was writing something or other, when the telephone rang. It was my agent. She asked me if I'd ever read a book called *The Pianist*? I said I hadn't, although I think I may have heard of it. She asked if I knew Roman Polanski. I said we'd met briefly once, in Moscow, but I doubted that he'd remember. Well, she said, he wanted me to consider adapting *The Pianist* for the screen.  Of course, I was immensely flattered and eagerly awaited the arrival of the book. That afternoon, it arrived by messenger and at once I sat down to read. I read it in one sitting, telephoned Polanski and said 'yes'. I may even have said, 'yes, please'.

There ends the pre-title sequence, which is meant to whet your appetite for what is to come and what is to come is an examination in part of why, in the first place, I should have responded to Polanski's offer so enthusiastically and, perhaps more importantly, why Polanski should have thought of me at all. The answers are, as you would expect, not altogether straightforward.

Some years ago I watched a television interview with the then Archbishop of Westminster, Cardinal Heenan. He was being asked about sin. Naturally, I was immediately interested because sin is to writers what illness is to doctors. Neither profession can exist without them.

During the conversation the Cardinal was asked how a human being is able to tell right from wrong. And his answer intrigued me greatly. He said, 'By informing our consciences of the difference.' He went on to explain that from a young age a person is taught the distinction between right and wrong to such an extent that, as time goes by, the conscience is so conditioned that it can, automatically, as it were, tell the difference. In other words, the Cardinal asserted, the conscience can be programmed like a computer. Hence, I suppose, when we feel a prick of conscience, we are having the same experience as when our computers refuse to function in the way we want them to, or when they send us one of those irritating messages telling us that we have done something incorrectly.

Now, I am no great expert on theological matters so I cannot comment on the Cardinal's pronouncements. What I can say, however, and with some authority, is that exactly the same criteria apply when a writer, especially a screenwriter, comes to deciding what he or she should or should not write.

Over the years, from childhood perhaps, a writer will, consciously or subconsciously, inform his creative mechanism – I hesitate to call it his conscience – as to what subjects and themes he or she responds to. This response is essential to the screenwriter.

There are two distinct strands to screenwriting. The first, and most common in the English-speaking world, is adaptation, transferring a book or a play or some other source material to the cinema screen. The second strand is pursued by those who write original material for the movies, stories they feel compelled to tell through the medium of cinema and no other.

Let me deal with adaptation because it is what I am most practised in. I have never written an original screenplay for reasons I will come to later, but I have, in a very long career, adapted for the cinema novels, plays, two of them my own, and works of non-fiction.

There are several ways in which a subject for a film may come to the screenwriter's notice. A producer or a director or a studio may present the writer with the subject and ask if it is something that may be of interest. Here is where the Cardinal's definition of sin applies. In my own case, I now know immediately if the book or the play appeals to my creative and technical process. I say I know now because I didn't always. When younger and less experienced, I was so thrilled and flattered to be asked to write a screenplay, and it was also so vital that I get paid for doing so, having a wife, three children, a motor car and mortgage to support, that I invariably said 'yes' to anything that came my way. Often to my cost.

Incidentally, the need for a writer to make a living is far from being a shameful one. Dr Samuel Johnson, the great English literateur and lexicographer, said, 'No man but a blockhead ever wrote except for money.' In other words, only idiots and amateurs write without expecting remuneration. And while we're on the subject, I fervently believe that writers should never be asked to subsidise producers, directors or film studios. All of them are much richer than any writer will ever be and if any of them ever suggest that the screenwriter should work for less than the union minimum or his usual fee, the writer should walk away as quickly as possible or, alternatively, pretend to be deaf.

I realise, of course, that in today's world it's very different from when I first started writing screenplays, and most writers just starting out will find that they have to write at least one screenplay purely on spec. But once a writer is established as a professional, he or she should never again be expected to work for nothing.

Those who suggest screenplays to writers, must, in my view, regard the offer in exactly the same way as they do when casting an actor. The actor – let us be daring and take for granted that he can act – has to be right for the character he's offered in every particular, or as near to it as one can possibly get, especially in his or her appearance. What an actor or actress looks like is vital to his or her success. I have known many cases where one is convinced of an actor's suitability for a part, only to find that the actor doesn't agree and turns the part down. That can be for a variety of reasons – often because the part isn't big enough or central enough, or sympathetic enough – but with the best actors it is because they know their own limitations.

It should be precisely the same for writers, although what the writer looks like, thankfully, is neither here nor there. But a writer, like an actor, has to be well cast. And, as I've suggested, a heavy responsibility lies with the writer himself.

It has been my lot to work over the years on several subjects concerning the Second World War and the Holocaust. I say 'my lot' because I have come to the conclusion that my preoccupation with this horrific period in history is something of a burden, an obsession, and I have tried to analyse why this should be.

It might be helpful to recount my experience in the hope that I can answer the questions I posed right at the beginning: why did Polanski come to me and why did I respond so positively? To this end, you must allow me to confide in you my own experience, to explain how my own conscience, to use the Cardinal's word, has come to be informed, so that it makes choices for me, and so enables me to know whether or not I will be able to fulfil my obligations.

I was born in South Africa, which, in my time, was a totalitarian state. I cannot pretend I was aware of that when I was growing up, but when I left South Africa at the age of seventeen and came to England, I became aware of it.

I was 5 years old when war was declared on Nazi Germany, and Cape Town was 6,000 miles from the centre of things. Yet I remember vividly the excitement of being a child during that time: the convoys carrying British and Commonwealth troops on their way to the Far East, the BBC news bulletins and, of course, Winston Churchill's speeches.

My father, an emigrant from Lithuania, was in his early 40s then, and had a lame left hand. Yet one evening he came home in military uniform, having enlisted that afternoon in the South African army. He had apparently passed his medical. My mother said, 'What did the doctor say when you showed him your bad hand?' 'I didn't show it to him,' he replied. 'He didn't ask, so I didn't show it.'

A belief in a just cause and the growing awareness of a great battle being fought against a barbaric enemy of the Jews informed my daily life. But in 1945, when the Nazi atrocities were revealed, I was taken with other Jewish schoolchildren to see the newsreels of Belsen and Auschwitz. Those dreadful images – the skeletons passing for human beings, the bulldozers shifting mounds of corpses into mass graves – have haunted me ever since. And I remember, too, a photographic essay in *Life* magazine, showing the bodies of the Nazi war criminals after they'd been hanged at Nuremberg. I can't deny the sense of satisfaction I felt at the sight of them.

Now, there may have been other children in the group that were taken to the cinema that day who were similarly scarred. But, as far as I know, none of them became writers and that is the critical difference.

I became aware, really politically aware, in 1959–60 when there was an incident at a place called Sharpeville, when black people protesting against the Pass Laws were shot in the back by South African police. I wrote a book as a result of that, my first novel. And I think that's what politicised me in that sense, against that kind of injustice, which Nazism and Communism were great examples of in the twentieth century.

The war defined my childhood, the Holocaust my adolescence. That synthesis has dominated much of my creative life ever since, which is why I have come to realise that I do not look for the themes I write about: they look for me.

It will be the same to some degree or another, for every writer. What he or she writes about will be dictated to them by forces outside of their conscious control. Of course, mistakes will be made. One's dear old conscience tries to say, 'no, don't do this one', but the conscious mind says, 'ah, but the director's a brilliant man', 'they tell me Nicole Kidman or Johnny Depp is going to be in the film', 'this will do my career some good' and, be sure of it, disaster will ensue. But if you obey without question your inner voice, no harm will befall you.

*The Pianist* sought me out as a direct result of a play I had written, also arising out of those obsessions and preoccupations, *Taking Sides*, which concerns the denazification proceedings against the great German conductor, Wilhelm Furtwängler.

In 2000, Roman Polanski saw the excellent Paris production with Michel Bouquet as Furtwängler and Claude Brasseur as Major Arnold, his tough, American interrogator. Since the play is about music and the Nazis, Polanski thought I might be the man to write the screenplay of *The Pianist*. So you can see that the subjects I write about form a sort of procession, one following the other. It is as simple as that. And it was for exactly the same reasons, because *The Pianist* belonged to my inner world, that I responded so quickly and so positively.

Quickly and positively, but cautiously. Writing about the Holocaust is a sensitive and often risky business and one has to tread warily.

What do such stories have in common, if anything? I can best answer by telling you a story that may help put into focus my aspirations, and I am sure the aspirations of other playwrights, screenwriters and indeed directors when they come to realise, in whatever medium, aspects of the tragedy that befell European Jewry during the Second World War. And this story is not about the Holocaust but about the Soviet Gulag.

In the early 1970s I adapted for the screen Alexander Solzhenitsyn's masterpiece, *One Day in the Life of Ivan Denisovich*. The novel was published during a brief relaxation of censorship shortly after Nikita Krushchev came to power. It was the first time a work of fiction about the Gulag had emerged from the Soviet Union and its impact was devastating, especially on communist sympathisers in the West, those fellow travellers who had been apologists for Stalin's terror. The result was that Krushchev immediately reintroduced censorship.

The novel describes, without complaint, twenty-four hours in the hero's life, a day of relentless cold, of back-breaking work under cruel guards and an inhuman system. And it is a masterpiece because what it describes is a good day in his life, as if in those circumstances such a day were possible.

The film was made in freezing conditions in northern Norway, in Röros, a small town on the same latitude as Nome, Alaska, where we built an exact replica of a Soviet prison camp. The film had Sir Tom Courtenay in the title role and was directed by a British-based Finnish director, the late Casper Wrede. Shortly afterwards, Solzhenitsyn published his first volume of *The Gulag Archipelago* and was savagely attacked in the Soviet press. On 12 February 1974, he was arrested, charged with treason and on the following day sent into exile.

Before settling in the United States, he negotiated with several European governments in the hope, it is said, of finding a tax deal that would treat his vast foreign earnings lightly. Among the cities he visited was Oslo. It so happened that opposite the hotel in which he was staying there was a cinema showing *Ivan Denisovich*. One afternoon he slipped across the street and saw the film. Afterwards he wrote the director a note in pencil. He had some criticisms, chiefly that the film wasn't funny enough, which rather baffled us since we had never seen much to laugh at in the book. But he also paid us a great compliment. He used what might be thought to be a supremely arrogant phrase. He said, 'You have been true to truth.' Those words have stayed with me these past thirty years.

I say supremely arrogant, because of course he was implying that the truth to which we had been true was his truth, the truth of his novel, of his own experience as embracing and embodying undeniable historical facts.

Well, as we all know, there is no such thing as undeniable historical facts. All history is subject to dispute. Revisionism has always been a fashionable way for an historian to make a reputation and a living. From the story of Creation in the Book of Genesis to the recent invasion of Iraq, history is disputed, interpreted, misinterpreted, falsified and ignored. Even the most conscientious and honest researchers are prone to error. Witnesses, especially eyewitnesses, are accused of faulty memories, of being self-serving, vengeful and often naïve. All of which tends not to illuminate the past but to obfuscate it, to make it more and more difficult to penetrate the events under investigation.

There is a further problem for the analyst of historical truth, which I can best illustrate, immodestly, of course, by quoting from my play, *Taking Sides*. A young American intelligence officer, in trying to placate a distressed witness, says to her, 'We're just trying to find out the truth.' To which she replies, 'How can you find out the truth? There's no such thing. Who's truth? The victors? The vanquished? The victims? The dead? Whose truth?'

Now, I don't happen to agree with her, but nevertheless that is what she says. I don't agree with her because I think it is possible to reveal the truth yet not necessarily through accounts written by historians, however brilliant or worthy, or by searching the archives for hitherto undiscovered facts. The truth, I believe – and here is a genuine paradox – can best be revealed through fiction. Because, to return to Solzhenitsyn, it is the individual artist's truth that allows us to accept the validity of the past.

My personal understanding of history has been immeasurably enriched by novels and plays and films. I suspect it may be the same for a great many people. For me, the most vivid insight into the Russia of the early 19th century was derived from Tolstoy's *War and Peace*. My understanding of the declining years of the Austro-Hungarian Empire came from *The Radetzky March* by Joseph Roth. My consciousness was first made aware of the evil of apartheid in the country of my birth by Alan Paton's *Cry, The Beloved Country*. To imagine Vienna in 1945, it is difficult for me not to be bombarded with images of Carol Reid's and Graham Greene's film *The Third Man*. The list is endless and I haven't even touched on the momentous achievements of Victor Hugo, Charles Dickens or William Shakespeare.

It is self-evidently impossible to tell the whole story of the Holocaust. But all the works I have mentioned have a shared approach: they focus on a particular character, episode or event and strive to discover the essence of what happened and by so doing contribute to the whole. They are epic tales if you accept my definition of an epic as one man or woman standing for many: Anne Frank, for example, standing for all the children lost, Schindler for those who saved Jews, Heydrich for those who murdered them. By using this epic form, they are able to express an accurate and vivid emotional experience. And because the makers were conscientious and serious they were, in that particular way, and in no other, true to the experience, true to the characters involved, true to the events they chose to dramatise. In short, they were true to the truth. Their truth. In dramatisations of events concerning any historical subject, but especially the Holocaust, the individual artist has come to be trusted as a lens, and it is his or her integrity that is the filter. We trust the artist to tell us the truth.

To explain further this contention I will try to describe how Polanski and I approached these highly sensitive issues. I was perhaps foolhardy to accuse Solzhenitsyn of arrogance. I have no doubt that you will now level the same charge against me.

There are, I believe, at least two rules that can be applied to all dramatisations dealing with the Holocaust. The first one is to shun any temptation to manipulate. Manipulation must be ruthlessly avoided simply because manipulation obviously is in itself a distortion of the truth. And because the events speak loudly enough for themselves.

The second rule, and perhaps the more important, and one that Polanski and I followed scrupulously, is that sentimentality must also be mercilessly shunned because the events are burdened with genuine suffering and therefore capable of provoking genuine feeling.

What conclusions, if any, are to be drawn from my experience as a screenwriter in general, and from my work on *The Pianist* in particular? Certainly, I have learned that the screenwriter's relationship with the director is at the very heart of filmmaking. But the screenwriter must learn, and it is sometimes a painful lesson, that he is not an equal partner, indeed he is somewhat subservient. Once the film goes into preparation, the writer is distanced from the centre of things. Some writers, I am told, visit the set and watch the filming. I avoid it like the plague. I would rather check-in at an airport than watch a day's filming.

I have to say, to Polanski's generosity and credit, he involved me in the editing process, which was, for me, unusual and highly enjoyable.

I have also learned, at times painfully, that the writer must be sure of the world he's writing about, and has to approach the screenplay with the same degree of commitment as he or she would any other work. I have learned that form is of secondary importance to content. What a film is about stands above all else. And the screenplay, besides supplying all the information that it needs to supply, must be enjoyable to read. And, finally, the director should shoot the film laid down in that document and no other. I talk, of course, of an ideal world.

# POV: Point of View

*Before turning to the specific screenplays which are discussed in depth, it may be useful first to consider some of the more general elements that inform the decision-making process when adapting a screenplay from another medium. These, by their very nature, are particular to each individual writer. Nevertheless, when the writer in question has enjoyed such consistent and significant success, whilst never intended as mandatory stipulations upon others, such a POV must be seen as offering potentially useful insights for other writers. During the question and answer analysis of selected films, such general information was invariably forthcoming.*

## Adaptation versus Original Ideas

*As you've had so many original ideas for your stage plays, why have you preferred adaptations for your screenplays rather than pursuing original ideas in that medium?*

When I began writing, the theatre and, to a lesser extent, television were the media where an impact could be made. I started with hour-long plays for television and later wrote for the theatre. Writing an original screenplay is the last thing I would think of doing. I regard myself first and foremost as a playwright. I have written novels, the biography of an actor, a history of the theatre, but for a long time now most of my original output has been for the theatre. If an idea occurs that excites me, it will be one that I think of as a play and in no other way.

I believe that to be because my imagination works best when I can concentrate the situations and the conflicts in the pressure-cooker that a stage becomes. And because I am given to expressing ideas and emotions through language in the hope of exciting the audience's imagination. It is, of course, one of the main differences between the theatre and the cinema. In the theatre it is no accident that the place where you sit is called an auditorium, which means precisely a place where you listen. Language is the key to the theatre. In the cinema, however, you are obliged to look, to view gigantic images projected on to an enormous screen. And this difference in adaptation, between language and image, is an ever-present conflict.

Of course films use language but it is of secondary importance. Nowadays, audiences seem to have such a short concentration span that story-telling in the cinema demands short, sharp scenes, each one with a new visual interest. This trend, I believe, certainly in America, is because of the commercial. No form that I know of places such stress on brevity. The product being advertised has to be sold in a minute or less and so the assault on our sensibilities is violent, brutal and, I suppose, thankfully brief. The commercial has enormously influenced the cinema, I believe to the cinema's detriment. But it is no good complaining, that is now the way of the world.

Also, in the theatre the playwright is god. Nothing can be done without the playwright's approval, from choice of director and actors to the choice of venue. Not so in the cinema. As we all know, the god of the cinema is the director, and rightly – although I sometimes think concentration on him is too great, the reverence for him too overpowering, and that is because, of all the media I have worked in, the cinema is the most genuinely collaborative. But the director reigns supreme and that is also the way of the world.

**Since winning the Oscar, have you been tempted to write an original screenplay?**

No, such a temptation might appear only if I had ambitions to be a director, which I haven't. The writer-director is a different breed, the true author in cinematic terms, and a rare animal. But there are writers who, when inspired by a story, will only think of developing the narrative for the cinema. I'm not one of those.

It also puzzles me why a writer should wish to hand over an original screenplay to the director in the knowledge that it will be altered – perhaps improved, but more often than not compromised. I love doing adaptations, that's what I believe I'm good at, so that's what I do.

## Producers and Script Editors

*You've enjoyed a particularly fruitful relationship with many of the producers you've worked with. Over the years, you must have come across the occasional down side.*

Some time ago, I was employed to write the screenplay of a very long and very, very difficult book, the most difficult screenplay I've ever written. And half way through I thought I'd stop and give the money back; and for me to give the money back, it really must have been terrible.

When I'd been about to start, the 'story supervisor' to the producer sent me twenty pages of notes about the book, outlining the most important things about the book and characters and so on. And I was rather taken aback because I don't like that. I hardly looked at it but I sent him an e-mail saying 'Thank you. I'm sure it'll be helpful', and I never looked at it again.

When I finished the screenplay and delivered it, they were over the moon about it. I subsequently had a three-way conversation with the producer, the 'story supervisor' and myself. The 'story supervisor' hardly said a word. He was cowed: firstly, because the producer was very enthusiastic about the screenplay and, secondly, because he had nothing to say. He was intimidated partly by the quality of the script, which I think is a very good script. But he was also intimidated by the enthusiasm that his boss had shown.

These guys only function when they feel they can exert power. I don't know what his background is. He may have been to a film school; he's obviously a very intelligent man; I'm not decrying his intelligence. But after I finished the screenplay – this is also important – I looked at his notes and his suggestions and they were useless. They were abstract notes: you know, 'perhaps you could use this as a way of telling the story.'

Now, we've all seen those notes that the readers do on scripts. They're dreadful. You know immediately which school they've been to; you know who's taught them because they have certain phrases; their jargon is of a certain kind.

I've now made it a rule. Somebody came to me recently with something and I said, 'It's interesting but I'll tell you, if you go with either of the companies you mentioned, you must tell them at once I will have no interference from story editors. I will only deal with the director.' I'm now able to say that. I wasn't able to say that when I was starting out but I can say that now. I will not deal with story editors. I just won't have anything to do with them. They know absolutely nothing because they're not inside the story. They view it objectively as if the film is already made and they're editing.

I've told them there's no point coming back to me unless that can be written into my contract. I will have nothing to do with that, I'll only deal with the director.

The 'story supervisor' concept seems to be part of modern life, consultants in every line of business who feel they must say something to show they're earning their money, often people with no comparable hands-on qualifications employed by other people to give opinions.

I said to Jeff Berg, my agent in America and a big player in the movie business, 'What do you feel, Jeff? Am I being ridiculous?' He said, 'PULL-EASE!!!' That was his response. Fortunately I've got their support so I'm in a position now to be protected and can speak from a position of strength. But I wasn't able to before.

In Hollywood the screenplay is regarded as fair game, not just by the director but by anyone involved in the film. So great is the desire to mangle the screenplay that it is tantamount to a disease of epidemic proportions. And I am sure that you, like me, can always identify what I call 'a script conference' scene. You can almost hear what was said. 'Wouldn't it be a great idea if we turned Hamlet into a woman?' You know the sort of thing.

As you may have gathered, my view on 'story editors', who are invariably twelve year olds and have wonderful university degrees, is that they should be lined up and taken off to prison and put in chains and starved.

*A lot of film executives insist on outlines and treatments before writing a screenplay now? Before your success, how did you deal with this?*

I didn't do them and I didn't get the work.

*What advice can you give a writer faced with that now?*

Well, they'd better do it but they have to be very, very careful. They mustn't write themselves out in the treatment. The excitement of the writing must remain in the screenplay. This is the heart of the matter.

15

I think it's very hard for a young writer. With a treatment, you start to write the story, you get involved, you think of the characters, it's down on paper and that's it. Then what are you going to do? To demand such a mechanical process is an appalling requirement. Or sometimes they say, 'Oh don't do a full treatment, just do a step outline.' You know, they say, 'Oh, just put down a b c – 1 2 3.' That's even worse because you're not even exploring what's happening in the scenes. Don't do it. It will absolutely upset your process. I'm sure of it.

**Where does this leave the young up-and-coming writer? It's so easy to deflate a perfectly good script. How do they negotiate their way through that?**

Well, I'm told that young people starting out now will encounter producers who will be powerful. In my view, they should fight that. Why is he a producer if he knows so much about the artistic expression of the film? I just think there's a conflict of interest. But that's just my view.

**When choosing your projects now, how important a factor is money?**

Well, I can give you an interesting little story. I loved W. Somerset Maugham's novella called *Theatre*, and I thought, 'God, I'll produce this, get the rights and write the screenplay.' And I phoned up at ten o'clock in the morning; and somebody said, 'The rights of this Somerset Maugham thing are very complicated.' So I stopped being a producer at five past ten.

Four or five years later, a young man called Mark Milln came to see me. He'd never done anything but he's very persistent and very clever and knows the way of the world. Of *that* world. He came to see me, sat down in my study and said I've got the rights to a book called *Theatre* by Somerset Maugham. I said I'd love to do it. He said, 'I haven't got a lot of money.' He had very little money compared with other projects I was being offered at the time and writing the screenplay would take six months. But I really wanted to do it. I loved the world it was set in, I loved the story. And of course I'd get money if it was made, as one always does. And I did.

If you get taken by the subject, there is no way you can resist it. And that turned into *Being Julia* with Annette Bening.

### What is the difference between working on a script with the director on board, as you did with Polanski, and working on it with a producer?

Well, the heart of the matter is that the producer shouldn't have anything to do with that. The producer should make it possible for the film to be made, he shouldn't be part of the creative process. It's the David O. Selznick syndrome.

Selznick was a remarkable man. He was the first of those great producer figures who had a real creative gift for movies and, in a way, invented a certain kind of movie. And he persevered with it in the face of great disasters and danger. He shaped movies like *Gone with the Wind* and so forth. It's a truly wonderful film. But Selznick ruined the producing business because he was a genius. He was unique: he was a brilliant caster, he saw exactly how a film should be, but he couldn't be bothered directing it so he got directors who did what he wanted. Now everybody thinks, 'Oh, that's what I want to be. I can't write, I can't direct, but I have wonderful ideas.' Well they don't always. There might be some about who can do that, but I doubt it. I've not ever come across a producer of that kind.

Polanski and I have a wonderful team with whom we've done *The Pianist* and *Oliver Twist*. The two producers make it possible for us to make the movie – raise enough money, see there's enough in reserve, schedule it properly – all the things that are required. They're just terrific guys and they don't interfere in the filmmaking. Sometimes they say, 'We can't understand this scene'. But that's after it's shot, not before, nothing before, and nothing in the script. That's my point. But I think we're talking about ideal circumstances.

**Once the film is packaged and you've worked solely with the producer, what happens when the director comes on board and has another vision?**

Generally speaking, as I said, I don't work solely with the producer, I only work with the director. Although recently I have worked with the producer on *Love in the Time of Cholera*. The director didn't come on till after I'd written the screenplay. And on *The Diving Bell and the Butterfly*.

If the producer's a good producer, he will employ that director in order that he should have another vision. Otherwise, the producer should direct the film himself. There's no point getting a director who will simply realise the producer's vision. I can't see the point of that. That would be very unintelligent.

Good producers will employ directors they think are good filmmakers in the hope that they will give life to what the producer and screenplay writer already subscribe to as written. So I've never discovered the conflict implied in your question though I'm sure it exists. It depends on the ego of the producer and it depends upon what kind of producer he is.

If he's a David Selznick manqué, there could be problems. There was conflict on Selznick's *Gone with the Wind* of an endless kind. And I knew one of the recipients: George

Cukor, the director. He was fired, now that's conflict. But I personally have not encountered that. I can't remember a director ever being fired or any of those sorts of things.

## Directors

Certain directors like to work with the same writer over and over again. This is not always advantageous though it may always be comfortable. But comfort in writing is a rare commodity and should be treated with suspicion. The director's spheres of interest may be very different from the writer's or much grander. Nevertheless the writer, out of loyalty or, as I say, a longing for comfort, will embark on the screenplay and the final result, the film itself, will almost always show signs of strain. And you will notice that when a film is praised by the critics, the writer is never mentioned. But should the film be condemned then the critics will inevitably say it is the fault of the screenplay. This is because of the perception of the director in the world of films and because of his position in relation to the writer's.

I've had a wonderful experience with directors during the last four or five years. I've worked with some of the best in the world: Polanski on *The Pianist* and *Oliver Twist,* István Szabó on *Taking Sides* and *Being Julia,* Peter Yates who did *The Dresser,* Norman Jewison who directed *The Statement*. And I'll tell you one thing they all have in common, these wonderful directors: once they've agreed the script, they're loyal to it and they don't deviate very much. And that's a remarkable thing in my experience. And, of course, I'm bound to say that's why I'm happy with the film. But in a sense so are the directors happy with it. Because they agreed it from the script and then they made the film from the screenplay.

There was one occasion on a film however, after my first draft, when the producer had suggestions. He didn't do it through me, he didn't come to me. Quite rightly, he went to the director who then sat with me and we went through these notes. And this director, on the whole, was in favour of the notes. His instincts were to side with the producer, not to side with the story or the film. And I think that was because they're brought up in the Hollywood system where the studios are very powerful and you don't make the film unless you do what they say. So that was one occasion. And I think in all cases, the original draft was better than the result that we finally settled for on that film. That's my view. It may be an arrogant view but I think it to be true.

### Is that because such interference upsets the rhythm of the story?

Upsetting rhythm, not trusting length very often, wanting things shorter simply for the sake of making them shorter. That's a very, very powerful impulse in moviemaking nowadays. 'Do you really need all this!' You hear that a lot. You have to trust the content of the scene to see if that works and, on the whole, I was disappointed with that particular director for that reason. He's a marvellous film director and his use of camera is quite remarkable but I do think that his sense of story was somehow compromised by his subservience to the producer.

### Presumably in your early career, there were people who interfered with your scripts?

I guess there were. It's so hard to remember. Let me think of some of the early stuff. Well, *A High Wind in Jamaica* certainly was chopped around but that was because it was

Twentieth Century Fox, Darryl F. Zanuck, and it was my first big film. But, on the whole, no.

You see, with the director being the crucial figure, once he comes aboard and the screenplay is agreed between you and the director, very seldom are there cuts except editorial cuts that make the film run a little bit more smartly or quickly or the pace needs to be increased. No, I haven't had great massive cuts done, ever. And I think that's something of a myth too. It might not be in television, but I don't know about that. Because there they have these things called 'story editors'.

**With the director, Mike Newell, coming on board** Love in the Time of Cholera *later, what kind of input did he have?*

Terrific. Mike read it and there were certain things he couldn't understand. He won't mind my saying this because our discussions have been endless. There's a certain element in the film – I won't go into it in detail because we're not dealing with it in depth in this book – which Mike could not understand. And I had to go on making it clear for him by adding lines and shaping scenes a little so that he would understand it. And he wasn't being thick, not by any means. He's a very bright man, a Cambridge graduate, so he's no dummy. And as a result, the producer felt that we made great improvements. The producer was, in that case, our sounding board.

And then Mike wanted to begin the film in a different way, which was perfectly acceptable, he just wanted to reverse some scenes: instead of starting outside, he wanted to start inside and then he went outside. It was just the usual thing, but in the editing he went back to the original screenplay. No,

21

Mike was terrific to work with. And very meticulous. He's got what I call 'actor's logic'. If you work a lot with English actors as I've done all my life, English actors find it very difficult to make an emotional leap. They have to know (a) he goes from there, (b) to there, (c) to there. It's got to be very logical: abcdefg. That's an English actor, whereas Russian actors can burst into tears for no rhyme or reason. They know how to do that, it's part of the Russian temperament.

And Mike has that kind of logical approach in his directing, in the storytelling. 'Is that absolutely true? Why do they do that?' And it's a great benefit to the screenwriter because he pins you down. Sometimes, you may have cheated a little, just a little, to get to the next scene. And he'll pin that down. He's very good at detecting that. No, I've been very impressed. I've had a lovely time with him.

### How would you advise the screenwriter who is fortunate enough to be doing an adaptation in collaboration with a director?

It's very unusual for a writer and director to be brought on board at the same moment. But if you can come together at that point, you should decide on a way forward. You can't decide every detail, that's impossible. You can only do that while you're writing. But you must agree the style of the movie and style is a very difficult thing to define.

John Gielgud once said, 'Style in acting is knowing what play you're in.' Well, it's the same with writing. You must know what story you're telling. Once you know that, you'll know how to tell it. But until then, it's very hard.

*In the early days of your career, did you ever experience someone coming on board who wanted the sort of wholesale changes many writers are confronted with?*

Yes, one particular producer was intolerable in that sort of way on a film. I was very unhappy with that because he wanted to control the whole thing and he didn't leave me any room at all. He imposed a lot. Yes, you come across that.

But the best things I've done have not had that element in them. And that, I think, is a symptom of not having those people who think they know everything, who think they control everything, who want to control. It's a question of power too, of course. I just think that producers should produce the film and the director should direct it and the writer should write it. That's a very simplistic view.

*How does the screenwriter deal with the sort of arguments or interference from unsympathetic directors that one can get caught up in?*

I've been very fortunate. I was thinking of *The Browning Version*, a film I did with Albert Finney, based on the Rattigan play. Ridley Scott, its producer, was originally going to direct it as well but then went off to do something else and Mike Figgis came aboard to direct it. And after my first draft, Ridley, Mike and I fiddled. But I was very happy for that to happen because Ridley is a very accomplished film director and Mike Figgis is a good film director. So I didn't have any problem.

I only have a problem in taking notes from: (a) people who've never made films before, because that's very often the way – you get them in financing operations and they don't know anything about films but they think they have a right to have a say; and (b) producers who are not doing their own job properly and then start interfering in your job. I resist that. But if they're proper filmmakers, I don't mind. Figgis and Scott are two very fine filmmakers so why not listen to them. They might just know things.

*I expect that's the biggest challenge screenwriters, established or not, will come up against, interference from unqualified people.*

Absolutely. People who don't know how to make films. But there's nothing you can do if they've got the money and are exerting that kind of influence. And they only need to make one successful film for them to think they can make all their films successful. But that's another problem.

## Screenplay Presentation

E. M. Forster, the English novelist and author of *A Passage to India* among many other splendid books, was once asked about the novel. What is a novel supposed to do? He thought for a moment and answered somewhat regretfully, 'What does a novel do? Dear, oh dear,' he said, 'well, a novel tells a story.' And so, of course, does a screenplay. A screenplay tells a story.

This begs the question, what is a screenplay? Is it simply a technical document or can it be regarded as literature in its own right? A while ago, the Royal Society of Literature, of which I was until recently Chairman, hosted a public conversation about the screenplay as literature between Sir Tom Stoppard and me; and although we gave a joint talk, we both successfully managed to avoid the issue.

How do you tell the story in such a very curious document? How much do you describe visually? Its technical demands are very odd with its numbered scene headings like 'Interior', 'Lecture Theatre', 'Night', and instructions like 'FADE IN' and 'CUT TO' and 'DISSOLVE'. It has to describe what it is and what's happening, and then, there's the dialogue. It is certainly a technical document and it has to satisfy everybody involved in the movie, from the actors to the director to the costume makers to the prop makers to the lighting cameraman. Everybody uses that one document to make the film.

I have always found most screenplays very difficult to read, especially those that have a sort of comic strip approach in the hope that you will imagine the film more easily. For my own part, my approach to screenplays is to tell the story as clearly and as interestingly as possible, remembering always François Truffaut's confession: 'All my films', he said, 'have a beginning, a middle and an end – but not necessarily in that order.'

I am a little on guard about over-constructing a story, flashing back and flashing forward, of glimpsing memory in short, sharp cuts, or asking for a split screen every now and then, we all know the sort of thing. I sometimes think that unfolding the events in that way is a symptom of the filmmaker's lack of confidence in the story he's supposed to be telling. Or perhaps it's simply an admission that there isn't any story to tell. Or it may even be a cry, 'Look, mother, I'm a filmmaker!'

I have a further confession to make: I am not very au fait with technical terms or indeed the mechanics of filmmaking. I don't know a dolly from a crane. So I try to tell what's happening in any given scene simply by setting out the action and supplying the dialogue in the hope that the reader will know exactly what's intended. And I stick rigidly to describing only what can be realised on the screen. I never say, for example, what a character is thinking or feeling unless it is absolutely clear from the action or dialogue. I never suggest music to accompany a scene or sequence. By being as economical as possible, I am simply trying my utmost to make the screenplay readable.

And when what our contracts call the First Draft is completed, we hand it over to the director. And then the fun begins.

**That may be difficult advice to take for less experienced writers who are following what they imagine to be other accepted guidelines in the screenplay format.**

Well, I'll tell you an interesting thing that happened. I got an e-mail from a friend who had commissioned a screenplay by a good writer but they weren't happy with it and didn't know how to get it right. As a favour, would I read it and have a word with the playwright. He's a playwright and now a screenwriter. Well, I was very reluctant but I'm very fond of this friend and the e-mail was very plaintive, so they sent it to me and I read it.

And I detected the problem immediately. What the guy had done – he'd obviously had a film course – he wrote too technically. There were lots of camera directions, there were lots of quick cuts in and out and not enough concentration on the story, on telling what happened. Also I have a feeling the story itself was not long enough for a movie but that's another matter. So I said I'd talk to him and agreed that he could telephone. He's a sweet man and he's not untalented, but he's just not focused on how you do a screenplay which is germane to what we're talking about here. And it's this over-emphasis in showing the reader of the screenplay that you're making a movie. That's not what you should be doing.

So I wrote to him and said, 'I feel very awkward talking to as good a writer as you in an analytical way, but I'm told you're keen to do it and so you should phone.' I had a long e-mail back from him, very long, where he was obviously at a loss about what the screenplay ought to be. And he's an accomplished writer; I'm not talking about a booby. He knows about words, but he doesn't know how to do it for the movies.

You should present a reading document that's good to read and not too technical. I avoid camera directions like the plague. They get in the way, and in the end they're not going to be the camera movements that the director uses, you can be sure of that. I can't emphasise it enough: if you put 'CLOSE UP', it's going to be 'LONG SHOT'; if you put 'PANNING', it's going to be a stationary shot. You know it's going to be different so there's no point in doing it. There is no point in telling the director how to shoot the film. He will have his own ideas which will override the screenwriter's. He will also have the advantage of having studied the set designs and of having chosen the locations.

You've got to find a way in the telling of the screenplay story where the visual is inherent in what you're describing. And you should never say anything that isn't clear on the screen. You can't say 'He's thinking "My God, how ugly this woman is!".' You can't do that in the screenplay. It's got to be clear from the dramatic content of the scene. And writers do that all the time – they write the description, 'He's low in spirits', but it's impossible to understand unless it's dramatised.

I've also noticed a phrase, 'We see'. I never use it. Some will say, 'It's a grey day. We see a shape come out of the…' Well, I never do that. I'll just say, 'A shape comes out'. I'll tell you what I also stopped doing, I used to put 'CUT TO'. Polanski can't bear it so I've stopped it. In the screenplay I did for the producer, Kathleen Kennedy, I simply took them out. Nobody complained, nobody said anything. So I've stopped that.

I must say, I've had to learn the hard way. I admit it. I didn't know all this when I first started writing screenplays. I over-wrote terribly. It's the combination of economy and not being obsessed by the technical requirements of a movie that make a good screenplay, or at least a readable screenplay. Good is another matter.

So there's an interesting insight into this problem of the screenplay as a document.

**What would you say to young writers who feel pressured into presenting scripts in what they are led to believe is the 'professional' manner?**

Well, you've seen Hollywood scripts. They are extraordinary: 'WHAM', 'BAM', 'SCRAM'! I would say just write the scenes. We don't need 'DISSOLVE TO'.

I was interviewed about the making of *Oliver Twist* and asked about Polanski. And I think I said a true thing about him: he doesn't sign every frame. He doesn't say, 'Look what a great film director I am,' that's not his style. He just tells the story and he has a particular vision and he uses it. But he's not showing off. It's not 'Look, the camera goes round and comes up somewhere into your ear,' you know. All you want is for them to tell the story and he does that wonderfully. So does Szabó, he's a good storyteller. Of course they have intricate camera movements but if I put that in a script, they'd be straight out.

*What do you say to young writers who come up with innovative shooting ideas who are invariably told it will never work and then someone else employs the same idea in another film and receives all the kudos?*

The distinguished British director Tony Richardson used to say, 'Always be second. Never be first.'

## Choosing Subjects

This question of the writer knowing the world he is able to write about is one of crucial importance. Some writers will be enviably versatile and have an apparently limitless range. Others will have a narrower field of vision. In either case, the writer must know with certainty that he can explore and develop the subject in hand. Writing a screenplay is as serious a task as writing anything else, be it a novel, a play, a poem or a history. In all these forms, the writer must, self-evidently, commit his entire being to what he or she is writing.

My advice to screenwriters, especially young, aspiring screenwriters, is always the same: be absolutely certain that you are able to write about the subject you've been offered. It must be able to reside within you and reside in that deepest part of you where creation is possible.  It is obviously different when the writer finds the subject for himself, comes across a story in whatever medium and thinks it will be worthwhile adapting as a movie. But in either case the decision is not to be made lightly. As I have said, but it is worth repeating, writing for the screen is a serious business.

I can understand one aspect of the original screenplay as an art form because of the times we live in. The meaning of the word culture has changed radically. *Haute culture* or 'high culture' has been banished to the sidelines, as though it were a sphere of interest only for elderly people, like me. Culture has come to mean pop music, television soap-operas and, of course, blockbuster movies. Culture is measured in numbers. How much a film took at the box office is the chief yardstick of its success. Popularity is equated with quality. And the cinema is now one of the most popular art-forms in the world. I discount television because television has become a medium good only for selling motor cars, detergents and politicians. And, of course, itself. Television's self-love knows no bounds. But films are seen in every corner of the globe in more or less their original form and the desire to reach great numbers of people – not only for commercial rewards but to be popular, though the two things are obviously synonymous – is compelling. And that is a great motivating force to screenwriters who have the compulsion to realise their work on the screen.

But what are they to write about? Given the enormous power of the English language and the American film industry, the temptation is to write what we may call mid-Atlantic movies, movies that are neither American nor European but are thought to be international. I have never seen one that works. The best films made by countries outside the Anglo-Saxon sphere of influence have always expressed the national character of the country of origin and are most often wonderfully parochial. The paradox is the more parochial, the more universal. Think of the Italian and French films made immediately after the Second World War. Or the British films of the 1960s.

**Is there a way of exercising the muscle that 'informs' the aspiring writer?**

There's a wonderful story about this which J. D. Sallinger tells. He has these terrible writer's blocks and he went to a lecture by Somerset Maugham in New York. And Somerset Maugham, who was a professional writer, got up every morning and said, 'If I don't have anything to write about, I just write I am Somerset Maugham, I am Somerset Maugham, I am Somerset Maugham; and eventually something will come.' Sallinger said 'I tried that. I wrote I am Somerset Maugham, I am Somerset Maugham, I am…'

I don't know if there is an exercise for such a muscle. I certainly don't write 'I am Ronald Harwood'. I certainly do not. (*Laughter*)

## Ideas and Starting Points

There are no easy rules, you know. That's the terrible thing. It's all very individual. But what I think can happen from knowing what another writer does is that it may give you a clue as to what you can do. You can't copy it. You can't re-produce it entirely as a carbon copy. But you know, 'Well, that guy, I see; he gets up and tries it as a novel.'

This has happened to me; you try it as a novel and it turns into a play. Usually I know when I get the idea what it's going to be, but sometimes you don't. So it's very hit and miss. There's a big feeling that writers have a sort of monolithic view of their world and their writing. I certainly don't. Oh, and there's confidence too. That's another thing people don't understand.

But you know, it's like being an athlete in a way, writing. You've got to keep fit. Keep the muscles going. Writing is like a discipline. You've just got to do it. Get up every day and do it.

***A few screenwriters treat writing novels as their creative fun time because the usual limitations don't apply.***

No, I don't have that view. All writing is identical to me, as long as I can express what I want to express. And that's why I'm choosy about the films I do, because I've got to be sure I can express what I want to express or be true to whatever it is that I like about the book or the play or whatever it is they offer me.

## Preparation

***Although you knew the novel* Oliver Twist, *how many times did you re-read the book before actually starting?***

I probably read *Oliver Twist* three times in my life: once when I first read it as a boy, then when I got a nice set of Dickens Complete Works and decided I'd read through all of Dickens because I hadn't read every book by that time but have now, and then once more when I did the film. I knew it very well for some reason. I didn't know all the details but I just knew it and so I only read it once more.

***And how does that compare with* The Pianist, *which was completely unknown to you?***

I read *The Pianist* once. What I do always is to read the book through and then I learn it. So I read it slowly and make an index. I make it like a non-fiction index of the book so that I can look up everything. My *Love in the Time of Cholera* index goes to something like forty-five pages. But that's my way of learning the book.

So it's not really reading it in the sense that you just page turn, I study it and that's how I absorb it. And it's no good having someone do that for you. I know writers who have a researcher do that for them. But my eye is my eye. And what I catch is what I catch. It's no good my researcher saying to me, 'Oh, that'll make a good scene.' Well, it won't make a good scene for me. It might for him or her, but not for me. So I don't really read it, I study it.

***Before starting work on the screenplays of your own stage plays,* The Dresser *and* Taking Sides, *how much re-reading preparation was required or were they so ingrained in your mind that it wasn't necessary?***

No, there I don't re-read. I try to imagine how I'd make it as a film. And then I go back to it, back to specific things. And I know what's got to be cut. You kind of have an instinct for that. But I don't re-read it in that way, no. Also, I've seen them quite a lot.

***What particular difficulty is presented when adapting a one-set theatre piece like* Taking Sides? *Presumably it varies with each different play, such as something like* Twelve Angry Men.**

It must vary from play to play. And *Twelve Angry Men* is a wonderful example because that is a very concentrated film, and they made a very good play of it.

Very few plays, of course, are made into movies but that's because they present a very different problem. Plays are so concentrated – usually in one space, in one time scheme, obeying to varying degrees the Classical Unities. These require that a play should always: first, have only one main action with no or few subplots; second, take place in one twenty-four-hour period; and third, take place in one location.

If you look at Shakespeare, you'll see he was really innovative because he broke the Classical Unities. In the opening Chorus of *Henry Vth*, Shakespeare says, 'we're going to smash time and place' in the Chorus. That is the destruction of the Classical Unities. But a really constructive destruction.

It presents obvious problems if the play you're going to adapt obeys those rules, and most of the best plays have something of that in them. They may not be entirely true to the Classical Unities, but most of the good ones are. *The Dresser,* for example, which I am now boasting about, takes place in the course of one night, as a play.

So that's one of the difficulties of adapting plays into films. Plays obey another set of rules whereas in films you're much more free. Films are more akin to a novel, you can go where you like, you can say ten years later, you can say fifty years later. In a play, that's very, very hard to do – the time lapse. So the difficulty lies with the concentration of the drama in the theatre.

Apart from two of my own plays, *The Dresser* and *Taking Sides,* and of course Rattigan's *The Browning Version*, I don't think I've been offered other plays to adapt. Oh, I was once offered a Chekhov play, but nothing came of it. They didn't get the money or whatever it was. But that of course has great possibilities because Chekhov has the whole description of landscape and so on. There would be ways of setting it within the estate and so on. There'd be ample opportunity for that. But it's certainly different from play to play.

# Opening In

You know this phrase 'Opening Out'. It's a dreadful phrase, and I'm guilty of it from time to time, where a scene or part of a scene is located out of context, often just for the sake of it, in order to relieve the perceived confines of a long interior scene. What one should really do is go into the play or book and see what's already there that can be expressed visually, see precisely what you can use of that and dramatise it for the film. That's what I call 'Opening In'.

I can illustrate this with *Taking Sides*. I knew I wanted to start with the music as it does in the play where they talk about the concert that opens the film. He says, 'The lights went out and Speer came round.' Well, as you're making a movie, you might as well see it. And it seemed to me a marvellous opening: hear the music, see Furtwängler conducting and see his connection with the Nazis. That was dramatising something that was already in the play.

And with *The Dresser,* I also thought that one should see some 'Opening In' because film gave us an opportunity to explore in a way that even the theatre can't. 'CLOSE-UP' is the art of the movie. You can see emotion and feel it and have one or two scenes outside. And so that's what we did. Since it's a touring company, you might as well see them tour.

I think the danger is when you think, 'God, we need to go out, we need to go up the mountains here.' They do that all the time and just for the sake of it. But you've got to be very, very careful. Sometimes the director has a visual image that is hard to vocalise. And so this phrase of mine, 'Opening In', I think is a valuable one. It is for me at any rate. I don't like legislating because every writer's different.

## Making Changes

*As you're a playwright as well as a screenwriter, let's deal with plays first. Do you consider making changes when they're in production or being revived?*

No, I don't change. I'll tell you why. Not because I'm arrogant, but because I can't get back into the state of mind that I was in when I wrote the play. And I suspect that all changes made a good deal after that time are always slightly ill-fitting. Do you know what I mean? It's not to do with arrogance, believe me. If somebody made a really terrific suggestion and I saw it as such, I would probably start to think about it. But the effort of going back into the state of mind one was in when one was writing – because it's a compulsive, obsessive thing, the writing of a play, because that's all you think about – to get back to that is very hard. For me anyway. Other people do it. I'm simply saying that's how I work.

*When thinking about a revival of* The Winslow Boy *twenty-five or thirty years later, Terrence Rattigan made some changes, not very much, for a modern audience's understanding. Would you consider doing that?*

I had a revival of *The Dresser* recently and they came to me with a couple of things they wanted to change. I refused that, but for other reasons. It was because, without wishing to sound unkind, most of them had done a lot of television and they were worried about audience understanding because that's one of the crucial things in television – 'will they get it?', 'will they get it?' But the sound of the words and the rhythm of the line should be of more importance. Of course they'll get it. It's the actor who has the insecurity about it. No,

I didn't change anything and, believe me, it's not to do with arrogance. The play has been played and worked. I'm surprised Rattigan made changes. But he wouldn't change the structure. Lines perhaps.

**But if it's played properly, they'll get it?**

They'll get it. If the actor finds conditions have changed and make it completely unintelligible, then, I would have thought, perhaps. But otherwise, no. When an actor says, 'I can't say this line,' I always say, 'You will when you're in character.' And it's true. When they understand the part more, they'll understand why the line's there. Because I don't write them arbitrarily, as it were. I have to think about it and test it and I re-write, obviously.

Interestingly enough, let me say something else about 'the state of mind' which we just touched on. When you come to do a film, it's actually easier to get back to 'the state of mind' because you're thinking about it in a different way, in a different medium. You're thinking of it visually. The theatre's the place where you listen, for language, but we have to look at a film. And so, that's much easier, in a way, to get back to 'the state of mind' via the medium of the movie.

**What's happening more and more in film, I don't know if you've come across this, is that writers have poured over so many drafts of a script to get it right and then star actors get hold of it and go through it, making serious major changes? This surely must destabilise the focus and the rhythm of the story?**

Well, I have not met that. I've been very fortunate in the last ten or fifteen years. I've worked with star directors and the actor knows he can't fool around with that director because he'll just cut it anyway. So the more important the director, the more the writer is protected. That's if the director is so minded. But I was lucky: Peter Yates, István Szabó, Roman Polanski all have theatre backgrounds so they trust the text.

**That can become a horror story when one's screenplay is in the hands of people who only have a Hollywood experience and do not trust the text.**

Oh absolutely. I'll give you an example. I went to see a film set around the turn of the century. Now I'm going to say this loudly and I'm going to broadcast it – it was appalling. And it was appalling for this reason: they absolutely neglected the accuracy of period. For some reason, the leading actor dispensed with the facial hair that was associated with the historical character he was playing. I don't mind that so much but in a scene at the beginning of the film he turns to someone in a theatre and starts publicly deriding the qualities of a play in terms of the most modern vulgarity. Now, who would have said that at that time? And so one's whole belief in the experience they're trying to give you is undermined. And I'll bet you that the star put that in. I have a very good ear for when a line has not been written. And I can just imagine the conversation, 'You know what he should say here…?' I can hear it from a mile away. So if there's somebody who actually respects the text on your side, the writer's side, it's much better.

# Actors

**Whether for stage plays or screenplays, do you ever write with actors in mind?**

Never, never, never. It's a rule, and I'll tell you why. Say I was writing for Maggie Smith. I would be so influenced by her delivery, by her attitudes, by her manner of acting, that I would compromise the reality of what I was writing. I have to be true to the character I'm writing. People have done it of course, and wonderfully. Noël Coward is a supreme example, someone who could write for Gertrude Lawrence, for himself, for the Lunts. He did it all the time, but that was part of another tradition.

The danger is that you write a theatrical piece and not a play. You imagine the actor playing it, you don't imagine the reality of the character. I get it quite often now. Hollywood actors phone and say, 'I'd love you to do something. You got anything for me?' And I say, 'It's impossible to think like that.' In being true to your central character, why should any particular film star necessarily come to my mind as an ideal? That's not the way I work. Others may do it, but it's not how I work. I love to keep the reality of the characters in my heart, in my mind. And I know them better than I know anybody else, obviously. I know everything about the characters I write; I don't know everything about everybody I meet in real life.

**Even when the project is on and they say, 'We have so-and-so. Can you write it for them?', what do you do?**

I can't do that. On *Taking Sides,* I told Harvey Keitel certain things. Szabó was very naughty and hid behind his, 'I don't understand, my English is not...,' so I had to deal with

Harvey, who's tough. He wanted some of the questions that I'd given to the young Lieutenant. 'Wouldn't I have said that?' You know, you get that kind of thing. But we got on and it was very enjoyable too.

### How do you cope with actors who are inclined to alter the writer's lines, choosing 'behaviour' over text?

In the theatre, I'd be very strict, I won't make changes. For those actors who want to 'behave', they have to learn to do it within the text. Neil Pearson, in the recent revival of *Taking Sides,* was wonderful as the American. He didn't change a line. He had all the behavioural things that you'd want from him. He was terrific. I wish they'd brought it into the West End of London; but I think it was too close to the first production. It was only a few years. But, I think actors have to learn to do it within the text – in the theatre.

In the movies, they 'behave' and they think that's acting. Some very big stars are guilty of behavioural acting that makes you think it's all very real. They do a lot of that, instead of speaking the lines.

From the writer's point of view, regarding text, it's only a problem if they don't say it. If they think they can get away with a bit of behaviour instead of a line, that's where the danger lies. When they think, I could just shrug here instead of saying 'I don't know.' The 'I don't know' may be very crucial to the rhythm of the scene. And good actors would never do that because they'd know what text is. Trained actors are absolutely wonderful with text.

### Before success came, were you ever made to alter a screenplay to accommodate a famous actor?

Yes, there was a famous moment on *A High Wind in Jamaica*. I finished the screenplay and Alexander Mackendrick, the director, wanted a few things done but he was pretty pleased with it. And we went in to see Twentieth Century Fox at their office in Soho Square, where it still is. And we went up to see the man who was running it. I can't remember his name but he had been the editor on *High Noon* and he'd been made Head of Fox in London.

And as we were talking, the secretary entered in quite a state with a seven-page telegram from Darryl F. Zanuck who was the Head of Fox. And the tenor of the telegram was as follows: 'I've got a board meeting in New York in forty-eight hours, and I have to show that I've got a lot of good projects going with very important people. Get the boys (that was Mackendrick and me) to change the pirate king in *A High Wind in Jamaica* to a pirate queen because we could then get Lila Kedrova.' She had just won the Oscar for *Zorba The Greek*.

Well, I didn't know what world I was in, never mind what to do. And Mackendrick said, 'I think that's a bit possible' in his Scots accent. 'Possible?' Whatever he said, I would have done. And so the Head of Fox said, 'OK. I'll give you secretaries. Can you do it tonight? Cause we got to get it off tomorrow morning. You better go home and get some rest, Ron, and we'll get you a car.' And I thought, 'This is movies.'

Honestly. 1962, I was twenty-eight years old and I'm getting four thousand pounds for the picture. To put that in perspective, you could buy a really nice flat in London for that in those days. It was an amazing amount of money. So I went home and had a rest and Sandy Mackendrick said, 'Don't worry, Ronnie. I'll be with you all through the night.'

41

So I got back there later and we were due to start at, say, nine o'clock at night. The secretary was there, I was there, offices, typewriter – no Sandy. Eleven o'clock – no Sandy. I said, 'Listen, we'd better get going.' So I did it, appallingly badly, but I did change the pirate king into a pirate queen. And Sandy never turned up in the end. He had apparently been side-tracked.

So that was my introduction. Talk about changing something, it was a bloody good baptism of fire. And then they got other people to fiddle with the script in America: Denis Cannan, who was a very well-known playwright of his day; and Stanley Mann. And that's the writing credit. But the main body of the screenplay was what I had done.

## Technology

I want to say something else about writing these days which is very important, and that is having a programme on your computer that formats the screenplay. The computer programme has been a remarkable tool for the screenwriter. I use one called *Final Draft* and it's just terrific. It should be an essential tool for all screenwriters, in my view. If you want to move a scene from one place to another, you just do it. In the old days, there would have been pages all around the flat, cut up and stapled. But this saves so much time. I couldn't imagine writing a screenplay now without using *Final Draft*. I use it for my stage plays as well. It just removes all the boring stuff and allows me to concentrate on the creative side of writing.

*That's something to be said to the steadfast bands of Luddites still holding out for pen and paper.*

It's wonderful. I print out a lot because it looks different when you read it on paper. I don't know why but it does. You see I love gadgets. Anything new, I'll buy. In the early 1980s when *The Dresser* was a huge success on Broadway and I had some money, I bought my first computer. And it took up a whole room with the printer and stuff spewing out over the floor. I spent eighteen hours with the handbook. And finally I made it, and I've never gone off it.

I remember Harold Pinter came down for the weekend and I said, 'Look Harold! You see if I want to get rid of a line, I just highlight it and I press delete.' And he said, 'If I want to get rid of a line, I just cross it out!' I reminded him when we had dinner recently. He now uses one through his secretary but he doesn't like anything like that. I think he still writes on an old typewriter, then she puts it on to the computer, and then he corrects on paper.

## Other Writers

*Interestingly, Harold Pinter directed a stage version of* Taking Sides. *As a playwright, does that side of his brain come into play when directing?*

No. Harold is a very extraordinary playwright. He's totally original. So what I write is absolutely nothing to do with his world, and what he writes is absolutely nothing to do with mine. He's an admirer of a great variety of writing which has nothing to do with his own writing. He doesn't make a comparison to himself. That's his world that he writes about. As far as directing is concerned, he just says, 'I'll do it.' He'll never interfere or say, 'I would have written it this way.'

I remember with *Taking Sides* he made two directorial suggestions but I agreed to only one of them. He thought that 'Adolf' should sometimes be changed to 'Hitler' which I did not accept; and at the end of Act two scene one in the play, the talk is about von Karajan, he asked to turn the two curtain lines around and I accepted that. My original was more abstract, and Harold thought his suggestion would make a better curtain line, and I bought that. I thought about it and it was reasonable and I bought it.

He thought that it would be more telling for the audience. He's got a wonderful sense of drama and that's what it's about. Where does the drama lie? It's that thing about 'And then?' in the story telling. 'And then?'. But I think that's the only suggestion he made and he didn't interfere at all in any other way and directed it brilliantly.

## Writing

E. M. Forster gave a series of lectures at Cambridge in 1927, now published under the title of *Aspects of the Novel*. And in one of the lectures he talked about plot and story. He said, 'To the story, you ask the question: And then?' And then, and then and then? 'And to the plot, you ask the question: Why?'

And he gave the following example: 'The king died and then the queen died' is a story; 'The king died and then the queen died of grief' is a plot. And when those two come together, you have proper literature, movies, plays. When you just have, 'And then?', the story, you have adventure. *Ivanhoe*, for example. You don't always know why people do things, they just do them. And there's a wonderful series of adventures.

It's perfectly legitimate, but it looses the heart of the problem. Which is 'Why?' Why do people do things? So when you asked me earlier about characters, I know why they do things, and I have to be sure that I dramatise that or make it filmic so that the audience understand it. It's no good it being locked up in me. That's no help to anybody. But if it's necessary for the audience to understand, one's instincts as a writer tells you that. As long as it's honest, it tells you that. So that's my view of the two elements of storytelling of the drama or films: 'And then?' and 'Why?' And you have to bring them together.

So in *The Dresser,* for example, all those scenes which may seem explanatory to us now as we look at them at a distance, objectively, in this way analytically, are there because you do want to know what happens to a touring company one step at a time – the train, getting to the theatre, the set up, playing the play, whatever. But you also have to know that Sir's in charge, it's his company. That's the 'Why?' of that. Why does he sit on the stage and say, 'Those boom lights are only for me'? Because he's the boss. That's the 'Why?' And it's dramatised.

While we're on the subject of writing in general, I once met Philip Roth, the novelist, in a bookshop and I said, 'Philip, how are you doing?' And quite excited, he said, 'I'm writing a book.' I said, 'What stage are you at?' He said, 'I'm not yet at the stage where what everybody says seems to belong in the book.'

I know what Philip Roth meant. You know that feeling? Oh, so-and-so said 'Good morning.' That's wonderful. I'll use that. There is a point when you become so obsessed with what you're writing that everything seems to belong to the world you're writing about. And the world you're writing about is the real world, and nothing else has happened of any relevance at all. It's rather interesting, it's psychotic. Absolutely psychotic.

That's why I say writers should never go to psychoanalysts. Because writing is psychoanalysis, writing is the therapy. If you're in trouble, you write it out. That's what you do. It's grotesque. I'm a compulsive writer. Harold Pinter isn't a compulsive writer at all. He might write a play, he might write a poem, whereas I have to write every morning, otherwise I'd feel bereft.

I think one has to de-mystify it too. Maybe there is a mystery. People think you're going to give them a clue to make their lives easier now about writing. Well, I say to young writers, 'Get up and write!' That's all you can do, and you'll learn by doing it. In general, that's writing.

**You've elected certain changes from the novel,** Oliver Twist**, to enhance the storytelling, tying things in. In an adaptation, where does one draw the line? Is anything fair game in telling that story?**

I don't think anything is fair game. As I said, by profession, I'm a playwright really, not a screenwriter. And so when you write a play, every line in every scene has to feed the centre of the play. You can't have extraneous things in a play. That's part of the discipline, the economy of writing a play. And I think I bring that to writing a screenplay.

Mike Newell noticed it recently. We were having a meeting on *Love in the Time of Cholera*. We had to do some changes because they'd seen the locations and all that, stuff he wanted added and subtracted. And he remarked on it, that the scenes are very tight, unusually tight for screenplays. That every line feeds into the centre. And I said, 'Well, it's just because that's my habit, my profession, as it were, my trade.'

But I don't think anything is fair game. I don't think you can go outside the confines of what the story demands. I don't know if that makes it clear. But everything has to feed the centre of it. You can't do it in a screenplay as economically as you can in a play because a screenplay has a much broader canvas very often. You can do it scene by scene in a play.

But anything that happens in terms of the scene that's going to come which I have to write is fair game. For instance, when Toby Crackit is reporting to Fagin about the last time he saw Bill Sykes, I added the line, he was seen 'swimming to London'. It's not exactly as it is in the novel, but it feeds into the centre and then will pay off in the next scene when Bill is seen fevered and delirious.

So anything is not fair game, but anything that feeds the story, leading backwards or forwards to the core, is fair game. But leading to the core of the story is what's crucial.

## When you write, do you have any particular audience in mind?

This may sound arrogant but I'll say it, if anyone writes for an audience, it immediately makes him a second-rate artist. And anybody who writes for critics makes him a third-rate artist. If you write for yourself, you stand a chance of doing something proper. That's my view. The moment you say, 'What's the most popular thing now? We'll do a cyber space robot picture,' or whatever, you're dead in the water as an artist.

Some people will say that's irrelevant, you can make a living if you do whatever they ask you to do. But I'm another generation; I'm in my early seventies. I was born in 1934 and I still have these perhaps pathetic aspirations for art. And that's my view. And the moment anybody says, 'The critics love this kind of thing,' you know they're even deader in the water than when they're writing for the audience. If this sounds very arrogant and old fashioned, but then that's what I am and that's what I have to live with.

## Where the Work is

*You're very unusual to have worked for Hollywood Companies or large Independents like Alain Sarde and Robert Benmussa, even before your Oscar. There are very few writers in the UK who manage to find such regular employment outside the country.*

Well, the British don't offer me anything. I've not been offered a British film for years and years. I can't remember when the last British producer or director offered me anything. They don't come to me. I don't know why.

All the subjects were lying about. Even *The Dresser*. No one in England said, 'Let's make it.' It was an Italian who came to me with it and got Peter Yates involved. Then we set it up in a small group: Tom Courtney, Albert Finney, Peter Yates and me. And John Heyman came in and found us a little money. We just took minimum payments. And then Columbia saw the value of it when they saw Albert and Tom and they came in. But we didn't get a huge amount of money. It's all documented in Jake Eberts's book about Goldcrest, *My Indecision Is Final*. How the deals were done. He goes into the money which I can't remember, but it wasn't huge. No British company came near me. In fact, everybody turned it down as I recall. But Columbia came in afterwards and bought us out.

But yes, I have mostly worked for companies abroad. And now I'm in a different area simply because of the Oscar. That's completely changed things.

# Pitching

I just want to say something about 'pitching'. It's a fairly new thing. I don't remember ever having been asked to pitch in my early days in screenwriting. But now they say, 'Well, would you talk to the producer? Would you pitch it?' And I say no because my theory about writing is that it's a discovery as you write; be it a screenplay or a play or a novel. You discover, about the people, about the world you're writing, as you do it. And to 'pitch' it is a phoney thing.

It's really to give the producers confidence which, if they come to you and employ you, they should have already. And the confidence they should express is in the money they pay you and in nothing else. And so I will not pitch.

And I know it's very difficult for younger writers because they're in a position where they're not powerful enough to say 'I will do this' or 'I won't do that'. But they should be careful about pitching. And I would always advise, as I've stressed before, if they can possibly resist it, never to do a treatment either.

***The trouble with that is you're speaking as Ronald Harwood the Oscar winner. For most writers, the people with finance, the commissioning editors, will invariably insist on them.***

Yes, I know that. But I say no. And I never did them. I said, 'I can't do them' and so I lost work I suppose. I know my own creative process very well, and there's no point in me damaging it. No film is that important. To damage one's own creative writing process would be insane.

Yes, I was asked to do treatments in the early days – it didn't happen much later – and I said, 'No, I can't do them.' I must have tried once and found this out. I can't remember the specifics of it.  But I must have done it and thought, 'That's the end, I can't do any more on this.' It's like writing a novel. You've written the novel in the treatment. So I much prefer somebody to say, 'How do you see the film? What's your take on the movie?' I'd rather give them that, though even then, I don't do that very much.

I've never done it because I discover by writing. That's how I learn about the subject matter and the characters. I don't make decisions up front. I'll write and say that doesn't work, I'll throw it out and try again. As I'm sure I've said to you, I'm not a writer, I'm a re-writer. I must have done eighteen or twenty drafts up to this point. Then, when it starts to flow, then, you know, I can go on. But the beginning is very hard to get right, and you just have to work at it. But I can't do it beforehand, I can't do it in the abstract. I have to work through it and discover the characters, and I can only discover them in the scenes they're in.

I'm sure there are other ways, but that's my way. And I strongly advise young writers to resist treatments and even step outlines. I do.

## The Writer's Place in the Hierarchy

*If the playwright's value is so obvious in the theatre, why is the screenwriter usually relegated to such a low status in the film world?*

I don't know. It drives me crazy, I have to tell you. It's really upsetting. Tom Stoppard described his experience of the writing of films as being there 'as the director's handmaiden'.

But I remember very well after winning the Academy Award, the look of relief on my agent's face when I said I didn't want to direct a movie. Because it's a pattern that happens: a writer wins a screenplay award, an Oscar, and immediately wants to direct movies because that's where the power is. The control is with the director, the screenwriter is very low in the hierarchy.

**You said in the theatre the writer is god.**

King. God. And in film, the director is god. But yet, I know this is a diversion, but it is interesting. I don't think a week passed when Roman Polanski was shooting *Oliver Twist* that he didn't call me. The smallest change, even of a costume, he'd check with me. And I've never had that before. It's to do with our friendship and our collaboration, but nevertheless, it is remarkable.

And another thing that happened on *Oliver Twist*, Alain Sarde and Robert Benmussa, the producers, phoned me after they'd seen fifty minutes of rushes in Prague to say how terrific it was. I've never had that before. But they just regard us as a team, and that's wonderful from my point of view.

**That's such a healthy situation?**

It's terrific.

# The Dresser

Adapted from the stage play *The Dresser* by Ronald Harwood
Directed by Peter Yates
Produced by Peter Yates, Nigel Wooll and Ronald Harwood
Starring Albert Finney, Tom Courtney, Edward Fox, Eileen Atkins and Michael Gough
Production Companies: World Film Services and Goldcrest
Distributors: Columbia Pictures

*The lives and relationships of those within a sadly depleted Shakespearean theatre company provide the backdrop for* The Dresser. *As the company tours the provincial theatres of war-torn England, the devoted dresser to 'Sir', the group's distinguished and tyrannical actor-manager, struggles to support the deteriorating star whose sanity comes to a crisis as Hitler's bombs rain down in a direct comparison to the world of King Lear that he is preparing to perform. This evocative, observant and hilarious picture of backstage life is drawn from Ronald Harwood's own acclaimed stage play.*

- The stage play was first performed at the Royal Exchange Theatre, Manchester in 1980. It quickly appeared in London's West End where it was an enormous hit, subsequently appearing all over the world. It is regularly revived.
- The film was made in 1983.

Nominated for five Oscars including Best Actor for both its stars, Best Director, Best Picture and Best Writing (Screenplay Based on Material from Another Medium); nominated for seven BAFTA Awards including Best Actor for both its stars, Best Director, Best Film, Best Make-Up Artist, Best Screenplay (Adapted) and Best Supporting Actress; winner of the C.I.D.A.L.C. Award for Peter Yates and the Silver Berlin Bear for Albert Finney at the Berlin International Film Festival; winner of the Golden Globe Best Actor Award for Tom Courtney as well as nominations for Best Director, Best Foreign Film, Best Actor (Albert Finney) and Best Screenplay; winner of the Mainichi Film Concours Award for Best Foreign Language Film for Peter Yates.

**As** The Dresser *was adapted from your own stage play, could you briefly discuss how the idea for the original story came about?*

I was a dresser for Sir Donald Wolfit, the famous English actor, the last of the great actor-managers. In 1953, I joined his company at the King's Theatre, Hammersmith where he was doing a Shakespearean Season and *King Lear* was the third or fourth play we did. And I was on 'the storm'.

'The storm' was never loud enough for him, he needed a hugely loud storm. And he got a water tank which was suspended from the flies and a broom handle wrapped with cloth and somebody to go inside, as it were, the tank and bang like hell to make more noise. And that task was given to me. I was the junior, junior Assistant Stage Manager, very junior, and I had small walk-on parts, no lines.

And on the first night of *Lear* at the King's Hammersmith, I did this and afterwards went into the corridor to have a smoke. My head was absolutely banging with this echo and re-echoing. And Wolfit came down from his dressing room on his way to do the Dover scene – 'No you cannot touch me for coining' – and he stopped. He also smoked so he was having a cigarette as Lear. And he said to me, 'Were you on the storm tonight?' I put this in the play. And I said, 'Yes, sir.' He said, 'You're an artist.' And the next day, he asked me to be his dresser because his other dresser was leaving.

His other dresser was an actor called Ronald Fraser who won the HM Tennant's Prize at RADA. We were all at RADA. I was still at RADA but I think Ronnie had left. He was a term or two above me. And when Ronnie left, I was then appointed his dresser. And I was his dresser from 1953 to 1959, on and off. I don't mean he had a company going all the time, but he did other plays and I dressed him then. And when he found out I was Jewish, he made me his business manager. I was twenty-one, I think. And I was very good at it too. It was a perfect choice: I acted, understudied, dressed, business managed for about fifteen pounds a week which was, even then, disgracefully underpaid. But I loved it. And I adored Donald. And that was the genesis of the play, my experience.

It's very difficult to make clear that I am not 'The Dresser'. Well, I'm clearly not. I'm camp but not that camp, and Donald is not that actor. Firstly, Donald would never have had that kind of dresser. He would never have had a gay dresser or anybody remotely gay.

I think it was John Gielgud who said to me when he saw the play in Manchester, 'The actor who plays Sir, you should always want to see his King Lear.' It's a marvellous piece of advice in the casting of the part.

There are bits of every other actor that I know about. The whole relationship between the stage manager and Sir is based on a relationship between John Gielgud and his stage manager which I'd only heard of at the time but I thought I'd put that in. Gielgud recognised it. When he saw it, John said to me, 'Oh, that's Alison, isn't it?' And I said, 'It is.' And he said, 'Oh yes. She'd never believe I was queer. Never. I tried to tell her; but she didn't believe it.' It was wonderful.

I was at a party one night, I think John Mills' birthday party, and Laurence Olivier came up to me and said, 'Is there anything of me in the play?' He'd seen it and loved it. I said, 'Yes, there is.' Sir calls his wife Pussy in the play and in the film too, and Larry used to call his wife, Vivien Leigh, 'Pussy'. So he was very pleased about that.

There was a famous actor-manager of that period, John Martin-Harvey, whose father was a boat builder, and I used that image in the play a lot. The idea of a boat being launched and the actor-manager being a captain, an admiral of the fleet, a captain of the boat. Norman's line, 'This isn't the death of Nelson, you know', echoes the sea theme. There's a lot about boat building and images of the sea.

So it's not Donald entirely, there are things that are Donald. I witnessed at close quarters a great actor preparing for a dozen or more major classical roles. He was a great King Lear, he made curtain speeches exactly like that, and he was tyrannical with the company. There is no denying that my memory of what took place night after night in Wolfit's dressing room is part of the inspiration of the play. But the actor-manager system was a paternalistic system. It was their money, they didn't have subsidy from the state, it was all private money. So they ran it and one did what one was told. And he was brutal about people getting in his way or his light and all that. So that's the background of that.

**You set the play during the war. Was that to show the old men needed to make up the company?**

No, it's *King Lear*. The war is to echo the storm in *King Lear*. This is a direct parallel to *Lear*. The reduction of the company to these old men is the reduction of Lear's retinue and Norman's the Fool. I remember thinking when I wrote the play, not the film, that I wanted the audience to see that analogous connection. Giving Madge the ring is to do with the three daughters – Cordelia, Regan and Goneral. They're parallels to *Lear*. And the war seemed natural to me when I first thought about it. The war has the bombing and the bombing was the storm, the pressure on Sir.

*You wrote the play, as you write all your plays, on spec, with no particular theatre company in mind.*

Yes, and you hope to God somebody will do it.

*And what happened?*

Well, I had a relationship with what started off as the 59 Theatre Company at the Lyric Theatre, Hammersmith. Michael Elliott and Casper Wrede were the two directors. I was a small part actor in that company and my wife was the stage manager. Casper Wrede was a Finnish-born director who'd studied at the Old Vic School. When I wrote my first play, *The Barber of Stamford Hill*, my wife said, 'Give it to Casper'. And I said, 'Don't be silly. It's a play about a Jewish barber in Stamford Hill. What would a Finnish-born baron know about that?' She said, 'Give it to him.' And I did, and he loved it and did it. He had a contract for two plays a year at HM Tennants television output at ATV – 'BinkieVision' we used to call it because of Binkie Beaumont who ran Tennants. He did it, and then I was put under contract. So I had a relationship with that company.

I didn't feel I could write theatre plays then because the British Theatre, in the late fifties and sixties, was all to do with English class structure and anti-authoritarianism. And I, being a foreigner, was out of that. I didn't have any interest, and I still don't, in the British class structure because I've never encountered it. It's in the British. It's not a solid wall, you have to be British to see those walls. Anyway, that's what I felt. Then in the late seventies, that began to change as the social structure of Britain became shaky. And then Mrs Thatcher came to power. It coincided exactly with my writing for the theatre. And the first thing I did was adapt a book of Evelyn

Waugh's called *The Ordeal of Gilbert Pinfold*. It was the first success I had in the theatre. And then *The Dresser* followed.

*Pinfold* was directed by Michael Elliott who was undoubtedly the best director of his generation. He did a very famous production of *As You Like It* with Vanessa Redgrave. Anyway, because *Gilbert Pinfold* was in a curious way so English – Evelyn Waugh being a great English writer whom I adored as a prose writer – Michael was more in tune with it than Casper Wrede. So Michael said he would do *Gilbert Pinfold*. Originally, it was to be done with Alec Guinness but he let us down and Michael Hordern did it and it was a huge success. It came to London to the Roundhouse.

I then talked to Michael about *The Dresser*. I said, 'I'm writing this play' and he said, 'God, that sounds interesting.' So when it was done, I gave it to Michael and he said, 'Yes, we'll do it.' And so we did it in their new theatre in Manchester, The Royal Exchange Theatre. It was a theatre in the round which had only just been opened about a year earlier. And that's how that came about. And I was very lucky that Michael did the play. He was a marvellous director.

**Both your original play and the subsequent film were called The Dresser. Did you have any sort of pressure from Columbia to change the name?**

No, none at all. Columbia came in very late. We'd already made the picture when Columbia came in. Goldcrest were the first producers and they didn't interfere at all.

**Your name appears as a producer along with Peter Yates in the title sequence.**

He just gave me that as a present. It wasn't contractual at all, putting my name up as part of the film. I had no involvement as a producer whatsoever.

**Did you have any interference from the finance people?**

No, none at all.

**That's quite rare, isn't it?**

Well, we had the same thing on *The Pianist.* We had no interference at all. It's rare because usually, when you deliver a screenplay, you deliver it to the producer who then delivers it to the company that's making it. And they might interfere. You know, they've got people who've just done a course on screenwriting at university.

**So this script is basically as you wrote it? There were no changes to it?**

Well, you're asking about something that I wrote nearly twenty-five years ago. But yes, we were very faithful to it.

**Screenwriters can get enormous pressure from producers and financiers to constantly change the story. Presumably, with something like The Dresser, your own play, you're able to argue, 'Look, it worked in the theatre.'**

I don't get into that. I really don't. And if I did, I would withdraw. I would just stop it. Because the guys who tell you those things know nothing. Absolutely nothing. They feel they have to make a contribution and therefore they say something. With the film, I had Peter Yates. As the producer and director, if I had encountered that sort of thing, he could say, 'No, I don't want that. I want to go with what Ronnie says.'

As I've already said, I've had this great good fortune of having directors who were loyal to what I've written. I've never had that kind of interference. The director may say something; that would be an entirely different creative decision. 'I don't want that, it's too long, can you come out of the scene more quickly' – those things I'd listen to. But if anyone wanted to change the story, I'd walk out. And it's not arrogance. It's because they don't know it and I do. It sounds arrogant, it ain't!

*You said you don't ever write with actors in mind. Does that apply even for the screenplay for* **The Dresser**, *when you knew specifically which actors had been cast? Were you never tempted, when re-working it for the screen, to think of things a given actor would be particularly good at?*

Never, absolutely not. That would be dreadful. Then you write theatrically or filmically when what you have to write is the truth. You can only write the truth of the character. And once you start adjusting for actors saying, 'Oh my God, he does that very well or he sings well or he dances well.' I've seen that happen in movies and it's appalling. You know the actor can play the piano so they put a scene in where he can play the piano. And it's pointless. It's not to the truth of the story which is all that matters. So I didn't do that at all.

And Albert Finney, of course, was young. Twenty-five years ago, he was probably forty-five then, which was a bit young for the part. Sir should be fifty-five or older. But Albert did a wonderful job. He had his hair shaved. He's got no false vanity about those things.

**What's the starting point with an adaptation of one of your own works? How much discussion at the beginning is there or is it entirely left to you?**

One of the rules I have is that you have to abandon the play. Now, I know one doesn't, but one has to think of it in terms of a movie. One isn't altogether successful because there will be longer playing scenes than you would normally have if you were starting from scratch. Nevertheless, films demand shorter scenes.

I think I asked Peter for the opening shot of *The Dresser* because I couldn't find an opening shot, and he said just start on the dressing table. That's what he wanted to do and it was terrific. Just as Roman gave the opening shot with *The Pianist*. I find it very difficult sometimes to get into the movie. But with *The Dresser*, I just wanted to tell the story, and I knew the story I wanted to tell. You know, when it's been in the theatre and you know where the laughs come, you know where the seriousness comes, you just rely on that. It's the same. I cannot remember anyone interfering on *The Dresser* except to ask us for that help with the BBC Announcement at the beginning. Columbia wanted it. They said it would be a help to American audiences. And I said, 'Terrific, that's a very good idea.' It was not a major thing, and it works beautifully because you just hear that voice in the background and it's fine.

We wanted to set the period very clearly. I don't think you should take it for granted that anybody knows anything at all, so you have to make it clear. So we put the BBC Announcement in to tell you that it was wartime, Roosevelt was President, Churchill was Prime Minister. And there are all kinds of establishing details in that opening shot.

**Did your screenplay mention any of the props seen in the opening sequence – ration books, etc.?**

No, I don't usually do that. I leave that to the director, except with Sir's inscribed silver tray which Norman polishes. That I noted to establish period, and also preparing the tin bath to establish the hardship of the touring actor which was a tough life.

All those things at the beginning are to give you a sense of the background of a theatrical tour. Obviously it's not generally known how touring worked so you want to tell the audience as much as possible. It's just storytelling. But the scene in the bath comes directly from the play at a later point. I simply moved it up front to show that the man was in crisis. You have to show Sir's suffering from a nervous breakdown or very near to it. So I brought the stuff that is talked about later in the play up front so that you got a sense of the development of the nervous breakdown.

The moment when the company is catching the train to the next town is very important. Peter Yates and I first met in somebody's house to discuss whether there was a film in this or not because, obviously, I wanted it to be made as a film. Peter had seen the play and loved it, but wasn't certain about whether it would make a movie. And we were having a general discussion, and I suddenly remembered an incident that I was told about – I wasn't present – of Wolfit stopping a train because his company was late getting to the railway station. And the story I was told was that he shouted, 'Stop that train!' and the train driver pulled the lever and it stopped. And the moment Peter Yates heard that he said, 'It's a film.' And it was after that meeting that we discussed casting and all kinds of people were discussed. Of course, Albert Finney came up. Tom Courtney was already on board. He'd played it in the theatre in London, and he'd played it in New York.

Tom nearly turned down the part in the play when we offered it to him because of the scene with Irene. He said it was wrong that he should be so vicious. It's much more vicious in the play. But when he played it, he realised it was precisely what was needed.

**It's interesting the way that you've played with the structure of the play, the way you've moved scenes around for the screenplay.**

You have to. You see, the play starts at a point where he's already had the nervous breakdown, and it seemed to me an audience in movies wouldn't take that so well. I had to move the build up to the nervous breakdown as the first act of the screenplay and that's what I did. Yes, that's what I call abandoning the play.

**The exterior scenes away from the theatre early on in the screenplay, such as the company catching their train, the street scenes, the hospital, etc., take the whole experience away from its theatrical origins and signal that the characters are always capable of being on the move and not bound within a single theatre-bound setting.**

Exactly. And that's what I mean by going into the piece because you have to discover what can be realised visually from the play itself. And it's wonderfully photographed, so authentic.

*In the railway scene, the touring company is travelling to Bradford. Is that just coincidence or did you choose Bradford because that's where the great actor-manager Sir Henry Irving died?*

No, I chose Bradford because that's where we were going to shoot it. Irving died in an hotel anyway, after playing Thomas Beckett, and the doctor who'd attended him who was also staying at the hotel where Irving collapsed and died, didn't recognise him, having just seen him in the play.

*How did you approach relocating both scenes and reported information from the confines of the stage play's setting?*

Well, I know that Sir's death has to be the end of this film, and so I had to tell the story that starts the process of his death. And that's why it's chopped up more. The play isn't like that. The first time you see Sir in the play is when he's in the dressing room. He comes in, having discharged himself from the hospital. So the back-story's frightfully important for people to understand what the hell's going on without spoken exposition. And as you've got a movie, you might as well tell it in visual terms.

If you read the first scene between Norman and Her Ladyship in the play, you'll see exactly what I did. I just took the stories from there and visualised them. No problem there. If you look at the speeches of Norman and of Her Ladyship, about him dreaming and saying 'I shall do something violent' and all that, that's what I've dramatised. I've just made that the front story.

The scene in the hotel bedroom where Sir is shown to be fearful of the coming performance is all spoken about in the play and it's brought forward to show the collapse. This was the last scene shot on the schedule.

Sir's line, 'I shall wake with the storm clouds in my head,' was also much later in the play but I brought it forward. That was a line Paul Scofield told me. I was writing the play when Scofield was doing a play of mine at the Haymarket called *A Family*. And I was watching the lighting rehearsal or one of the technical rehearsals, and Scofield came by and, it was amazing, he said, 'You're writing a play about us, aren't you?' and I was absolutely alarmed. And then afterwards he asked what it was about, and I told him. He said, 'Oh, Lear. When you play Lear, you wake with the storm clouds in your head.' And I made a note of it. It's in the play as well as the film, of course.

And the line, 'I know what they mean, moral grandeur,' that's a line Edith Sitwell used about Wolfit's Lear in a letter to him. I used 'moral grandeur'. It's a lovely phrase.

Later on, when Sir spits on his hands before attempting to carry Her Ladyship, she says, 'I do wish you wouldn't do that. You remind me of a labourer.' That's an Ellen Terry line. She used to say that to Irving. Sir Henry Irving used to spit on his hands before he picked her up.

And we did the lighting rehearsal scene to dramatise something that a worldwide film audience could not possibly know about – boom lights, etc. Wolfit had following lights. And that was all learned by me at Wolfit's knee. He always had two boom lights, one at each side of the stage with someone on them following him.

And Wolfit's make-up for Lear. I tried to reproduce it as accurately as I could. I used to watch him every night. He always started with the eyebrows, soaped them, and then put number twenty, which was a white stick, on them. And then combed them against the grain so they stood out as older men's eyebrows do. As mine do now.

And I put in a Wolfit line, 'And the broad straight line of number twenty down the nose gives strength to the face.' I don't know what he meant by it but that's what he said.

But Sir's eventual first entrance on stage – the terror in that shot is wonderful – that's very un-Wolfit. Wolfit had no terror of going on stage. He couldn't wait. He'd never have had a breakdown, he loved acting.

### Did you write things down at the time when you were his dresser?

No, I have a theory that if it's important, you'll remember it. I never make notes of that kind. I do when I'm writing, 'Oh God, I'd better remember that.' I do that. But not at the time. I never keep diaries. I have kept diaries, but not very good ones.

You see, our generation – Tom Courtney, Albert Finney and I – just caught the end of all this. They were part of the new world, and I was a bridge between the old world and the new world. I spanned both. And Tom had played on television in *The Master Builder* with Wolfit.

I added an exterior scene early on showing a fire being put out following a bombing raid. That was pure invention on my part. It was to show that the destruction around Sir was part of his breakdown, the bombing and the constant anxiety about the war.

This was followed by a market scene that was something Norman talked about in a long speech in the first scene of the play, so it may as well be dramatised. It was all described in the play, Sir jumping on his hat and taking off his clothes.

And Peter's use of music in this movie is so good. It's by James Horner. The tendency is to put in as much as you can, but he just spotted it exactly right. In the scene where Sir runs away from the market, there's the most beautiful musical entry, with the horn. Just the solo horn. It's lovely.

**So you had an additional input into the production, you suggested the composer.**

No, it wasn't input. It was just they were thinking of names. And I think Peter had heard of him and knew about him. No, I had no input. I brought up the name because I knew James Horner as a little boy. His father, Harry Horner, was a very good friend of mine. Harry was a distinguished production designer who'd won two Oscars, one for *The Heiress* and the other for *The Hustler*. No, anybody who makes a good suggestion should be listened to.

I also included the scene when Sir is admitted to hospital, which is all described in the play as well as the scene between Norman and Her Ladyship which is also in the play, but in the film it's done on the move. To describe it, I just put 'Exterior. Street – Evening.' Peter's such a clever director, the camera is so unobtrusive.

**How much do you describe a particular scene?**

I try to keep that to a minimum because it's going to change when they get the location.

I also dramatised the scene in hospital where Sir is faced with sedation, which is described in the play. God, Albert was good.

And I added a scene with the front-of-house manager which was not in the play, in order to show the uncertainty and consequences that Sir's precarious condition has on everyone else.

Also the scene when Sir tries to flee from his preparations for *King Lear* and is observed in the corridor by the rest of the company, that's what a film does wonderfully. You can't do that in the theatre.

**The scene in Sir's dressing room after he has fled the hospital is quite a long scene in the play.**

Which I simply trusted. And it's pretty much as it is in the play.

**On the theatre's press board extolling Sir's company's revues, your name appears as the critic for the Portsmouth & Gosport Express.**

They did that. Nothing to do with me. That was production business. I hate those kind of jokes. Others rather like them and I can't bear them.

**When writing a film about the theatre, it's very easy to have all of that shorthand that people in the business know about. Did you find when you were doing this that you had to go back and change things, knowing the public wouldn't understand it?**

No, I don't think so. I tried to make it clear through the action of the play. I put in the scene about Brown & Polson's in the market. It's not in the play, because, as you rightly say, you can't rely on the audience knowing our shorthand. But I don't remember encountering that as a block or as something that I had to overcome.

You see, I don't think it's so much a play about 'the business'. It's set against that background and you just have to make it clear. I don't know if people ever said 'I don't understand that.' I don't think it ever cropped up.

**Whether consciously or unconsciously, the film has totally avoided theatre in-jokes that the audience wouldn't understand.**

Well, I don't have an outside eye when I write. It may be a fault but I just don't have an outside objective eye. I don't think, 'What will the audience think of this?', 'What will the director think of this?', 'What will the producer think of this?' I don't have that in my mind at all. I'm inside it, and I want to write the story. And I want to be as true to the people in the story as I can be. And so what the characters say, they say. I don't bring any censorship. I don't censor my own work. I'm not very good at that. Once I start to do that – it may not be true for everybody, I'm only talking personally, other people might do it differently – once I start to censor, because I think, 'Oh God, will they understand that or not?', then something false enters into the characters or the storyline.

Alan Ayckbourn said a very, very interesting thing. He didn't say it to me, I think I read it or may have heard him say it. When he was stuck in a play and he couldn't find out why, he'd have to go back until he found where he told the lie. And the moment he found that he'd told a lie, he re-wrote and made it truthful and the play went on. And I thought that was a very accurate observation about writing. Because at some point, you may, for the sake of ease or for the sake of what you think is moving the story on, distort it a little. And it will block. At some point, you'll hit the brick wall. And you have to unpick. So, it implies that Ayckbourn, like me, doesn't have too good an outside view of what he's doing. But I would never dream of thinking, 'God, Peter Yates or Polanski, they won't like this scene.' I just don't have that. I think other people may, and they do it very well. But I don't. I can't.

***It's very accessible for the audience.***

If it's truthful, I think they do get it. They wanted me to change the line 'he's been about a bit' to 'he's been around a bit' because Americans say 'been around a bit', but I wouldn't have that. And Peter supported me on that.

You see, it's interesting, you hear 'calling the half'. It's a phrase that theatre people would use. But there's no need for explanation. You just use it. Once it's real and in the truth of the scene, I don't think it's a problem. I really don't. I'm sure intelligent people work out – 'half', it must be half an hour.

And 'trouser-loonie'. That's an old slang now gone entirely for under-dressing the costume with street clothing. But it was a perfectly accurate one, not made up by me.

It's all accurate – the opening of the house for performance, the orchestra. Wolfit always had a little orchestra in the pit. I love all that theatre atmosphere. I tried to do all that in *Being Julia* too, with the buskers and things going on outside the theatre and the Gallery queues.

And the lines, 'There will be no extra payment for tonight's performance. Your contract is, I believe, play as cast' for going on as understudy in a major part and 'Good fortune attend your endeavours' were all pure Wolfit.

***Would the orchestra actually play a Gilbert & Sullivan piece before*** **King Lear?**

Oh yes. Always. Always the wrong music.

*The superstition of quoting from* Macbeth, *the Scottish tragedy, is another example of perhaps an 'in' thing, a little-known theatre tradition.*

The play was revived recently at the Duke of Yorks, Peter Hall's production, and they applauded that scene. 'The Scottish tragedy' is now a rather well-known bad luck thing, isn't it? It wasn't then, I don't think. In a way, this is rather uncompromising in helping the audience along. It just does what it does.

This is really a 'show must go on' story, you know. That's really what it is. Someone once said that, disparagingly, about the play and the film. And I said, 'That's what it is, of course it is. How terrific!' And an American critic said that it was really about a Jewish mother and her recalcitrant child. Norman as a Jewish mother – the critic was trying to find a connection to me, I suppose.

*A lot of actors work out the back-story for their characters from the script. Do you use that process when writing? For instance, on the company's tour, you mention Bridlington and they're on their way to Bradford, which isn't far. Did you work out a possible route for the company's tour?*

I didn't do it that way. It could have been anywhere. It didn't have to be near because they made huge journeys. There's a line in the play about coming from Aberdeen to Liverpool. I've done that journey on a tour, it took all day. I used Bridlington because it's funny. I find the name funny, but others might not.

It would never occur to me to get the geography of a tour right. Simply because you did travel. You tried to get them – I know from being Wolfit's business manager – you tried to book a tour that was pretty logical. But you couldn't always get the theatres. So you had to take what you could.

Aberdeen to Liverpool was the worst journey I've ever done. There's a line in the play which Sir says, 'A journey I recommend as punishment for deserters'. It's an appalling journey. No, Bridlington's just got a good name, hasn't it. It's a funny name.

**How much of the back-story do you work out, either in your head or on paper?**

None at all. I just carry that with me. You mean do I make notes or anything?

**Yes. Do you think about where they were before? About their character? That sort of thing?**

No. The character is born in the writer, isn't it? This is the most difficult thing to describe in writing. Years ago, I was friends with J. B. Priestley; we talked about this. He created hundreds and hundreds of characters in his novels. And Jung did a chapter or an essay on Priestley's characters because he created archetypes. And Priestley said to me – and this is late in his life, about four or five years before he died and I was staying with him up in Warwickshire – he said, 'I can't do it any more. I can't create these people any more. I used to do it like that.' And I know in my own case, I just have the character inside me. I can't describe it. It just is. I don't have to think; I know everything about him or her. So when you say, 'Have I worked out the back-story', I don't have to, I just know it. That's a good way of saying it: I know it, like I know my own life.

If someone said, 'Where did Norman go to school?' when I was writing it, I could tell you. Or if someone said, 'What sort of parts did Sir play when he was not a leading man?', I could tell you that. Or 'What was his father?' – well, that comes into the play, so I knew all that, and his mother was browbeaten. I could tell you all those things because they're just in me. And I could do it for any of the characters. I can still, when I write a play or book, whatever, I can do that.

### What an alarming loss for Priestley or any writer to be unable to do that any more?

Well, it was very near the end of his life. And he couldn't write that way anymore. He wrote essays and things and he tried to write fiction. He wrote a detective story which was not very good. Good plot, but the character thing had gone from him. But then, he had invented hundreds and hundreds of characters.

Two great writers of that kind are Shakespeare and Dickens: their timeless, famous, wonderful characters. And I suspect if you asked Dickens, 'Do you know their background? Have you worked it out?', he'd say, 'No. That's how they are. I've got them in me.' I know. When I was working on *Oliver Twist*; the characters are spectacular, perfectly formed human beings.

### Can you say something about the casting process?

I can tell you how that came about. All sorts of people were suggested. Orson Welles phoned me and asked if I'd be interested in him doing it. I said 'yes' and never heard from him again.

**So you obviously got involved with the casting of this film?**

Only at the beginning, just with the two main parts. Then they came up with suggestions for the others, and Peter would ask me. But I didn't have a great input, not like in the theatre where I could say 'no' and they wouldn't cast them. We had a lovely casting director, Noel Davis, now dead. Noel and I had been actors together in 1954 so we went back a hell of a long way. And they knew that world as well as I did, they knew what was required. Peter's older than me, and Noel and I were roughly the same age, I suppose. And they cast it bloody well. Wonderfully well. So I didn't have much involvement. I interviewed actors with Peter. We sat in his flat and people came to see us. But there were no disputes. I can't remember any anyway.

Albert didn't want to do it at first. But, as I knew him, I got the script to him. He finally agreed, and it was a very good decision for him. And for us.

It wasn't that he didn't like the part. It was just that he may have felt he was too young for it, and he probably was right. But he overcame that in the performance. Nobody ever said he was too young. And he had his hair shaved, and he might have padded up, I can't remember. Then he went on to do *Annie*. Later, when my wife and I were in Los Angeles, we went for a walk with him, and he had no hair at all. He'd had it shaved for *Annie*.

**You wrote additional dialogue for the scenes in the film that take place backstage.**

Oh yes. What I was trying to do was give a film audience the double life that happens in the theatre, the backstage life. And the storm was all very accurate. And the props were very good. And it's so well shot.

**As you were so close to it, did anyone from the Art Department ever consult you about 'the storm'?**

Oh yes, they consulted me. The Art Department always consult the writer. They ask impossible questions. Wolfit had a roll-top desk. I must have told them that. They did on *The Pianist;* they did on *Oliver Twist* as well. But British designers and prop people are the most conscientious in the world.

And with the storm, that's absolutely what Wolfit did. He had a man in the tree rocking backward and forward. He nearly killed Wolfit one night. The man was drunk and he fell forward and hit Donald on the back of the head.

**Can you say something about dealing with unforeseen problems that arise during filming?**

I can give a very good example. There is a good cut on the line 'Fetch Madge'. There was a scene from the play that I'd written in the screenplay between Sir and Her Ladyship, his wife, where she puts the pressure on him about retiring. And it was all shot and it was very well acted. But when we came to see it, I saw a rough cut, somewhere there was a problem. And Peter was very, very hesitant to suggest to me that we cut the scene, and I think I suggested it. I don't know if I'm taking credit for something I shouldn't. I think they said, 'Perhaps we should lose the scene,' and I think I said at once, 'Cut it.' I saw it was absolutely essential for the film. And they were very relieved because it's what they wanted to do, but they were careful with me. But I wanted what was good for the movie. It was a shame for the actress playing Her Ladyship because she lost her best scene.

But that cut, 'Fetch Madge', is originally after the scene with Her Ladyship. And they must have fiddled it so that it looked like a sharp cut to when he opens the door to her and says, 'Fetch Madge'. It works terribly well, and it solved the problem. But I remember it being a very great problem at the time, in the cutting, in the editing.

*Where did the idea come from for all the actors to say goodnight one by one outside Sir's dressing room after the performance? It's very effective.*

I wanted it to be like curtain calls, slightly theatrical, and so did Peter.

*You said you thought* The Dresser *wouldn't be made now. Is that due to the 'dumbing down' of cinema audiences that one hears about?*

No, I don't think so. I just think the more that commercials influence movies, which they do, the difficulty of writing the longer scene, using perhaps a little more elegant language than is normally done in movies, would make things more difficult. It just occurred to me watching it again. Don't you feel the same?

*Who will be the audience of the future if people only have teenage soap TV to cut their teeth on for dramatic guidance?*

This is the problem. They're not taught Shakespeare anymore. Well, now they are again, these things come and go. I think we've got that back from the curriculum people. But it's a worrying development. What will films rely on in future if not spoken scenes?

I think it's rather bold, keeping so much of the Shakespeare in and the backstage thing. That would be difficult now. But Peter and I still get letters about this, and praise, from youngsters really.

Perhaps this film wouldn't be made now. The language is quite high-falluting, and I think now producers wouldn't dare put money in it. I don't know. Maybe with the right actors, it still could be made.

Incidentally, I was told Al Pacino said *The Dresser* was the best adaptation of a play he's ever seen for the movies. I think it was Al Pacino, I don't want to put words in his mouth. But if so, the man's an intellectual giant. (*Laughter*)

# *Taking Sides*

Adapted from the stage play *Taking Sides* by Ronald Harwood
Directed by István Szabó
Produced by Yves Pasquier
Executive Producers: Rainer Mockert, Maureen McCabe, Sir Jeremy Isaacs, Rainer Schafer, David Rogers
Starring Harvey Keitel, Stellan Skarsgård, Moritz Bleibtreu and Birgit Minichmayr
Production Companies: A French/British/German/Austrian Co-Production
MBP, Palaladin, Maecenas, Twanpix, Jeremy Isaacs Productions, SATEL, Great British Films, Studio Babelsberg, Enterprise Films, Spice Factory, BR, MDR, ORF, France 2 Cinema, Canal+, FFA, Filmboard Berlin-Brandenburg (FBB), MDM, Eurimages, European Union Media Programme
Distributors: Alamode Film (Germany), E Stars Films (China), Guerilla Films (UK), Mikado (Italy), Mondo Films (France), New Yorker Films (USA), etc.

*Based on the true story of Wilhelm Furtwängler, arguably the most eminent conductor of his generation, who is brought before the American Denazification Committee after the fall of the Third Reich. When Jewish artists were compelled to flee Hitler's Germany, others went voluntarily into exile in protest; Furtwängler, however, decided to remain. And though he helped to provide a safe haven for many Jewish musicians, at the same time he served as one of the Nazi's foremost cultural assets. Ruthlessly pressed and humiliated by his American Army interrogator, the esteem in which he is held by his countrymen remains undiminished. This story presents its balanced evidence, leaving any answer to the question it raises to its audience.*

- The stage play, written in 1993, was first performed at Chichester in 1995 following an unusual delay for the recuperation of one of its leading actors from illness. It was subsequently performed in London, Paris and New York.
- The film was released in 2001.

Nominated for a European Film Award for Best Actor (Stellan Skarsgård); winner of Best Director and Best Screenplay at the Flaiano Film Festival 2002, winner of five Mar del Plata Film Festival Awards including the ADF Cinematography Award, Best Actor (Stellan Skarsgård), Best Director, the Kodak Award and the SIGNIS Award; winner of the Hungarian Film Critics Award (István Szabó); winner of the Valenciennes International Festival of Action and Adventure Films Jury Prize (István Szabó); included in the Official Selection Berlin 2002, out of competition; in the main Selection (Gala) Toronto 2001.

**Once again, as the source material for this screenplay stems from your own original idea, could you start by telling us something about its conception as a stage play?**

The play came to me in the mid 1990s when I happened to be up in Manchester directing one of my own plays. My wife came up to join me and she had brought a book that she thought might interest me.

The book was called *Berlin Days, 1946–48* by George Clare, the author of *Last Waltz in Vienna*. Clare was a young Austrian refugee who'd come to England at the age of twelve in about 1936. By the time the war ended, he would have been twenty-one and the British Intelligence people were recruiting German speakers because they had a lot of interrogations to do in Germany and Austria. In this memoir he recounts his time spent as a young British intelligence officer immediately after the war in Germany. Papers concerning the conductor, Wilhelm Furtwängler, happened to pass across his desk before he was obliged to hand them over to the American authorities in whose zone Furtwängler's activities fell. But Clare described clearly and in some detail the case against the conductor.

And as I was reading, a play was born in me. Not the exact shape or form, but the drama itself. I can't explain it any more clearly than that, except to point out that my own obsessions instantly recognised the value of Furtwängler's story. The ambiguity of his case was immediately intriguing. And, arrogantly, I had an instinctive belief that my own understanding of the events could shed light on Furtwängler's dilemma.

He was never a member of the Nazi party but was Hitler's favourite conductor and had been honoured by both Hermann Göring and Josef Göbbels. He made anti-Semitic remarks but saved many Jewish musicians, albeit only the most talented. The ethical choices facing him, an individual artist in a totalitarian regime, spoke directly to me. Perhaps it also had something to do with another obsession, my upbringing in South Africa under another totalitarian regime.

It was performed first in Chichester, then came to London and New York and it's been played all over the world in various languages. The film has come as a result of that.

I called the play and the film *Taking Sides* because I want the audience to take sides. I hate propaganda films, I hate being told what to think, I hate being recruited to causes. I think audiences are very intelligent. We underestimate our cinema audience all the time. We think they're only capable of short ten-second shots like commercials. But they're capable of listening, just as a theatre audience is, and they're capable of understanding arguments. And that's what we've done in the movie. I want them to come out and argue, 'Was he guilty?' And I want them to ask the basic question, 'What would I have done in his place?' Everybody will have hoped they would have behaved beautifully and morally and correctly, but the facts are that very few people do.

The Americans and the British wanted to make an example of the leading members in a great many professions: law, the theatre, films, music.

Almost everything Furtwängler says, he actually said in the denazification proceedings that followed the investigation which is the subject of the film. I think there's only one speech that I invented for him. And all the other characters are inventions. Furtwängler is the only true, real, historical character. The others represent actual people who were there but are not the real people themselves.

He was an extraordinarily original conductor. And the feeling that he brought to the work is, in my opinion, unique. There are people still about who knew him, principally his widow, Elizabeth Furtwängler, a very beautiful and enchanting woman. She came to see the play in London. She's the only witness to these events that the film used. I tried to find records of them. I had people searching all over Europe and in America to see if there were records of these interrogations, and there weren't any. I don't know if that's sinister or not. There simply weren't any. And I was very relieved because it meant that I could invent these characters and, according to her, it's fairly accurate.

It's a very ambiguous case. He was very comfortable in Germany, he was very well paid, he had a great orchestra. You know, for every bad thing against Furtwängler, there's a good thing: he was Hitler's favourite conductor, but he helped Jews. He helped many, many Jews escape. But he certainly played in Nuremberg on the eve before the Nuremberg Rally. He played on the eve of Hitler's birthday. He was certainly not a member of the party. He stayed because he believed, perhaps naïvely, I don't want to judge him in this way but this is what he said, that he had to be with his people, that he wanted to help them through these hours of dreadful trial and tribulation.

*Different writers would have approached this subject in a multitude of ways. When you first became aware of the Furtwängler interrogations and the idea of taking art and making political capital out of it, how did it strike you?*

Well, it just sprung at me. I can't say it was difficult. I read it and I thought, 'This is a play.' And I knew exactly what I wanted it to be about. I liked the moral dilemma. And it's grey. It's very, very grey. So that came to me. And I love interrogation.

### Did you aim Taking Sides *at any particular audience when you were writing it?*

No, as I said, I don't think like that, I honestly don't. And I don't think of a message. I just think of the moral dilemma. I wanted everyone who watched it to say, 'How would I have behaved in those circumstances?' That's all, it's a modest ambition. And I think it's part of the power of the play, and maybe the movie, if people say, 'How would I have behaved if I was Hitler's favourite conductor, if I had this wonderful orchestra? Would I have got out? Would I have resisted these pressures if I'd been invited to Berchtesgarten or the Reich Chancellery?' That's what I wanted to do. I wasn't aiming it at anybody.

### How did the screenplay come about?

I smoke rather heavily and cigarettes, of course, are crucial to this film being made. I was at Sir Georg Solti's house. He couldn't bear smoking in the house. It was a cold November night and I went out on to the terrace to have a quick puff. And there was another man, quite elderly I was very glad to see, standing in the corner, chain smoking. So I thought, well I've found a fellow sufferer, and I went up to him and I introduced myself. And he'd just seen the play which was running in London. His name was Peter Diamond, and he was a great musical entrepreneur and impresario. He was the first director of the Edinburgh Festival. He'd known every leading musician in Europe for the past fifty or sixty years. He'd known Furtwängler, he knew Richard Strauss, he knew everybody. And he said, 'Are you going to make a film of it?' I said, 'I'd love to make a film of it but nobody approached me.' He said, 'I know someone who'd love to make a film of this.' And it was through him and his contacts with Yves Pasquier that this film came into being. And it was all due to cigarettes.

Yves is a remarkable man, and it was a very happy collaboration. He persisted for many years to try and raise the money. It was a hell of a struggle.

The film opened in Toronto, unfortunately on the 13th of September 2001, two days after the New York massacre. And it just disappeared, of course it did. But Pasquier, again with great perseverance and persistence, stuck with it. And it was released in America in late 2002 or early 2003 and in Britain in the winter of 2003. It's been a struggle, and if not for Yves and Rainer Mockert, the Executive Producer, we'd never have got it shown.

### When adapting the screenplay, did you need to do any additional research?

I probably did have geographic things I had to research. I don't remember doing much more. I used the books again that I had. I was very lucky because Szabó, who comes from eastern Europe, from Hungary, he knows that world very well, so the setting of it was easy. And, of course, Ken Adam, the designer, was vital. He comes from Berlin and he knows the period very well. So, I didn't have to do much research.

### You were very fortunate with the casting of your two leads.

We got Harvey Keitel, which was a great coup, and I also think one of the great good fortunes we had was casting Stellan Skarsgård. Because he's not obvious casting, he may even be a little young for the part. And he's certainly not a look-alike in an absolute sense. But what he brings to the part is the presence of a star, which is what Furtwängler was. When he entered a room, Furtwängler put the temperature up several degrees. There are many accounts of it: of him coming into a rehearsal which was not his own and the orchestra suddenly playing better. Something to do with his presence. I remember reading one account of him coming into a room where everyone was talking with their backs to the door, and the moment he entered the conversation died. They all turned and were silent as he came into the room. He was a great figure. And Skarsgård brings to it that kind of gravitas which great conductor's have. They are the centre of the world. They are, as someone says in the film, dictators of their own worlds.

And I think the test of that was when Elizabeth Furtwängler saw the film, she deeply admired his performance. And it's not, as I said, because he looks like him or is the right age or anything, but it's something in his personality that absolutely matches that star quality that great conductors have.

When Stellan stood before that orchestra for the first time and lifted the baton just to scratch his ear, the orchestra burst into music and it nearly frightened the life out of him. But after that, he calmed down, and he does the conducting wonderfully.

**When adapting your own play to the screen, do you find you have more control than another writer would?**

It depends upon the director. *The Dresser* and *Taking Sides* were both done by directors who loved the original piece and respected it. Obviously, they had suggestions to make. And they're more cautious when it's the screenwriter's own play. But I don't think you're any more in control. It depends on how well you do your screenplay.

**When Yves Pasquier came to you, did you do a draft screenplay to get the others on board to move the project along?**

No, I think they got Szabó involved on the play. Ken Adam, the designer, came later. But Szabó became involved when he'd seen the play in Budapest or Vienna, I can't remember. He saw it and liked it, and when Yves came to him he said he'd love to do it.

Then we met in Budapest and we discussed in general terms what I wanted to do and what he wanted. I don't think he even took notes then. He doesn't trust his English all that much, and so he had someone to help him, a very, very nice woman, Gaby Prekop. She is spectacular at scripts. She's very, very good. And she made suggestions, whether it's too long, because you can't always judge that, the length of a scene. You know, it should be shorter than in the play but you don't know how short. We discussed that. And I think I did two drafts, my draft and Szabó's draft, and we may have changed one thing later. But it wasn't difficult, it was never agonised.

**In the writing, were you ever tempted by influences outside your original theme: for instance, to comment on contemporary political or social views or were you ever under any pressure to allow for 'political correctness', that sort of thing?**

No. I tried to stay true to period, what we knew then and not what we know now. If they called a homosexual a 'poof', that's what I put in. I would not be politically correct or make any concession. No.

**Was there any pressure on you with Taking Sides to cut it or to make it shorter for distributors?**

No, I don't know about that. You'd have to ask them. They never came to me. Once it goes into the editing process, the writer's not consulted. Except with Roman Polanski. He's the only director I know who asks me to come and see the editing, if I like this or that. But that's to do with our collaboration. Usually, once the film goes into editing, no one comes near me. And I wasn't asked to see it until it was a rough cut. That was in Paris. And if I did make a suggestion, Szabó is inclined to object to it. That's his area, he was very covetous of the editing. So is Polanski to a certain extent. They all are. Because that is where the film is made.

The putting together of the film is a vital moment: if we shot enough stuff, does that cover it, all those things. That process is, for me, delicate and sensitive.

I know they cut one huge scene which I loved and I was very, very upset about it. And when I asked about it, again, there was some sort of tricky problem. There was a scene between the Major and Emmi's mother which was not in the play at all and I loved the scene. And I thought I'd written it well and I thought it would play well. But some problem arose and they just simply removed it. There was no way of saving it. And it may be to the good of the film, I don't know, because I never saw it in context. But I did ask about it. So you get that as well.

*With* **Taking Sides,** *did the possible encroachment on similar territory to a film like* **Mephisto** *tempt you to alter or expand in any way your original premise or emphasis? Especially with Szabó directing?*

> No. I was just delighted that Szabó said yes to this. I knew it was his world. No, that didn't bother me at all. And I think it is rather different in certain ways. Because *Mephisto* is a black and white story, obviously, given the title. The man, the actor, is corrupted by the Nazi regime. In the Furtwängler story, it's much more ambiguous. So it didn't bother me, no. But I was thrilled that it was Szabó because he knew that world better than anybody as far as I'm concerned.

*You chose to start the film with a series of scenes not in your play. First, it opens in the middle of a concert.*

> Yes, as I said, the concert is talked about in the play. Furtwängler was conducting a big concert in Berlin, there was a bombing raid and what followed was described in the play. And I thought when writing the screenplay that that would be an ideal opening although I knew it would be very expensive and probably upset Rainer Mockert.

*Then you added the destruction of the Nazi swastika.*

> I put the coming down of the swastika, the Nazi emblem, in the screenplay because I was trying to echo that moment when the Reichstag was taken by the Russians, and there are lots of newsreels of that stonework coming down.

*Did that idea come early on?*

> Immediately. That was my first thought about how to begin. Once I saw that then I could get on with the script.

The other danger is to become too attached to the play. Every line suddenly becomes a golden thing, you know. You don't want to disturb it. But I think I'm good at that. I can abandon the play. Adapting novels is different. It's more difficult for an author of a play to abandon his own play than it is to abandon someone else's, I'm afraid.

**You also show the appointment of Major Arnold, the American Prosecutor, who's already taken up his post in the play.**

Again, this scene is described in the play, but I thought it proper to see it in the film. And that General is a real general, General Wallace, who was in charge of these groups that were investigating prominent people in Nazi Germany.

It is a crucial moment in the film when he watches the archive material that the General shows him, and especially the film of Belsen, of the corpses being shoved by bulldozers into pits, a scene which has haunted me all my life and, I think, is the reason why I write so much about that period.

**In a story dealing with several nationalities, how did you solve the dilemma of a language convention?**

Of course we cheat a little bit. The Germans who speak German to each other, which they don't actually do, speak in English with a German accent, which is perfectly acceptable. It's part of a convention that you do that. It's always very difficult when there are two or three languages involved in a movie to decide what is the language of the film. I know when we did *The Pianist,* which I did after this, which was obviously set in Poland, we had the same problem. So we said for that film, English is Polish and everybody else spoke whatever language they spoke in their original language.

Here, everyone speaks English, and I think having the German actors was a great help because it gives it an authentic tone.

**Yves Pasquier, the producer, was keen to do something where dialogue was important. He was conscious that serious dialogue is an important part of cinema and should remain so in order that the audience, who should not be underestimated, has the opportunity to understand it.**

I absolutely agree. And I think the modern trend which is so influenced by commercials that everything has to be in short, sharp, brief images is so pervasive and overwhelming now that I was very pleased that we were able to keep long dialogue scenes, longer than usual at any rate. I think that just made a different kind of film and a film which people have to listen to as well as look at.

**Do the actors consult you much? About what it's all about?**

Much more in a play because I go much more to rehearsals. I can't bear going on the film set. It is very boring, unbearable. There's nothing for the writer to do. In the theatre they ask questions, yes. Even recently, so many years after *The Dresser* was first done, they asked questions. So did Peter Hall, the director. Not major questions. He knew most of them have been solved. It was just a question of whether he understood what the intention was. I don't get that much in movies. Occasionally.

They had a reading of *Taking Sides* and Harvey had a lot of questions, but he comes at it from another angle. He is a method actor, and it's different for him. The director sometimes asks me when he's been asked a question he can't answer. So he'll say, 'I'll think about it,' which means, 'I'll talk to the writer.' But, no, it doesn't happen a lot. Film is such an interesting business. They do it in such short bursts. They haven't time to ask questions.

### Is a theatrical background a help for actors doing an adaptation of a play?

I don't know about Harvey. Stellan was a stage actor, a leading actor for the National Theatre of Stockholm. And I think Harvey may have started with the stage, I'm not sure. But I like having stage actors because they're much better at text. If you get a pure film actor, very often the text isn't understood. For them, that's just what they say but it's the sub-text that counts.

Annette Bening is wonderful. She has a theatre background and she understands what text is. You have to dig, you have to find, you have to discover. And she's terrific. But I've often noticed with just plain, ordinary film actors, I don't think they go into that. But then they can 'behave' very well, and sometimes film is about behaviour.

### You wrote in some additional interviews with several members of Furtwängler's orchestra.

That whole sequence, with the various musicians, in the play of course, is only talked about and it's talked about by one man, Helmuth Rode, the second violinist, played by Ulrich Tukur, a marvellous actor. In the play, it is a very, very long part and tells much of the background of Furtwängler and the orchestra which we dramatised in the film.

I divided that up into several musicians because it's more filmic. In a film, it's very difficult to do a very, very long speech just on one actor. That's not what film does very well. So that's why we have the story of Furtwängler and his relationship to his orchestra told by several of the musicians. And some of it, when I did the movie script, I took from a newsreel documentary about Furtwängler where you hear people talk about him, how they responded to him as a conductor.

**You also created a Russian character for the film.**

In the play, you don't see any of the Russians. But István and I had a long conversation about this in Vienna, and we decided it was absolutely essential we introduce one. But I must pay tribute to István here because his insight into the Russian mentality, into the Russian view of imperialism, as it were, as opposed to the American view, was absolutely crucial to making these scenes work. And we were very, very lucky to get Oleg Tabakov who was a great Soviet actor and is now a great Russian actor and, I think, gives a thrilling performance in the film as Colonel Dimshitz, Cultural Commissar for the Russian Zone in Berlin.

**Such people as the Dimshitz character, a former head of a museum, were important in the Intelligence of the Soviet Union and they had a distinct advantage when the Cold War started because of their grasp of art and culture, which gave them a jump on the Americans.**

The real point about this is that the totalitarian regimes believe in art, and they believe it to be powerful and important. Democracies don't believe in art. But in this case, the Americans wanted to get the artist, the Russians wanted to get him back as a great conductor. That's the crucial difference: the desire to control art, to make art entirely political. That is at the heart of the story of this film because Furtwängler has just emerged from a totalitarian regime himself, as the Germans are just coming out of the most horrific experience under Hitler. So the conflict between the two attitudes of the imperial powers, as it were, is vital to the story. And I'm very pleased we introduced the Russian and that István Szabó was so magnificent with his insight into how that worked.

**The Russian Zone took in the historical part of Berlin where the opera was situated.**

They had in their control, I believe, three or four orchestras, including the opera, and they offered any one to Furtwängler. But he didn't want to go. He was deeply anti-communist, which does not make him a fascist or a Nazi, but he didn't want to go into another totalitarian situation.

**The film also shows the differences in the cultures of Europeans and Americans.**

That's much more emphasised in the film than it is in the play. It's something that Szabó wanted very much to stress. That the American culture and the European culture has a great divide. Without pointing fingers. The difference between popular culture and *haute culture* is immense. And I think we did that rather well, I have to say; or at least Szabó did it rather well.

**This is an exercise in tolerance, allowing the audience to adopt the argument of each side and finally both sides in pursuing its moral journey.**

That's why the play is called *Taking Sides.* Because I have never said which side I'm on, as the author of the play or as the screenwriter of this film. Every interview I've ever given, that's what they ask me, 'Do you think Furtwängler was a Nazi, do you think he wasn't?' And I say, 'I refuse to answer.' And I will take this position to my grave.

The great accusation made against Furtwängler was that he didn't leave Germany. Why did he stay? And Solti, when he saw the play and we had dinner afterwards, said to me, 'You know, you missed a very important point.' And I was rather taken aback. He felt that one of the reasons that Furtwängler did not leave Berlin was, in Solti's words, 'He had a jewel in Berlin.' And that was the Berlin Philharmonic Orchestra. And it's very difficult for us to understand, but for a conductor to leave his orchestra is like a father leaving his children. And I wish I had known that when I wrote the play because I would certainly have made a point of it. But Solti was absolutely certain that was a great element in the reasoning.

**You added two other scenes that were not in the play: a small local audience listening to a concert in a bombed-out hall followed by a scene with American soldiers relaxing at a dance.**

This was very important to me, because in the hall there is nothing said until the very end. But it's the cut that's important, because you have the Schubert and you go straight to the Cole Porter.

Then in the next scene – it was hinted at in the play, but only hinted at – the envy of the Major for the young people, his loneliness and their apparent togetherness.

**There is also a scene by a lake.**

Yes, exactly. The 'opening out/opening in' dilemma again. And I think we managed that here. It's a wonderful location.

Because Berlin was an embattled city. There wasn't much countryside; it had all been bombed out. In the play, it's a Sunday evening back at the office. And of course, in the play, you can't go outside so these scenes are all done in the office in the one set. That would have been ridiculous in the film. If you wanted a day out in the sun, you had to go somewhere. Maybe a café would have been better, I don't know.

I also think this is beautifully edited. I think one should pay tribute to Sylvie Landra, a French editor, who cut this film with Szabó, of course, supervising. But there's something wonderful in the rhythms of this particular scene, the way she cuts from very close to medium shots and then wider shot. And I think that's really remarkable. What is required is that the rhythm of the scene is protected by the editor, and I think Sylvie Landra did an incredible job in doing precisely that. She protects the integrity of the scene.

## Because of the subject, music is an essential presence in the story.

In the play, the last piece of music you hear is Beethoven's Ninth Symphony. And I regret that he chose the Fifth here, because, when I was writing the play, I listened every day, prior to writing the final scene of the play, to five or six recordings and I left Furtwängler's for last. And when I got to the Furtwängler, it was like hearing another piece of music. It was so extraordinary: the tempo, the dynamics. But I think István decided that he wanted something better known, something that people could recognise instantly. And the Fifth Symphony is what we start with and what we end with.

It's interesting about the music. When I first got interested in the play and I was trying to get recordings of Furtwängler in England, just before going to France to write the play, I couldn't find any of his recordings. I couldn't get hold of anything. My younger daughter, who's a composer, was studying composition at the Julliard School of Music in New York. So I telephoned her and said, 'Please go out and see if you can get me some Furtwängler recordings.' And she went to a very well-known record shop in New York, and she went up to the guy running the classical music department and said, 'Do you have any recordings of Wilhelm Furtwängler?' He said, 'We don't keep the recordings of Nazis in this store.' So I was rather shocked by that. Eventually I found them, somebody ordered them for me. And I wanted to listen to a whole series of recordings of Beethoven's Ninth Symphony particularly, which I did.

I have to say that Frau Furtwängler must now be very pleased that I wrote the play and then the film because you can now get his records throughout America.

### Herbert von Karajan plays a prominent part in the discussions during the interrogations.

Von Karajan's is a very interesting story. He joined the Nazi Party twice, once in Vienna and once in Germany. I know the first thing he did after he was denazified, which was done very, very quickly – it shows his genius – he employed a Jewish secretary. That was just after the war. I thought that was a master stroke.

I saw him conduct Mozart in London twice and I couldn't bear it because you couldn't listen to the music, you could only watch von Karajan. He was a great star and he showed off on the podium. And even the greatest conductors I've seen – Solti among them, many of the great English conductors – they somehow blend with the music and allow you to listen. And certainly Furtwängler did that. You can see any of the movies of Furtwängler that they made, the newsreels. Always, he's unobtrusive. He's there, but unobtrusive. Von Karajan wanted you to look at him. And so I have a great reaction against him.

I think the interesting thing is Furtwängler's attitude to him. He called him 'Little K'. According to Frau Furtwängler, she never heard him call von Karajan that, but it's very, very well documented that he did. But the fact was that von Karajan was a Nazi star. He was encouraged by the Nazis and he was used against Furtwängler as a weapon. As Major Arnold says in a scene, 'If you won't do it, we'll get von Karajan.' And I think Furtwängler was made insecure by that.

### But Furtwängler was Hitler's favourite conductor?

That's perfectly true. Hitler admired him, he thought he was the best in German music. There's no question about that. And that was beyond Furtwängler's control, I presume. But he did conduct on the eve of a Nuremberg Rally; he did conduct on Hitler's birthday. So these were difficulties for him although he never joined the Nazi Party.

### The Nazis were very attuned to art as power.

Göbbels and Speer, between them, represent a kind of genius, not to be admired of course, but it was genius what they did. And Lene Riefenstahl captured it superbly on film. There's no question that those are great, great films about dreadful things.

It's very interesting that she couldn't work again really. Whereas Bertolt Brecht, who championed Communism, an evil regime, which he knew was evil, who had allowed his own fiancée to be taken by the party and destroyed by them when he could have intervened, knowing all of the leading party people, Brecht goes on being played all over the world. I just find that intolerable.

### Your play drew some criticism of the character of the American Major.

It's interesting. When the play was first done, I was criticised for making the American Major too brutal, too aggressive. Certainly in London and in New York, I was criticised for drawing a 'grotesque caricature'. And now we know that he ain't. He just isn't. Not in the light of the invasion of Iraq. I've seen a documentary in which an American officer says, 'Right, let's just shoot the guy, take him away and kill him' – much more brutal than Major Arnold, for God's sake, who was a democrat really.

When I did the research into this, I softened it. But the American Occupation Forces were deeply, deeply aggressive towards the Germans. They were shown the Nazi archive films, they had seen the evidence of the concentration camps, and they were angry. And I had lots of letters from men who had served in these units, the unit that Major Arnold served in, saying that I should have gone further. But most of the critics felt I had in some way caricatured the Major. But, in the present circumstances, after 9/11 and the Iraq invasion, I think they're coming round to feeling that maybe I was not so unfair to the Americans.

But the point is that the men from the interrogating section, represented by Harvey Keitel's character, were mostly from Milwaukee because they spoke a kind of German that could be understood. They were not cultured, and they were deliberately chosen because they were not cultured. The fact was that they wanted the people under investigation to be measured by their actions, not their artistic achievement. I have a letter from one who saw the play, not the film, who said, 'I wouldn't have stood for what Major Arnold stood for.' No, those guys were extremely tough.

## What information exists on the interrogations themselves?

The only witness is Elizabeth Furtwängler because she was there. They lived in Berlin while he was being interrogated and he used to come back terribly depressed in the evening. I had people look for official documents in Hamburg in the Bundesarchiv, in Washington at Arlington, but nothing exits.

And she was very nice about it when she saw the play in London. She asked me if I'd got records, and I said, 'No, I made it all up.' And she was very complimentary, so I was rather touched by that.

## You said all of Furtwängler's dialogue is his own except for one speech.

I took most of his statements from the denazification tribunal. Everything Furtwängler says in the play and the film he actually said, except one speech. The 'What kind of world do you want?' speech towards the end of the film is the only speech I wrote that I have no record of. But it was to make clear the difference in the two cultures. And he stresses materialism there and what he regards as the new world that's coming. And it frightens the life out of him.

## Brecht went through a similar experience during the McCarthy era ten years later.

It's usually totalitarian states that are insecure and conduct themselves like this. Democracies don't need to. They're secure in the people that put the government in power.

I think they behaved properly here. But in the 1950s, in the McCarthy period, I think Americans have a very black period in their history. As a great democracy, they should have felt more secure, and the film does echo this.

97

### *You make an alarming point about the plots against Hitler.*

It's very interesting about the plots against Hitler, and there were several. The plot that ended in June 1944 was a climax to a great many plots by officers and others to destroy Hitler, and they all failed. The books, by high ranking German Wehrmacht officers, that have recently come out about the conspiracies against Hitler are really fascinating. They, none of them, ever complain about concentration camp corpses being bulldozed into pits. They complain instead about the strategic decisions Hitler made, that he was driving Germany to a disaster in military terms.

The thing that has long, long puzzled me and no one can really answer is that, by using the railways as the Nazis did for the transportation of Jews across Europe, they undermined their own military ability to move troops. It's one of the most extraordinary things that no one at the Wannsee Conference, the minutes of which were taken by Eichman and which exist – you can read them and they made a wonderful HBO film about it called *Conspiracy* – there is no mention of this. No one says, 'Well, wait a minute. We've got to move armies. We've got to get people to the east. We've got to get people back. Reinforcements, etc.' No one said this. They accepted that this was a *fait accompli*, that the Jews had to be transported to Auschwitz and to Belsen and to Dachau and wherever. It is one of the great puzzles to me why they were so insistent on that, and at such a cost to their own strategy.

**The Nazi system also seemed oblivious to the link of the dependent and connected integrated German–Jewish culture of Science, Literature and Music, which it did all in its power to destroy.**

I could not agree more. That is the greatest destruction that Hitler perpetrated.

What you say about the integration is very interesting. Many of my friends here are refugees from that period, from 1936 to 1938. It absolutely shocked them because they were the most integrated Jewish population in Europe. No one accepted the Jews more than the Germans, and then this terrible division was driven into the society on a maniacal level. And it's still one of the great puzzles, and one of the great, great tragedies of Europe. The Soviet Union also suffered this because they got rid of their middle class in another way, their bourgeoisie – the Jews were a part of the bourgeoisie – and, of course, you depend on a bourgeoisie for culture. That's where the heart of culture lies.

I hope that this film has some contribution to make. I never want to overstate the case with these kinds of things, but as anti-Semitism is again on the rise, I think it's important that these films are seen – films like *Taking Sides, The Pianist, Schindler's List* – because they remind people of the great tragedy that occurred in 1933 to 1945.

**This story offers a chilling challenge to the consciences of all artists.**

Well, this was in my mind throughout the writing of the play. How would I have reacted if the head of state had telephoned me and said, 'Mr Harwood, you are my favourite playwright, I'd like you to come and read your plays to me.' I'd have said, 'No, I'm sorry. I don't approve of what you're doing.' Oh really? I hope I would have done that, but I don't think I would. I was a great opponent of apartheid, but at a distance of six thousand miles. I was never in danger. No one threatened my wife, no one threatened my children, no one threatened me. So it's easy to be brave, at a distance, geographically and historically. It's very easy to have a view of how one would have behaved, fifty or sixty years after the war. I think these are important questions for all of us: how would we have behaved? And, of course, it's asked at the end of the film.

**There was a very interesting use of archive film of the real Furtwängler concert at the end of the film.**

That is a piece of pure Szabó. He found this archive material. Furtwängler leans forward and shakes Göbbels hand and then wipes his hand with a handkerchief. István then rocked it and it's repeated several times, the wiping of hand with the handkerchief. Somehow it tilts the balance a little bit. I'm absolutely sure it tilts the balance in favour of Furtwängler and doesn't leave it ambiguous enough. I've had that all the time with questions I've had in Q&As in L.A. and Britain. It's *Taking Sides* just a little bit. And I don't like it. It does look like Pontius Pilate.

The play just ends with Arnold saying, 'Turn it off.' And that just seemed to me a subtle way of illustrating the battle between the new world and the old world.

**What happened to Furtwängler after the events of your film?**

He was denazified after two days of hearings. Immediately, Yehudi Menuhin, who was in London, of course, and Benjamin Britten travelled to Berlin to play with him, to show solidarity, that they had no question of forgiveness but that they accepted him again into the musical community of the world. And I think that was a most marvellous gesture.

Menuhin saw the play in London – it must have been about a year before he died – and took us to dinner afterwards. And I asked him, 'What was it like to play the Beethoven Violin Concerto with Furtwängler conducting?' And he thought for a moment and he said, 'Like floating on air.' The most wonderful tribute to a conductor, I think.

### Furtwängler said something that made a great impression on you.

Furtwängler had a very bad downbeat. He couldn't bring the orchestra in very well. He didn't like to. And somebody said to him once, 'Maestro, why don't you give a more positive downbeat? Obviously you can do it. Why don't you do it?' And he thought for a moment and he said the most wonderful thing. He said, 'An orchestra must play when it has no alternative.' And that's true about all creative art. I know, as a writer, you should write only when you have no alternative. You can't make yourself write, you can't want to write. You have to write when there's nothing else you can do. And it's true. I think it's the most marvellous insight into the creative process from Furtwängler. 'An orchestra must only play when it has no alternative.' And it's the most beautiful expression of creative art.

I think *Taking Sides* may help the politicians; I'm not sure it helps the people at all. If art was a protection against barbarism, the Holocaust would never have happened. Germany was a most cultured nation, so art wasn't a protection. Barbarism won. But that's not to say that artists and people involved in making movies and plays and writing music and books shouldn't keep trying. That's the point.

# The Pianist

Adapted from the memoir, *The Pianist* (aka *Death of a City*), by Wladyslaw Szpilman
Directed by Roman Polanski
Produced by Alain Sarde, Robert Benmussa and Roman Polanski
Executive Producers: Timothy Burrill, Henning Molfenter and Lew Rywin
Starring Adrien Brody, Thomas Kretschmann, Frank Finlay, Maureen Lipman, Emilia Fox and Ed Stoppard
Production Companies: R.P. Productions, Heritage Films, Studio Babelsberg, Runteam Ltd., Agencja Produkcji Filmowej, Beverly Detroit, Canal+ Polska, Canal+, FilmFernshFonds Bayern, Filmboard Berlin-Brandenburg (FBB), Filmförderungsanstalt (FFA), Interscope Communications, Mainstream S.A., Studio Canal and Telewizja Polska (TVP)
Distributors: Bac Films (France), Wild Side Vidéo (France), 01 Distribuzione (Italy), A-Film Distribution (Netherlands), Alfa Films (Argentina), Amuse Pictures Inc. (Japan), Bergvik (Iceland), Europa Filmes (Brazil), Focus Features (USA), Frenetic Films (Switzerland), Gateno Films (Peru), Impuls Home Entertainment (Switzerland), Tobis StudioCanal (Germany), Transeuropa Video Entertainment (Argentina), United King Films (Israel), Universal (UK), Universal Studios Home Video (USA), UFA (Germany)

*Taken from the memoir of Wladyslaw Szpilman who recorded his survival during the Second World War. A renowned pianist, he played the last live music heard over Polish Radio before the Nazi invasion. During the brutal occupation, he eluded deportation, eventually escaped the devastated Warsaw Ghetto and struggled in near isolation to stay alive, entirely surrounded by the enemy. His ultimate salvation came from the unlikeliest source – a German officer who helped him hide during the final days of the war.*

- The memoir was first published in Poland in 1946 under the title *Death of a City* but was soon suppressed by the Communists until the dissipation of the Soviet block when publication again became possible thanks to the efforts of Wladyslaw Szpilman's son.
- The film was released in 2002.

Winner of three Oscars including Best Actor, Best Director and Best Writing (Screenplay Based on Material Previously Produced or Published) along with four other nominations for Best Cinematography, Best Costume Design, Best Editing and Best Picture; nominated for an American Screenwriters Association Award; winner of two BAFTA Awards with five further nominations; winner of the Palme d'Or Cannes Film Festival; winner of seven César Awards plus a further three nominations; winner of a European Film Award plus three further nominations; amongst numerous other awards.

**What drew you to The Pianist *and how did you get*** ***started on the project?***

Well, as I've already said, it found me. Roman Polanski had seen the wonderful French production of my play, *Taking Sides*, in Paris, and from that, thought I might be right for *The Pianist.*

In the sixty odd years following the Second World War, there have been countless plays and films dealing, in one way or another, with the industrial slaughter of the Jews. Among the most memorable for me were *The Diary of Anne Frank*, both as a play and a film, *Judgement at Nuremberg* with Spencer Tracy, *Ghetto* by Joshua Sobel, Stephen Spielberg's *Schindler's List*, and recently, as I mentioned, *Conspiracy*, starring Kenneth Branagh as Heydrich, dealing brilliantly, I thought, with the Wannsee Conference where the Final Solution was discussed and decided.

*The Pianist* also deals with a dreadful historical event. You can't start glamorising it, you can't start trying to soften it. You have to tell it as you believe it is. And there is no ultimate truth of it because you can't explain that to anybody, so the truth is very difficult to get at. But whatever the truth is within one on that subject, you have to be true to that truth.

A decided lack of sentimentality was especially evident when I first read *The Pianist*. Szpilman wrote of his experiences but as if they had happened to someone else. He simply described the terror without comment, without reference to his own suffering or courage, without saying, 'Wasn't this appalling?' or 'Wasn't I lucky?' And I found it so interesting because, years before, researching *Ivan Denisovich*, I had been obliged to read several accounts written by survivors of the Gulag, accounts which had been smuggled out to the West. All of them, without exception, were little more than personal complaints, railing against the fate that had condemned each author to such horror. Solzhenitsyn's novel was entirely without complaint and, as I said, described a good day in Ivan Denisovich's life. So it was in *The Pianist*. Szpilman kept his distance from his own suffering.

There was another element in Szpilman's book that spoke directly to me and that was the appearance near the end of the German officer, Captain Wilm Hosenfeld, who saved Szpilman's life.

It was known that Polanski had turned down an offer from Steven Spielberg to direct *Schindler's List*, which is set in the Krakow ghetto from which Polanski himself had escaped at the age of six. His parents and sister were taken off to the camps; his father and sister survived but not his mother. His reasons for rejecting Spielberg's offer were that the events would have been too close to him, the people too familiar. He had known most of them and some were still alive. But *The Pianist* offered a means of expressing his own feelings about the horror of his appalling childhood.

We met in Paris where he lives and to my astonishment, in no time at all, discovered that we agreed on the form and content of the film. I also discovered in the course of our first conversation that he too kept his distance from the past, and when he recounted some of his memories it was as an observer, not a participant, which accorded precisely with Szpilman's own amazing objectivity.

The most important thing about the book which we were determined to capture in the movie was the point of view: Szpilman's distance from his own story. That was absolutely crucial to our approach. I think that's the first thing I said to Polanski when I met him. 'We've got to keep that distance.'

A few days later, he decided we should go to Warsaw, mainly because he wanted us to look at sickening archive footage shot by the Nazis and to inspect the place where the Jews had been walled in and then sent to their annihilation. For three successive days, we sat in a viewing theatre to watch the grainy black and white record of the brutal destruction of Warsaw's Jews, most of it never shown to the public at large, it's so awful. They were a deeply depressing few days but we were, without being wholly aware of it, beginning the process of creating our own truth to which we would have to be true. Looking back, I suspect the archive footage was of more value to Polanski than to me because when he and the production designer, Allan Starski, came to reproduce the ghetto they were able to do so with ruthless accuracy. But it somehow brought the whole event into me in a way that was difficult to do from scratch. It was a very good reference.

I returned to London and began writing the screenplay. No, that's not strictly accurate. I found I didn't know how to begin. Polanski would call me from time to time and ask how I was getting on. I lied and said it was going swimmingly. But at last, I was forced to confess the truth. 'I don't know how to begin,' I said. Polanski exploded. 'For God's sake,' he cried, 'the book's called *The Pianist!* Start with him playing the piano!' And that was it. That's what I did. It's so simple when you hear it. And from that moment the screenplay began its journey.

I was determined to preserve the author's approach as observer. But, with Polanski's agreement, I was also determined not to use a voice-over, not to have Szpilman as narrator. This, of course, presented problems. Szpilman is alone for much of the story. He has no one to confide in. So the emotional content had to emerge from the action without any help from us.

My main task was to turn Szpilman and his family into characters who lived and breathed. In the book, they are more or less symbolic figures – mother, father, sisters, brother. So I delved into the book in great detail, trying to discern clues to these people in the hope that I wouldn't create stereotypes. And it's odd that Szpilman is much more forthcoming about many of the other characters he describes and it was as if he was being reticent about his family because the memory of them was too painful.

In due course I delivered the screenplay. Polanski made very encouraging noises but added, rather ominously I thought, 'Now we lock ourselves up until we're totally happy.'

To do this we repaired to a house near Rambouillet, south-west of Paris, where for four weeks we were locked up together and worked every day from 10am till 6pm. But – it's very difficult to describe what he wanted – he wanted precise details of what he was going to shoot, but mostly he was very concerned about historical accuracy.

We began our work, at Polanski's insistence, on the end of the film, not the concert with which he was completely satisfied and never questioned but with the scenes concerning the German officer. He didn't want many changes but that's where we began because what I think Polanski was doing was finding a way for his imagination to enter fully into the story so that he could always keep in mind our final objective.

We'd act out scenes aloud and when he wasn't sure I understood exactly what he wanted, he'd draw the location or the prop or the camera angle. He is a gifted artist so his sketches were enormously helpful. When a problem arose and I'd make a suggestion that wasn't to his liking, he'd react as though I'd insulted his wife. 'You crazy? That's terrible!' he'd cry. 'Let's have a coffee.' And when I suggested something of which he did approve, he would be equally extreme: 'That's great, my God, that's great. Let's have a coffee!' We drank a lot of coffee.

In retrospect, I see now that we were not simply finalising a technical document but trying to ensure that there was no falsehood or bogus emotion in our account of Szpilman's story. You would be hard pressed to find two less sentimental men than Polanski and me and any hint of it we both instantly recognised and excised.

In search of our own truth, for much of the time as I've said, Polanski was dredging his own memories for details and incidents. There was one in particular I remember. I had accurately reproduced the moment in the book when a Jewish policeman saves Szpilman from boarding a cattle truck bound for Treblinka. Szpilman describes himself running from the scene. 'No!' Polanski said. 'I'll tell you what happened to me, it'll be better.' Apparently he too was saved in a similar manner but when he'd been pulled out from the crowd and started to run, his saviour hissed, 'Walk! Don't run!' And so we changed it. In the film Szpilman walks slowly towards the gates while the Germans herd his family and all the others into the trucks. I knew it was a reality I personally could not have invented.

Despite the subject matter we laughed a lot, making dreadful jokes in bad taste about Jews, Poles and Germans. It was the only way to get through. A month to the day later, we finished. Once back in Paris, he presented me with a gift: an espresso coffee machine.

There were no further changes to the screenplay. Polanski allowed no interference from anyone. As a matter of fact, if an actor wanted to change a line, Polanski would call me from the location or the studio floor and ask my opinion. Inevitably I said my line was better and in every case Polanski agreed and refused the change.

Enormous care was taken with the casting of the Szpilman family because Polanski wanted the six of them to have a believable physical resemblance, and this I think we achieved. And then there was something a little more subtle concerning accents.

For the purposes of the movie, English stood for the Polish language and the Germans spoke in German, which we sub-titled. So the dialogue I wrote for the Poles was neutral, that is to say I had to avoid slang and English colloquialisms or any attempt to make the lines sound as if they were translations. But how would they be spoken? What accents were the actors to use? Polanski decided that they should find or be given an unidentifiable accent, a sound that was impossible to place precisely. This, as far as I know, has never been remarked on by critics, which is exactly how it should be. The effect, as we hoped, was unnoticeable.

There are curious side effects from creating fiction out of historical subjects. For example, there are always experts and critics who know more than the filmmakers or the playwright. Theatre critics are particularly skilled at telling you what play they would have written on the subject if they could write plays which, of course, they can't. Then there are the meetings with witnesses, especially Holocaust survivors or their children who are either grateful or hostile.

One case was particularly interesting to me. After *The Pianist* was shown in the United States, an article appeared in *The Wall Street Journal* written by a son of Holocaust survivors, attacking the film for including the Poles who had helped Szpilman and the German officer, Captain Wilm Hosenfeld, who eventually saved him. The writer's main thrust was directed against the German officer whose presence in the film, the writer asserted, distorted history and was meat and drink to apologists and, indeed, to Holocaust deniers. I was rather shocked by the reaction. In the first place, the incident was true. Neither Polanski nor I would have dared invent him. As it later transpired, Szpilman was not the only Jew saved by Captain Hosenfeld. In the second place, as I indicated earlier, he was one of the main reasons I was so captivated by the book. It seemed to me then, and does so now, that Hosenfeld's courage and humanity sounded a note of reconciliation in which I believe passionately. I have the good fortune to have my plays and films taught in Holocaust studies in Germany where a great effort has been made to face its terrible past. I believe reconciliation to be absolutely essential if the history about which I and others have written is never to be repeated.

### How different is that experience, being locked away with a director for several weeks, from the normal writing process?

I'd not done it before, I have to say. But it cemented not only Roman's and my friendship, but our collaboration. And when we came to *Oliver Twist*, we didn't lock ourselves up. We took ten days to do what we did in four or five weeks because we knew each other. And there were very few changes in *Oliver Twist* in comparison to *The Pianist.*

It depends on the personalities of the two people involved. And we just happen to be friends from the first day we met. That's how it was.

### Polanski's direct personal knowledge of the subject matter must have been unique in your experience.

Roman was a wonderful touchstone because it happened to him. But in Krakow; this was set in Warsaw. But I always had him as my yardstick. He was only small when the war broke out. When they invaded in 1939, he would have been six. But he has a remarkable visual memory.

**Szpilman's memoir relates impressions and events, but isn't at all forthcoming about character. How did you get past that?**

In the book, mother, father, brother and two sisters are simply mentioned like that. They have no character at all. They're not developed in any way by the author. So that was my main task, to give those people character. His own character comes out because that's what the book's about, it's about him. But the siblings and the parents are not touched on. So when you ask about character, I didn't think about what their backgrounds would be. They came alive to me as I wrote them. They're just alive, inside one somehow. It's awfully hard to describe the presentation of character in plays and films. They're there or they're not there. I don't know how else to describe it. But that's what I had to do.

**But whatever the process, it's crucial to the laying out of the story. It's the whole resonance of that family.**

Precisely, and you can't teach that. That's the gift that you have or you don't have. But people who want to write screenplays had better have that gift.

**Considering all the films that have dealt with this period, it's surprising that we have never before seen it from the point of view of such a detailed degeneration from normality to brutality.**

The closing in, that was very much Polanski. He knew it and we plotted that very carefully – the closing in, the regulations that were issued to the Jews and so on. I did an awful lot of background reading about the historical incidences that lead to the invasion of Poland by the Nazis. All that's accurate, of course.

*There are wonderful establishing details: the BBC
wireless broadcast, the family's celebration meal,
thinking Poland is saved by Britain's declaration of war
on Germany, with the father saying, 'All will be well,'
and then the cut to the Nazis marching through the city.*

That's my favourite cut.

*The early scene where the family is deciding where to
hide their money is very revealing about each of them,
their personal attributes.*

Exposition is the hardest thing to hide but there's brilliant
exposition in that scene, I must say. You get that one of the
daughters is a lawyer very easily. Szpilman's brother was the
most difficult character to write, that sort of constant nihilistic
view of the world.

We also did the very clever thing of getting their diction,
neither American nor English, but slightly foreign. We had a
special coach do that.

*Was it an actual newspaper report, the one about
'Emblems for Jews', read by the father to the family?*

Yes, we had very good people in Warsaw providing us with
any information we needed. We'd phone through or I would
ask Roman to find out – because obviously he speaks Polish –
and he would come back to me. And I adapted it for the
length of the scene. And it's pretty well accurate.

Newspaper reports are shown in the same way as today's
television news.

This is very much Polanski. Because he remembered the
reading of newspapers. That was the way they got
information and that's what gives it authenticity, I think.

### What sort of thing did Polanski bring to the writing process?

Roman and I improvised the scene with the piano buyer. I'd written it and he said, 'Let's try and get it more lively.' He wanted a different kind of vitality to the scene, which I was very happy to take from him. And so we improvised it. He played the piano buyer and I played the other parts. He was brilliant as the piano buyer. And when it was pretty good I took notes and then I wrote it that evening and that was it. That was in the film.

### You gave Dorota the line 'It's too absurd' when she sympathises with Szpilman as he's being moved to the ghetto.

I kept wanting to use the word 'absurd' because I wanted that to have a contemporary echo to the Theatre of the Absurd, to the madness of the world. And, although I don't think it is a period word for that, it seemed to me good for this purpose.

### How much invention did you need? For instance, the building of the ghetto wall?

The wall going up is in the book because it was a crucial event. I put that in the very first draft, I remember. They see the wall, that's how it is, there's no other way to tell the story. I think in the book, Szpilman walks round and sees the wall being built, I can't remember precisely. But there's no way other than just doing it and we did it. It tells you the story, that's all.

And the demented woman looking for her husband during the walk in the ghetto, that's all taken directly from the book. The waiting at the gates by the tram crossing is all graphically described in the book. I didn't have to do anything. So is the scene where Szpilman plays the piano in the restaurant for the smugglers and black marketeers. I think I invented the character who talks about building a bridge over the tram crossing in order to give information that's probably in the narrative of the book. It's wonderfully directed by Polanski.

I wrote the scene in the printers at length and Roman wanted it written at length. And then he filmed it at length and cut it afterwards. He cut it in the editing. He actually called me over to France to come and help him cut it. And I can't remember what we cut but I went and sat with them while they cut it. That's totally unusual, a director bringing a writer in on the editing.

### In writing that scene at length, did Polanski have a pre-thought-out plan?

No, I don't think so. We thought we needed a longer scene. And then he shot it at the length I wrote it. Then, when he came to edit it, he thought it was too long and that's when he decided it needed to be cut.

### How did you go about creating the life inside the ghetto?

All that detail of the dead bodies on the streets is all taken from those three days of watching archive material. It's wonderfully filmed. And parcels being thrown over the walls from the other side, that's in the book.

Now, the boy trying to get under the wall and being prevented from the other side is also from the book. But I wrote it as it is, and then we had a long discussion about whether you should see the other side of the wall. I wrote it exactly like that because it's only seen from Szpilman's point of view in the book but he could hear the beating on the other side. And we decided – it was one of the key things, I

113

think – we decided that this is how you kept your distance. This is as close as we get. I don't think we even see the boy's face, just being objective about what was happening instead of going into close shot.

Then the scene where Szpilman flatters the Jewish policeman in order to save his brother, 'They told me you were an important man,' that's all invention. A lot of the dramatisation was in order to find a way of giving information without its being too obviously exposition information. You had to dramatise a scene where the information could legitimately be given. And that was tough. I found it so.

**When you were writing, did Polanski at any stage give you any idea of the kind of designs he wanted for it or did he just give you a free hand?**

A free hand.

**Presumably the setting with the bridge is very accurate, with the road and the tram underneath?**

Oh, very accurate. And the film cameras; we wanted film cameras. We watched these three days of archives and the extraordinary thing is how many films they made of these things. Extraordinary. They must have had cameras everywhere, so we put that in the shot as they cross the bridge.

**Were all the actors in the family actually Jewish?**

No, I don't think so.

*I remember reading somewhere Spielberg saying how, when they did* Schindler's List, *the actors playing Nazis and the actors playing Jews were very much split apart.*

Polanski might have done that. What we wanted in the family was a look-alike family and they've all got a very good facial resemblance. The shape of faces.

Roman has a theory that everyone in movies is only there for one reason, and that's because of what they look like, not because of how they can act. It doesn't matter how gifted they are. If you look at *The Pianist,* it's very interesting how he's cast the family. He'd cast Adrien Brody, which was the lynchpin of that casting. And then everybody else has a physical resemblance to him. That was Polanski's theory. And they all had to speak in the same way. He had voice coaches to do all that. So if they don't look right, they don't get the part. And he's probably right.

*Was the father's speech over the dinner table, saying American Jews should have done something to bring America into the war to help, taken from the book?*

No, we brought that up. We wanted to hit that hard.

*The scene where the Nazis raid the house opposite the family seems all the more violent and shocking by keeping its limited perspective.*

It's described in the book but this is a crucial scene in the film of keeping one's distance. We see what happens from this side of the street and from this angle. We never go into the other room. It's watched from the family's point of view; it's all from this side. In a Hollywood movie, you would have gone in that room, seen close shots of the faces looking horrified. We resisted that and I think that's what gives it great power.

**Was that actively discussed, not going into the room across the road?**

In the screenplay it's described as we shot it. It was always like that. We were determined not to do it the usual way, not to shoot cover from another perspective. It was discussed at our first meeting. And 'No voice-over', I remember saying that. The temptation is enormous when you've just got one man throughout a whole story.

**So basically you and Polanski had the same vision throughout.**

We did. We didn't have conflict at all. We knew that we had to tell the story as objectively as we could. And once you put a voice-over in, you're dead because it's no longer objective. I'm not against voice-overs in principle. I think they're good from time to time. But it does mean that you have a subjective point of view. We didn't want that. And we didn't want flash-backs. We didn't want to invent a constant friend that he could talk to. And that was quite difficult. I think it was one of the reasons I couldn't get started. But once I did start, I was fine.

There's not an awful lot of dialogue in the picture. There is dialogue, but not a lot. It was to tell the story, visually and pictorially, that was the challenge and I think we did that well. And we don't dwell on the emotion of it. Either you get it or you don't. And you know, when it was first shown, it was criticised for that.

**The scene where the family waits for the train to deport them is a very powerful milestone in the film.**

This is another scene that I wrote at length that they chopped in editing. I think Polanski just shot in sequence and then edited it as it is now. It was the placing of the moment, when the family are reunited, that was put later.

The most difficult speech I had to write was in the scene about the girl who smothered her baby so as not to give away their hiding place to the Nazis.

And the brother's *Merchant of Venice* quote. We don't tell you where it's from, you're supposed to know it comes from *The Merchant of Venice*. But if you don't, it doesn't matter. But the Hollywood studio executives – I don't want to be too hard on them and they do make some terrific movies – but they do like things to be explicit. And explained.

Now the moment where the father buys a caramel and cuts it up for every member of the family, their last supper together, that was in the book. Those are things you can't invent.

And the lines I'm most proud of in the film are where Szpilman tells his youngest sister he wished he got to know her better on their way to the train that will take the family to their death.

I've already talked about the moment the Jews are being shoved onto the trains and a Jewish policeman pulls Szpilman out of the crowd and tells him to get the hell out. I followed the book and said, 'The man says to him run.' But when we were working through it in detail and Roman told me what happened to him – the chap shouted 'don't run' – I could never have invented that. In that terrible situation of German guards, armed guards, people being shoved into cattle trucks, that would never have occurred to me to have been so cool about it. And Roman put that in and I think that works terribly well. Pure Polanski, from being there.

And he is wonderful, Polanski. He doesn't put any of the family in the front of the freight wagon when we see them being taken away, except for the father. There's no emphasis on it and that's the last you see of them. It's just very well done.

And after the family is taken away on the train, from then on, it's really almost like a silent movie. And the images have to match the action. The deserted ghetto is an obvious example.

Now Polanski surprised me with the scene where Szpilman hides under the piano stage. Because when he shot it, I didn't know it was going to be upside down. But I think it's quite wonderful.

And the taking down of the wall, that's good storytelling, I think.

The scene with the arbitrary shooting of workers, that was in the book. But in the book, he doesn't run out of ammunition and reload. We put that in.

I found all the scenes on the building site were difficult to write because there's so much prose information from the book and you want to do it in character.

But I must say, what I love about Polanski is that he doesn't tell the story in the straightforward way. He doesn't spell it out. You find it.

### From the moment the family is deported, was it a conscious decision to go for short progressive vignettes with very little dialogue?

No, I just followed the storyline of the book. I didn't make a conscious decision. And what I didn't know was how many dissolves Polanski was going to use. He dissolves, you know, and that's a good time lapse. I was always worried about time lapse, that it should seem long. But the dissolves did it for me.

***In a film with such demands, where the main character is seen to physically degenerate, did they try to stick to a sequential order in shooting the story?***

They had to film Adrien Brody, who played Szpilman, thin. I don't know whether that was first or second. They must have done him thin first. I think he was on a diet before we started. And the others, but they weren't on the strict diet he was. It was so depressing for him. And long period too. God, he lost a lot of weight. It was very hard on him.

In the story, Szpilman's decision to escape the ghetto seems almost foolhardy in its bravery.

People accused us of having a very passive character to whom things happened, but here Szpilman makes his own decision. It's small, but it's all you could do in those circumstances. And that decision, a dangerous decision, changes his life. So when we were accused of saying 'how lucky he was', Roman said to me, 'How do you think I survived?' He was lucky.

The scene where the Nazi guard searches the grain sack and doesn't find the hidden weapons, that's luck, isn't it? That's straight from the book. He didn't find the gun. It's down to luck and the stupidity of the Germans.

And the scene where the work party are returning to the ghetto and are just beaten by the Nazi officer rather than shot. That was pure luck. That character was a mad sadist as he was in the book.

**Once Szpilman escapes from the ghetto, it becomes a different kind of storytelling. Almost exclusively imagery rather than dialogue.**

Yes, starting with his throwing the Star of David armband in a milk churn. I think that sort of detail was left to Roman on the set. I don't think I would have written in that churn.

And then walking the street outside the ghetto at night, there you have to tell the story with pictures only. There's no other way of telling it. It was harder. But we just kept it very simple.

At the house of his friends, Szpilman has a bath. That is my invention because I have a cleanliness fetish and it's one of the things I'd want immediately under those circumstances. Washing away where one had been, and the burning of the clothes of course.

And we were extremely lucky with Krzysztof Pieczynski, the actor playing Gebczynski, the man who helps Szpilman to a new hiding place. He's frightfully good. So unsentimental, that's what I love about it. It's wonderful when you have an actor who doesn't have a huge part but brings absolutely everything to it. Wonderful. The world, he brings his whole world to it. Just lovely.

Then in the first safe house, there's more Polanski brilliance. His framing of the shot when Szpilman is lying down is very original. You see the feet first, and you don't pan up to the head. It's just quite unexpected and brilliant in its simplicity.

Seeing the brutal response to the uprising in the ghetto was shot very realistically, as if the audience was actually witnessing it from a safe distance.

That was the first uprising in the ghetto. It's very accurate because it's all taken from the newsreels that we saw. It's a famous piece of film that we re-staged. And the sets are bloody good.

And you see, the machine gunning of those who surrendered, Polanski's dissolve is wonderful there. Not a cut, but a dissolve. Which I didn't write in, of course; these were editing decisions. And that's precisely what I mean about not writing too much of the technical matters into the screenplay because they're decisions, first, for the director, and then, for the editor. You know, one's inclined to write the transition in, but it's not necessarily the way to do it.

Time lapses are very, very difficult things in movies. When Dorota visits Szpilman, it's a short scene but it's got the dissolve in it so you have a sense of time passing.

And again, when Szpilman is warned to leave the safe house, the constant points of view of Szpilman. We don't break it, we don't go downstairs. It's very subtly done.

Incidentally, when Szpilman is placing the chair in order to jump out the window if the Germans come for him, it's quite differently described in the book, but Roman didn't believe it so we did it our way instead.

It's interesting that the woman neighbour at the safe house who discovers Szpilman and tries to give him up was a Pole. They were pretty much the most anti-Semitic nation in Europe at the time. They were very happy to get rid of their Jews.

Then when Szpilman is looking for another safe house, that's all our invention. And a pretty good invention, I think. The girl, Dorota, isn't in the book at all. We invented her as a way of giving a certain kind of information, a bridge between normality and then the horror. In the book, there were other people he stayed with. He was passed from one family, one friend, one ally to another. But you can't do it like that. We wanted something personal and dramatic. So as Szpilman rests, he sees the girl playing the cello. And that was Roman. I knew when he said it to me that it was a brilliant piece of invention. This is a filmmaker's piece of invention, not a writer's. This was put in after the first draft. It's wonderful, a pregnant woman playing the cello. It's just pure filmmaker's vision. And the actress, Emilia Fox, is a cellist too which is a great help.

**Szpilman becomes dependent on Szalas, a new contact charged with looking after him, who turns out to be an appalling, self-serving character. Was he real?**

Yes, that's from the book, but those sort of people exist in all our daily lives. Andrew Tiernan, who plays Szalas, is so good, such a believable character. And his trick of opening a bottle of vodka is a typical Polish thing, which only Roman and the other Poles on the set knew. You could knock the cork out of a Polish vodka bottle by hitting it on the bottom. You can't do it with an English bottle. And, again, the scene ends with another wonderful dissolve.

**When the girl discovers Szpilman lying dangerously ill from malnutrition, there's another particularly wonderful cut.**

That was my invention, that cut. I remember Roman doubted it would work, but it did. You go from the man listening to the girl's suggestion to get a doctor, and then straight to the doctor and it works very well.

***The next milestone comes when Szpilman has to flee the safe house following the fighting on the streets.***

The dates are crucial in the Polish historical memory. That's the Polish uprising. Large chunks of the book were ignored obviously because some of it is repetitive of course, passing from one safe house to another.

***And was there really a hospital just across the road from Szpilman?***

The fact was that the hospital was absolutely opposite and the Germans were bringing many of the wounded from the Russian Front there.

***When Szpilman is searching for drinking water in the abandoned hospital, he finally  resorts to drinking water from a hospital fire bucket.***

There were much closer shots. It was more graphically described in my screenplay and in the book, the flies in the water. But Roman or the editor, I can't remember, thought it was better just done more obliquely as we had done for the rest of the picture. You could see just enough of it.

And we had wonderful special effects. Like the burning of the pile of bodies across the road from the hospital. It's wonderfully cheated, it all looks so real.

***Would the reintroduction of the imagined 'musical' themes that Szpilman experiences, such as in the hospital, be at your discretion?***

No, at Roman's. I never write music into a screenplay. I probably said, 'He practices with his fingers,' but I wouldn't have intended music to be heard. Never, never, never. My God, one of my golden rules. A lot of screenwriters do. They say 'Music builds'. I don't do that at all. You cannot tell, until you've got the picture, whether you need it or not. But some people believe they can, but that's something I can't do.

**When Szpilman is finally forced to flee the sanctuary of the hospital, he sees for the first time the complete destruction of Warsaw.**

That is the famous shot. It's described in the screenplay, and that is how Roman filmed it. And it has now become, I think, a rather famous shot.

**Where on earth did you film such devastation? Is it a set?**

No, what they did – it's a wonderful story, this – they were looking for a place they could destroy. And they looked all over Europe. They thought they'd just have to get Adrien to go there. And our producer, Robert Benmussa, was having a meeting with the Mayor of Berlin who said, 'But I've got Russian barracks we want to get rid of. In East Berlin. It's round the corner from you.' They wanted to destroy some abandoned Russian barracks. So we blew them up. Yes, it was perfect. The desolation.

**Then comes the remarkable sequence when Szpilman is discovered by the German officer who asks him to play the piano that's in the bombed-out hiding place.**

Played by Thomas Kretschmann, he's bloody good. Yes, there was a discussion here about how long the music should be. I said it should be short and Roman said, 'No, you must play it at full length.' And he was right. And it's his cutaway that's wonderful. As the music plays, you go outside to the chauffeur waiting in the cold. That was Roman's cutaway. It's an editorial decision. It only happens once but it's enough to break the long piece. But it does work because it has that humanising effect. Absolutely.

All of that comes from the book. Of course we must have fiddled with it a bit. But what the German says, what he brings him, the evacuation – it's all in the book, and I just simply edited it and elided it.

And then seeing that same German officer imprisoned by the Russians as Szpilman's colleagues return, passing by him. That is absolutely from the book.

### Did they find out anything else about the German officer, about what kind of war he had?

No, Szpilman's son found out much later. In the 1990s they found out who he was. He had saved other Jews.

Szpilman's book was first published in 1946 and it was called *Death of a City*. But the Communists banned it because it was too much about Jews and not enough about Poles. Then when Communism fell, Szpilman's son, a dentist who lives in Berlin, had it re-published and edited it and probably made a better edition of it.

And during the course of that, he was making enquiries and stumbled across another Jew who knew about this German officer. And they found out that his name was Wilm Hosenfeld and that he'd saved two or three other Jews. And they found his family in Germany and there was a picture of him with his family. And Szpilman identified him and said, 'Yes, that's him.' And when the film came out and they gave it rave reviews, The *Mail on Sunday* sent a reporter to Hosenfeld's decendents – a grandchild or maybe even a daughter, I don't remember.

**We then see Szpilman playing for Polish Radio again and seeing his old musical colleague.**

That's one of my favourite bits in the whole picture. That moment. A lovely moment, between the two of them.

**And you just wrote, 'he plays the piano here'.**

I didn't specify the music, no.

**You mentioned that you'd only had one query from your producers over the original draft of your screenplay.**

Yes, this was the only question I had from the producers. I wrote the piano concerto in, at the end of my very first draft. And they said, 'It's very expensive,' I said, 'I know' and Roman said, 'We'll have it.'

And the closing title sequence is the best title sequence, for those long titles, ever done in a movie, in my view. To Chopin.

# *Oliver Twist*

Adapted from the novel *Oliver Twist* by Charles Dickens
Directed by Roman Polanski
Produced by Alain Sarde, Robert Benmussa and Roman Polanski
Executive Producers: Timothy Burrill and Petr Moravec
Starring Ben Kingsley, Jamie Foreman, Barney Clark, Harry Eden, Leanne Rowe, Edward Hardwick, Mark Strong, Alun Armstrong, Ian McNeice, Liz Smith, Timothy Bateson and Andy de la Tour
Production Companies: Runteam II Ltd., ETIC Films, Medusa Produzione, R.P. Productions, Runteam Ltd
Distributors: Sony Pictures Entertainment (USA), Summit Entertainment, A-Film Distribution (Netherlands), Columbia TriStar Films de Argentina (Argentina), Filmax S.A. (Spain), Medusa Distribuzione (Italy), Monopole-Pathé (Switzerland), Pathé (France), Pathé (UK), Pinema (Turkey), SPI International (Czech Republic), Shaw Organisation (Singapore), Tobis Film GmbH & Co. KG (Germany), Toshiba Entertainment Inc. (Japan), TriStar Pictures, UFA (Germany)

*Oliver Twist is Charles Dickens' classic novel about a charming orphan boy whose life seems to depend entirely upon the whims of fate. Abandoned early in his life, Oliver seems doomed to life in a workhouse, where he is farmed out to a local undertaker and is regularly underfed and mistreated. Hoping to improve his lot in life, Oliver runs away to London, where he falls in with a gang of petty criminals led by Fagin and the young pickpocket, the Artful Dodger. His relief at this new situation is short lived when he meets Mr Brownlow, who sees Oliver's true character and potential and seems determined to intervene with destiny.*

- Dickens began the serial publication of *Oliver Twist* in 1837 in *Bentley's Miscellany*.
- The film was released in 2005.

Nominated for two Young Artist Awards including Best International Family Film and Best Performance in an International Feature Film (Barney Clark).

Note: Although the novel favours the spelling 'Sikes', it occasionally also uses 'Sykes'. As the latter was preferred for the screenplay, that is the spelling used for the purposes of this book.

**When you and Roman Polanski decided to do** Oliver
Twist, **the setting up of the film must rank amongst
the quickest on record. How did it come about?**

Well, this is exactly what happened. We were looking for a
year for another subject for a film after *The Pianist* and we
wanted to make something that would appeal to children as
well. And I read a lot of fairy stories and none of them made
any sense to me, nor to Roman I have to say.

I was being interviewed by a young woman for a
newspaper and I'd said to my wife, 'I don't want any calls,'
obviously. And suddenly my wife came into the room and
said, 'Ronnie, you'd better take this call. It's Roman.' So I left
the young woman and went through to the kitchen where
my wife had taken the call. And Roman said, 'Ronnie, I'm in a
restaurant. I'm just finishing lunch.' It must have been about
four o'clock in the afternoon. He said, 'I have only two words
to say to you: *Oliver Twist*.' And I said, 'Terrific'. I came back
into the room. The interviewer didn't say anything to me,
which struck me as odd as she'd heard my wife say, 'Roman
Polanski' and I had said, 'Terrific' in some excitement. But she
didn't pick up on that at all. She could have had a tiny little
exclusive, but she didn't.

After she left I then called Roman back and said that we
ought to announce the film because it's in the public
domain. And we talked to our agent, Jeff Berg, in California,
and Berg put it into the trades the next day – that was on a
Friday – and by the Monday we had a vast number of
companies around the world, thirty-five I think, wanting to
be part of it in financial terms. And that was that. It was all
very quick.

**That's the combination of you and Polanski, obviously, having worked on The Pianist.**

I rather think the other way round, Polanski and me. Yes. (*Laughter*)

**Has that ever happened to you before, where a project's come together so quickly?**

No, never. Not at that speed. I've never known it. It may have happened to Polanski on *The Pianist*, but that would have been before I came on board. Although I think he may have had problems getting the money for *The Pianist,* but it was all there in principle by the time I was employed. So I don't know what his experience is, but certainly mine, I have never known anything like the setting up of *Oliver Twist*. It was amazing. It was quite a big movie. I think the budget was sixty million dollars.

**Was there any reason for choosing the Oxford World's Classics version to work from?**

No, it was on the shelves. I had other versions but I didn't want to mark them up. They were nicer editions.

**What was it specifically about Dickens that appealed to you?**

The great genius of Dickens' storytelling and the power that he has – 'what happens next?', 'what happens next?', 'and then?', 'and then?' He is a modern novelist in that way. His plots are wonderful, you know. *Great Expectations*, for example, glorious plot. And *Oliver Twist* is superb. If I was asked to tell the story of *Oliver Twist* to a kid in as few words as possible, this is what I'd say: 'It's about a little boy who takes charge of his own life, escapes from terrible trials and dangers and emerges triumphant.'

I've always thought Dickens to be one of the great novelists in the English language, and now that I've worked on him for the first time, I have no doubt that he is the greatest of English novelists. He was in his twenties when he wrote *Oliver Twist*. It's an amazing achievement. Charles Dickens was a champion of the underdog and he wrote social novels. *Oliver Twist* is a novel that is savagely critical of the poor laws in England at the time – the workhouses, the way orphans were treated, the way the poor were treated. That's what inspired him. He was a young, thrusting, ambitious novelist and he had this huge instant worldwide success with *Oliver Twist*.

And this is the coming together of two extraordinary imaginations that make the film powerful. Both Roman Polanski and Charles Dickens are magical storytellers. The thing with a Dickens novel is you have to turn the page. You want to know what happens next. So it is with a Polanski movie.

### Did you decide the film's running time initially? Was it left up to you?

No, nobody gave me a running time. I have a very good in-built clock and I would go for two hours. That would be my instinct. And that would be so many pages, and I'm pretty good at judging that. It's not a gift, it's just an internal clock that I have.

### Have you always had that, even when you were younger?

Yes, I think I did. I just knew. I remember with early television plays, I read them aloud and timed them. But then I got into the habit of it and I knew roughly how many pages to go for.

**As a writer, is that awareness of a project's correct length a general thing that might apply whether it's a novel or a novella or whatever?**

Well, I think you should know roughly what length you're going for. This was going to be a major feature film so I knew it was going to have to be two hours minimum, although in the old days it would've been an hour and a half. So I would have gone between ninety minutes and a hundred and twenty minutes. But it wasn't in my mind. I know that when I get near the end, if it's running to a hundred and forty pages, I've done something wrong and so I would have had to cut. I can't remember if I went through all that with this, but I don't think I did. Difficult to remember these things. One should keep notes, shouldn't one?

**The scale of the novel is epic, far too much for any film. How did you decide what to leave out?**

I knew that the first decision we had to make was what we were going to leave out. It's nearly a four hundred and fifty page novel after all. Well, I always hated the back-story. Even as a boy, when I first read the novel, I couldn't bear it. I thought it was simply a Victorian conceit, too far-fetched – that Oliver discovers that Brownlow was his grandfather and that there was a dead mother, that awful sentimental, coincidental story. And so when I came to do the movie, it was the first thing I knew I wanted to cut. I knew I had to make a big cut and so that was it.

We made the decision just to tell the story of Oliver Twist, from the moment he enters the workhouse to the end of the story in the novel. We kept Brownlow, of course, but we lost all those implausible back connections and sub-plots.

### Did you discuss taking out the back-story with Polanski?

Yes. When I went to see Polanski for the first time about this movie in Paris, I said I wanted to cut that and he absolutely agreed and there was no further discussion. I thought it couldn't work with a modern audience and so we cut it.

### That decision to remove the back-story opened the way for a style that stressed realism over Victorian sentimentality. Was that part of your initial discussions with Polanski?

No, Polanski and I never discussed it. It was simply a direct result of cutting the back-story. Because of that, we removed the sentimentality, which also is not part of Polanski's or my temperament. That cutting of the back-story resulted in the triumph of realism over sentimentality.

### Oliver Twist is probably the most universally familiar source material you have adapted so far. What's the process, the starting point you use in choosing the scenes and storyline for the story you tell?

Well, as I've already said, the most important thing in a long work like that or any work is what you leave out. That decision is crucial because once you've decided that, then you know the A to Z of the story. So taking out that back-story – the second family and when he's taken into shelter by various people – once I got rid of all that, then I knew I just told Oliver's story: from the workhouse in the Midlands to London to Fagin to the escape to Mr Brownlow and so forth. You just know the arc of the story. I can't remember having any difficulty with that.

And then, my own sense of storytelling comes into play. And Roman's, of course. Concentrating on what tells the story.

**Is there a physical method, for instance mapping it out on a piece of paper?**

Not in this instance, it's in my head.

**Did working from a version of the novel illustrated with Cruickshank's original sketches have even a subliminal bearing upon your inspiration?**

It didn't to me, but I'm sure it's of help to a director. The sketch with Brownlow meeting Nancy on London Bridge. Yes, it's very nice to see but I wouldn't have imagined it like that. I'd have imagined him higher up, I don't know why. But it's good atmospheric stuff. I described it all lower down because I wanted the tramps and the homeless. You hear them in the background. I remember after they shot it and we were doing the sound, I had to write lines for them. You don't hear them clearly, but Roman's very insistent that the extras have proper lines so they don't just go 'mumble mumble'. But I liked it down below by the water's edge, I thought that would be very atmospheric. And it may have been influenced by the picture, but I don't remember it being so.

**You've captured so many elements of the novel that none of the previous screenplays have included.**

Well, we put in two things that are not usually included in *Oliver Twist* film adaptations: one is Toby Crackit – as far as I know no one ever put him in before – and of course the Fagin gaol scene at the end.

*And you've included a host of minor characters from the novel who are not usually portrayed. For instance the early scene where the Chimney Sweep wants to purchase Oliver as an apprentice for £5 and which leads to a Magistrate scene which is never normally included.*

No, that's right, I've never seen that before. And it's very important because that is where Oliver changes his own future, by his own intervention in the scene with the Magistrate. It seemed to me vital. It is odd that others have left that Magistrate scene out because it's crucial to the story. It is the moment that Oliver takes charge of his own life by saying, 'Don't send me off with this terrible man.' It's not just a picaresque novel where things happen to him, he actually drives his own life at that moment. He's not just a victim, he actually changes his future. And he makes other decisions, he tries to escape from Fagin and various other things.

*You mentioned that you were very familiar with the book before you began work on it. Had you seen any of the other film adaptations?*

I knew the David Lean film, which I was terribly disappointed with when I saw it for the second time because I thought Alec Guinness' performance was a sort of caricature. And I knew the musical, of course, which I think is a wonderful musical. But being a musical, it's soft centred and has none of the hardness of novel in it. Nevertheless, I knew that very well. I think *Oliver* is terrific. I was at the first night of the musical in London. So yes, I knew the subject pretty well.

**Dickens wrote Oliver Twist *in episodes. Did this present any difficulties in maintaining the story's through line for the adaptation? A change of style, that sort of thing.***

I never noticed a change of style. There are some very odd things that are not truthful in the novel, that is to say that Oliver always talks in an upper-class accent. If you read the dialogue, it's always, 'Yes, sir' and it's very polite. We changed that a bit in the film. I don't know why Dickens did it, perhaps heroic figures couldn't be seen to be working class. But if you take the reality that he'd been brought up in a workhouse, he'd have spoken whatever the rough accent was. So it's odd that he speaks in this very grammatical way.

**Do you ever write a title sequence for your films?**

No, I leave that up to the director. There isn't a title sequence on *Oliver Twist*, nor was there on *The Pianist*.

**Have you ever been asked to write one?**

No. They can put that in on the opening shots if they want to.

**Presumably the lovely etchings in the film's opening title sequence are not your suggestions.**

That's all the director's and designer's stuff. I love all that. And the music written by Rachel Portman, it's lovely. She's very clever, to give each of the main characters a theme.

And it's a very beautiful film to look at, beautifully shot. Pawel Edelman is a marvellous cameraman. And also the muted colours, that's very Roman.

**In losing the book's back-story, you had to decide where to start your story.**

Yes, the important thing with *Oliver Twist* is where it begins. I originally started the film much earlier. I started it in the workhouse with Mrs Mann and Mr Bumble, the Beadle, coming and taking him off. And there were scenes with Oliver and a little boy who was dying. It's all in the first chapters of the book. And everybody liked all that and Roman and I were very happy with that. And then they came and said, 'We have to take money out of it.' It was too expensive. And so I phoned and said, 'Let's start with Bumble taking Oliver to the branch-workhouse.' So that was a later start than I originally planned. And, it was very interesting, when Roman and I were discussing it. I said, 'They can come walking towards us.' And Roman said, 'No, no, with their backs.' He is marvellous. It's a much more interesting image. Marvellous. Mine was such a conventional idea, but his, it's beautiful.

**This version really hits hard the idea of Oliver as a boy completely at the mercy of the world.**

I know. That's to do with Roman. I think he felt a great autobiographical sympathy with Oliver, this boy cast out into the world and then making good. Falling among thieves and all that.

**Was there much cut from your original script?**

What, afterwards? No, no, no, because Roman won't allow that.

**So the opening was all you adjusted?**

The opening, I took out. It must have been five pages or something, but it was enough because it saved them a week. And there was some problem – I can't remember the detail now – a holiday in the Czech Republic where it was filmed that coincided with that first week of shooting, so if we could move that out, we got a clear week. And then we started at the point in the story where we agreed it would open.

**When writing, did the young age of the central character ever affect the depth of what you gave the character to act?**

No, not at all. I knew they'd have to find a kid, and that's always possible. There are some very talented people around. I obeyed the story. It's his birthday in the story and that's what I obeyed. I'm terribly faithful to it. I probably said this to you hundreds of times in our conversations. One of the jobs of the adaptor screenwriter is to protect the heart of what you're adapting. Otherwise, there's no point in having that story. And Polanski absolutely agreed.

And Polanski's enthusiasm to the world is childlike, he's open to things. And when he's directing the children, he is wonderful with them. He treats them as adults, first of all. But he enters their world. He has a capacity for a child's mind, a child's imagination, a child's view of the world.

If you're going to do that novel, do that novel. And so, we obeyed those things, the truth of those things.

**Why a Midlands accent for the workhouse?**

We did that on purpose. That was a decision, a joint-decision I think. We discussed it and worked out the seventy mile radius from London and decided we wanted it somewhere in the Midlands. And the accent works very well.

**In the scene where Oliver faces the committee in the workhouse, was the number of characters you included at your discretion?**

Well, in the book it says there's the man in the white waistcoat, there's the chairman of the board, I don't think he's given a name, there's the parson, and I suppose we just added two or three others. I probably said in the screenplay, 'The Charitable Board sits round the table.' I don't think I specified the number.

**How did you decide to show the daily grind faced by the workhouse inmates?**

I put the Oakum Scene in. I didn't know what 'oakum' was and I remember researching it and thinking, 'God, that would be marvellous.'

> **Oakum** – the loose fibres obtained by unpicking old rope, a common penal occupation in prisons and workhouses. These were then sold to the navy or other ship-builders and used as caulking when mixed with tar to seal the lining of wooden ships. Picking oakum was done without any tools whatsoever and was very hard on the fingers.

I also liked the line, 'You're serving your country.' I put that in and Roman never questioned it. And I described the kind of operation in some detail, picking the oakum out of old ship's ropes.

**Oliver is chosen to utter his famous line, 'Please Sir, I want some more' on behalf of all the other inmates when he unfortunately chooses the shortest straw.**

Yes, it's in the book. But I put the drawing of the ropes to relate to the oakum, you see. I didn't have straws.

And when Oliver approaches to ask for more, for anyone unfamiliar with the book, Roman turned it into a good suspense moment. And Barney Clark plays it awfully well. He's terrific.

**None of the adaptations to date, including yours, give the character of Noah Claypole, who plays a much larger part in the novel, anything more than his initial scenes with Oliver. What informs such a universally agreed decision?**

That's because you have to cut and you have to make it much more linear. I think it would be very difficult, and pointlessly so, to re-introduce a character from the early story so far into the later part of the story, and one who then becomes such a crucial factor. He follows Nancy and all that. It's all part of that tie up of a Victorian novel that everything belongs in the plot.

Incidentally, Chris Overton, who plays Noah Claypole, is awfully good, I think. During the production, they made a film of the children interviewing the grown-ups, and he interviewed me because he wants to be a writer. And it was a terrific interview, he was really good.

**Mr Sowerberry seems more sympathetic and more of a potential ally to Oliver than he is in the book.**

I think he's quite sympathetic in the book, but I did make it a little more that he was a sort of ally because he comes up with this idea of Oliver appearing as a 'mute' at childrens' funerals. 'He would make a delightful mute, my love.' But, of course, that's just because he wants something from Oliver.

*So many versions either briefly mark Oliver's journey from the countryside to London or else just cut straight to his arrival. You made a virtue of suggesting the whole experience in montage – his being frightened, alone and at the mercy of uncaring people, and all from Oliver's point of view.*

Well, that's like a novel. The point of view is crucial in a novel, and so it is in a film.

I can say something about the montage. We tried several ways of doing it, and Roman really solved it in the shooting of it. He shot a lot and then put together a sequence. It wasn't so much written by me, though I had all the scenes. I had him drinking water but I didn't perhaps have it in the order we finally see it. Roman designed it as a sequence, and beautifully I think.

*So technically, do you write the individual scenes for the montage in the shooting script?*

Yes, I did. But it was never a 'shooting' script in the precise sense of the term. It was always the screenplay. For instance, I had the scene with the coach passing Oliver on the road to London, but not where it's actually placed. Roman fiddled with that. That's the lovely part about collaboration.

And the scene where Oliver is refused water and driven from a property, finally collapsing in the road, is a marvellous punctuation. It illustrates the basic question: how would a child, alone, find food and water enough to survive such an arduous journey?

I don't believe the scene with the Old Woman who takes him in and feeds him has ever been in other adaptations. It's a beautiful scene, beautifully written by Dickens and wonderfully played by Liz Smith. She's lovely and a wonderful actress. Truthful. And what a glorious image, the rural cottage on the roadside. And there are some cuts. I wrote that scene at much greater length, and Roman filmed what was written. But he shortened it in the editing, and it's quite right that he did. It works beautifully.

There are a number of characters who are kind to Oliver: the Magistrate in that scene with the Chimney Sweep, the Old Woman, Mr Brownlow and Nancy. They're the crucial figures who are kind to him and want nothing from him and are actually human. And Mrs Bedwin, the housekeeper, of course, but that's a minor one.

### Can you say something about the difficulty you experienced with the transition from Oliver's journey on the road to his arrival in London?

I had difficulty with the time lapse. We read that passage. I had to read it from the book to Roman aloud, how that transition works – when he gets to the outskirts of London, the market, meeting the Dodger. And you have to show a kind of progression there: he gets there, then he wakes up in the market. And I had quite a lot of trouble with it. But we found it very neatly in the end, but it wasn't as easy as it looks. We had to work at it to find a sequence.

Roman loved the description that Dickens gives of Oliver on the church steps, asleep, and waking up in the market. So ours is a kind of cheat: they're setting up their stalls, we see him asleep and then you have the noise of the market. It works very well and it looks so easy, but you get into a kind of rut with sequences like that with all sorts of difficulties.

But I must say, the introduction to a bustling London is quite wonderful. That was very much my construction, I have to say. I don't want to take credit where I shouldn't but I had that explosion of London in the very first draft that I ever did, my own first draft, and it was never changed. It was always there. Bang, that explosion with St. Paul's in the background. That was put in later, of course, digitally. And it's the best St. Paul's you'll see because the other films give it the wrong shape. Have you noticed? Too narrow, but now with digital stuff you get it so exact.

Our memory of Victorian London is entirely Dickensian. He gave to the English language and to all the people who came after a vision of London that was entirely his. I don't know if it was entirely true, but it was entirely his and it's the one we've accepted. When I say 'we', I mean everyone. Dickensian London means narrow streets, dirt, people lying in doorways, buildings bearing down on you, all that is Dickensian.

**You've kept a lot of the thieves' slang, such as 'beak' (a magistrate) and 'trap' (a policeman) which other people tend not to use.**

And 'wipes', we didn't say 'handkerchiefs' because it would be odd for them to use such a formal word. You have to. Roman and I were very arrogant about that. We thought Hollywood gives us American slang which nobody here knows and they make no concession to us, so we'll do the same thing. We may have paid a penalty for it, of course, but that's what we did. It is the period language and it is very important.

Roman and I are both insistent that you obey the period. In *Titanic*, for example, the Kate Winslet character made a rude gesture that was very modern. It's 1912, you simply don't do that. It's not on, and we would never do that.

The language is part of the atmosphere and character of the book so you have to keep it. You have to trust it, and it usually works. And we didn't want to dumb it down. The French producers, of course, didn't have any idea what the characters were talking about but they were very agreeable, they were perfectly willing to go with us on that.

**The look of nineteenth-century London is wonderfully realised, with Polanski's brilliant crowd scenes on its streets, packed with individual dramas and realities.**

Well, London was a city that was thriving, flourishing, the richest city in the world as well as the biggest, so you have to capture that. And with Allan Starski, who won the Oscar for *Schindler's List*, we had a great, great production designer. Even the names of a lot of the shops are authentic. Berry Bros & Rudd is there, John Lobb, and they were very thrilled.

And Roman will have had all the fights choreographed, he's marvellous at all that. And the whole thing of the dubbing of it all. I had to write dialogue for the crowd in the dubbing sessions, for all those scenes as well, because he doesn't like it to be general, he likes it to be specific. You can't hear it now, but I did.

**The casting of the people in the streets is very good indeed, actors you don't always see.**

That's right, and you know why? Because Roman doesn't live here, he just takes the face. So if agents try and sell an actor that they all like or someone that we've all seen a hundred times, he doesn't fall for that. He just goes for the face.

**Did the depiction of Fagin enter into your initial discussions with Polanski?**

Not at all. Polanski and I have been asked this often. We never discussed it. In fact, Polanski was very dismissive in an interview when somebody asked that question – not as politely as you did, but quite the same question. He asked, 'Did you and Mr Harwood discuss how you would approach Fagin?' And Roman was really angry, he suddenly flew. He said, 'We're both men of a certain age, we both have a sense of the world. There was no question of discussing it.' And he got rather cross. I don't know why he did. I never questioned it, I never asked him. But no, we didn't.

**So the portrayal was left entirely to you.**

No, it wasn't even left to me, it was really left to Dickens. It's in the book and we took that. But we didn't discuss the anti-Semitism at all.

**Did the constant references to Fagin as the 'Jew' present any problems for a modern adaptation?**

No, but it's really fascinating. I think only one character, Bill Sykes, once calls Fagin a Jew. Otherwise it's only in the narrative by Dickens. It's in none of the dialogue and that's what I followed. Dickens says 'The Jew' all the time, but never his characters. The characters don't turn on Fagin and say 'You Jew' or anything. Nothing of that sort.

I did point out to Roman that no one says 'Jew'. No one says it in the book, so no one says it in the movie. Not at all. Sykes says, 'you avaricious old skeleton' rather than 'you avaricious old Jew'. It's very interesting, that. It's only throughout Dickens' narrative that you constantly get the word 'Jew'.

*Presumably that was perfectly acceptable to the society reading it at the time.*

Oh, no question. There was no question about it. But Dickens felt guilty about it afterwards apparently, because he had several Jewish friends. And he tried to correct it in a later novel, *Our Mutual Friend*, which has a character, Mr Riah, who's a 'decent Jew'. And a Dickens' scholar said to me, 'It comes out much worse than Fagin.' The 'nice Jew' was some kind of condescension, I imagine. Patronising.

But, curiously, Polanski and I, both Jews of course, never discussed how we were going to treat it. So there he is, Fagin. We know that he was a Galician because they were red headed. We worked out all kinds of things about him, but we never discussed the anti-Semitism aspect of it at all. We just kept true to the character.

For the sequence demonstrating picking pockets, we had a man come in and teach them. He's a magician, a lovely chap – his father came up to me at a do the other day and said, 'My son helped your *Oliver Twist* kids.' In that sequence, Rachel Portman introduced a very clever kind of Jewish element to the music there.

*So it's only hinted at in the music?*

Yes, but you'd have to be quite clever to get that.

*Fagin seems to be very much looking after the children rather than threatening them.*

But that's right too, that's also in the book. They're his livelihood so he has to look after them. I think it's Polanski's addition, Fagin laying the table for the kids when they come back from their stealing. And that's the thing you remarked on, him taking care of the children. Fagin has a very important line, it's from the book, 'This is a pleasant life, ain't it my dear?' He's so contradictory: he's kind to Oliver, he's beastly to Oliver, he betrays Oliver and at the end he wants to misuse Oliver.

**And by the end, Fagin is tacitly complicit in the plan to murder Oliver.**

Of course, self-preservation comes into it then. But he's beastly to Nancy. He mistrusts her because she so dislikes him. Because he put her on the streets as a whore, I should think, at the age of twelve or thirteen.

**Did your screenplay suggest any of Fagin's mannerisms? Ben Kingsley has a wonderful thing of occasionally not looking directly at the people he's getting information from? It's brilliantly observed.**

No, that's all him. I didn't describe that in the screenplay at all. He's so good, Ben. Absolutely terrific.

Dickens' scholars were very pleased with the interpretation of Fagin. I had several letters, one from a professor of English somewhere in Canada who is a Dickens' scholar and who thought we'd done Fagin pretty well. And it's because we obeyed the book. We just simply followed him as he appears in each scene of the book.

**Did you re-visit the David Lean version once you'd finished your final draft?**

Yes, when we'd locked the script, after the final draft when it was finished. Polanski said, 'Let's watch the David Lean.' And he's got a huge screen in his office and we watched it. And it's like a German expressionist film: the scudding clouds and dissolves and things. And then the performance by Alec

Guinness. We were totally shocked. It was like a *Der Stürmer* caricature, which was amazing in that it was made just after the war with the news of the Holocaust coming out. It was just odd to me. But that might have been Polanski's and my sensitivity to that particular interpretation.

Alec Guinness was my neighbour for many years, and I once broached him on it and I think he was embarrassed about it afterwards. He told me that Lean didn't want him for Fagin originally. After playing Herbert Pocket for Lean in *Great Expectations*, he had to show that he had the depth for Fagin, so he asked Lean if he could have a screen test. And he paid a very famous make-up artist and did the test and that's how he got the part. I think that's the story. But Lean always had a sort of love–hate relationship with Alec and vice versa.

**The second Magistrate scene following the picking of Brownlow's pocket outside of the bookshop and the chase through the streets must surely be its best portrayal ever.**

Well, the chase is very, very well staged. It's an epic sequence in the book. Dickens does a huge description of the pursuit, much longer than ours.

And Dickens hated magistrates. That's a real Dickensian scene. It's the heart of Dickens, those kind of ironies. And such a marvellous name for a magistrate, Fang. 'Or my name's not Fang.' I had to put that line in, of course.

**That's a good example of what the adaptor has to do in order to establish things that appear only in a novel's narrative.**

Well, just to give the information. Otherwise you don't know his name is Fang, and it's such a marvellous name.

There's also another invention here, my invention I think. A discarded calling card that reveals Brownlow's Pentonville address is handed over to Nancy when she pretends to be Oliver's sister trying to learn his whereabouts. Otherwise they don't know where Brownlow has taken Oliver. In the book, they look for him over London, but that didn't seem right. A card seemed a much easier and simpler way.

**Polanski's direction perfectly compliments the unsensationalised realism of the screenplay's approach.**

He's wonderful like that, Roman. He's wonderful with a camera. He doesn't show off at all. And yet, he'll delicately frame a character against the window light. Beautiful.

In the scene when Oliver wakes at Brownlow's and then collapses onto the floor, Roman's awfully good. When he falls, you don't go to a close shot of Mrs Bedwin waking up. You just take it, you're just observing what's happening. He's marvellous at that. He never stamps every shot, does he? He doesn't say, 'Look, this is a film by Roman Polanski, and I'm a clever director.' And, of course, it's far more interesting.

**Without all the back-story information from the novel, Oliver's arrival at Brownlow's must have required some considerable further invention on your part.**

Yes, I included a scene that added the motivation which was crucial in demonstrating Brownlow's reason for keeping Oliver. I added this because, without the back-story, there is no reason for that at all because there's no blood connection. So I put those lines in about 'being drawn to him' as well as a back-story that I'd invented – a very little, minor thing – that Brownlow was a 'do-gooder' to these young people that he found. And it works well, I think. And Oliver has that effect on Nancy too. She's drawn to him at once because he's polite and there's some goodness in him. And no one has ever questioned that. No scholar or anyone has said, 'Where did that come from?' But it is absolutely essential to the storytelling that they're 'drawn to him', something in him.

And sometimes the lines that I've pointed out that I'd written – about him 'having something in him', that draws them to him – tie up very well with the actual story too, with the actual lines of Dickens.

We also added a scene from the novel that's not in any of the other adaptations, but Roman and I liked it very much. The one where Brownlow discusses his collection of books with Oliver and then asks, 'How would you like to grow up a clever man and write books? Wouldn't you like to be a book writer?' And Oliver replies, 'I think I'd rather be a book seller, sir.' It's an in-joke by Dickens.

And I don't think other adaptations have used the scene after the boy delivers some books to Brownlow's. Oliver is asked to fetch him back. And in our film, unawares, he is very nearly caught by Bill Sykes in the street, adding a wonderful tension. Normally, after the book delivery, Oliver is just seen taking the books directly back into the city.

*Following Oliver's capture, there's a scene in a small room in which he's been locked up where Fagin visits in order to give him some sound advice. In the novel, this is dealt with in a brief narrative which you dramatised and expanded quite brilliantly for the screenplay.*

I thought it important for Fagin to make this contact with Oliver, for similar reasons to those of Brownlow. It was meant to be an echo of that. That was in my mind. I don't think it was in Dickens' mind, but it was in mine.

**_That lends potential to Fagin being a father figure._**

Which he absolutely is. He is to the other boys, of course. In the novel, his advice is simply described in the narrative. So I had to make that up, Fagin's 'the greatest sin is ingratitude' speech. I turned what was all described in the third person into dialogue.

**_And Fagin's recollection about hanging is a wonderful precursor to his own._**

Yes, that's my line too. 'They hang you for anything, these days.'

**_Why did you expand on Dickens' narrative?_**

Because I think it's vital that there's a real connection between Oliver and Fagin. And that Oliver can say at the end, when he goes to see him in prison, 'You were kind to me, sir.' And later, after Oliver's bullet wound is dressed following the bungled robbery, again I had to dramatise the novel's third-person narrative into a speech there as well. The relationship is very important between Fagin and Oliver.

Another interesting thing, the 'japanning' scene – cleaning the boy's boots. I did not have that in my first draft, but Roman loved it. I don't know why, he just wanted it and so I put it in. It didn't bother me, but it wasn't something I'd put in. I think I put stuff in about going to go see the house in Pentonville, but he wanted that 'japanning' scene. It's all that hanging thing with Charlie Bates making his gallows gesture. That came from Roman and that also evokes the hanging scene, of course.

Roman also loved another scene, where Sykes threatens Oliver with the gun. I did have it in, but Roman adored that scene. He always talked about it, when Sykes says, 'You know what this is?'

### Why is the delightful Toby Crackit left out of so many adaptations?

I really don't know because he's a marvellous character. He's a wonderful character. And Mark Strong plays him so well. God, he's brilliant.

### You rarely get it in films of this period, the importance of a light, of a candle at night. This film makes the audience more aware of it than anything I've ever seen before, with that wonderful line, 'Don't leave us in the dark.'

That's Dickens, of course.

I loved that scene at Toby Crackit's, preparing for the robbery. If Roman had obsessions about other scenes, I had one about this, about all the little details of thieving. This is Dickens showing off too, his knowledge of the underworld and so on.

### In the book, there's a series of robberies, but none of them at Brownlow's house.

No, it's not in the book, that's our invention. That was my idea, I think. It was hard to tie the robbery in, it was hard to make a fitting piece of it. They rob somebody else's house in Dickens, but I changed that. And why not? They'd 'cased the joint', as it were, so that worked quite well. And it also adds a potential element of doubt in Brownlow's mind about Oliver's character.

**With so much technical detail to housebreaking taking place, does your script spell it all out or just indicate that they approach the house?**

Oh, no, that's all spelled out, 'Toby goes over the wall first. Bill passes Oliver up.' And Roman's wonderful at these practical things, how you get in and all that. It's absolutely real, he doesn't cheat at any of that. The execution of it is very realistically done. And the wonderful lightning effects Roman put in. God, that was good. It's lovely being a screenwriter. All you put in is 'rain', and they do the rest, don't they?

**The Lean film doesn't really go into the robbery, the musical shows the bungled burglary at an anonymous house where a tray clatters and wakes everyone up, and in the George C. Scott film, it takes place somewhere way out in the country.**

Well, that's more like what's in the book. I've never seen the George C. Scott film, but in Dickens, Oliver is shot by residents of the burgled house whereas we thought it added a more interesting element if it was done deliberately by Sykes. And as they escaped from Brownlow's, we set up the threat to Oliver very economically: 'We've got to get rid of him or he'll squeal,' 'We've got to do him in,' all that.

**Was it your invention, Sykes tumbling into the river?**

Yes, I think so. And Roman was so clever showing the passage of time: the dog, the rain, and Sykes asleep.

**In the novel, other characters discover Oliver lying in a ditch and tend his wounds.**

Yes, but without that back-story, I had to invent all this. I don't think much of ours is in the book. And I had to write Fagin's speech about having a 'remedy as old as time' in order to tie up with the last scene.

Then the scene where Nancy tries to go out and is prevented by Sykes; they play that wonderfully, I think. When they screen tested for Nancy using that scene, I played Fagin and Jamie Foreman played Bill. Leanne Rowe is awfully good as Nancy, and quite rightly young. In the Lean picture, whoever it's played by, she's in her thirties I should think. And of course Jamie Foreman's Bill Sykes is a marvellous performance.

He's wonderfully perceptive, Bill Sykes, when it comes to Nancy. It's a marvellous character thing in Dickens. He reads her absolutely accurately.

And the line, 'They're as close as Cain and Able,' everybody thinks it's Dickens but that was my line. But, 'Look at him. What a shame it is. With his face, he could pick ladies pockets in church,' that is Dickens but from an earlier scene. I used it later because we loved the line.

**Some of the scenes in Oliver Twist *are very scary.* Since it was intended as a film for children, did you ever tone back any of the novel's violence?**

No, never. I always think that Roman saying that he wanted to make a film for children was misleading because I don't think this is a children's film myself. I think it's a young adolescent film perhaps, but people younger than twelve might be quite frightened by it. I think that was just something he'd said in passing and then we absolutely forgot it because it was never in my mind.

*There's absolutely no way one could depict Nancy's killing without it being anything other than a brutish act.*

We changed that on the set. I happened to be there when they were filming the scene, and Roman wasn't happy with the way it was in the script. So we shortened it, we greatly shortened it and re-jigged it, much to the advantage of the scene.

But there was a lot of discussion about that at the time. I had the blood coming under the door and there is a shot of that, very brief. And I wanted the blood spattered over the dog. And there is a bit, but Roman cut it very, very short. That, I think, was a discussion with the producers.

*It was a PG (Parental Guidance) in the UK and more blood would have put it up a rating.*

Yes, but I liked all that. I mean, if it's gore, it's gore. But it wasn't how we finally did it. It was very, very brief.

*After the killing, Bill Sykes escapes to the countryside, which is perfectly bleak mid-winter after the lush greenery of the earlier scenes. Was that deliberate?*

I don't know but, God, I think that's the best shot in the whole picture. The shot of Sykes alone on the field. But I didn't write any of the seasons in.

*And following the murder, there's the brilliant scene where Toby Crackit turns up to report the events to Fagin. Whilst everyone is in a state of fearful confusion, he's utterly unflappable in the worst of circumstances.*

And so cheerful. He's so thrilled that they're all in the newspaper. There's a hint of it in the narrative of the book. But that's all invention, reading the actual newspaper article aloud. It's not in the book at all.

And when Sykes appears, that was something I fiddled with. It's not the Dodger who attacks him in the book, it's actually Charley Bates who does it. That change was a sort of playwright's playfulness.

### The chase of Sykes and Oliver across the rooftops works very well.

It's terrifically well done in the book, and it's terrifically well done in all the movies. It's a sort of foolproof sequence, isn't it?

There's a mistake in Dickens incidentally in this scene. During the pursuit, someone calls out, 'In the King's name.' And there's no possibility of irony there, it's simply a mistake by Dickens, but his editors didn't pick it up either. The queen was on the throne by that time. It's a very, very odd mistake.

### It's very realistic the way Sykes is caught up in the rope before losing his footing, leading to his hanging.

That I'll tell you about because it doesn't work in the book. The way Dickens describes it could not possibly happen, and Polanski and I worked hard at trying to find a way that would be believable and naturalistic. Polanski worked at it and then found a way, and I just described it. It's to do with the way he puts the rope around him and the way he takes it off. He's got one bit under his arm so he can get across. In Dickens, it's described as round his neck from the beginning, which wouldn't have worked. And just as he's taking it off, and the dog appears, he slips. We worked it absolutely spot on.

Then, finally back with Brownlow at last, there is a wonderful touch of Roman's. He put Oliver in glasses. We see him reading and that says so much: that he's been there a bit, he's settled in. It's absolutely beautiful.

**The traditional film of Oliver Twist *ends with his safe return to Brownlow. What prompted the continuation of your story?***

This is very important. Right, I ended my first draft just as you said. I thought that's where we'll end it. And then, when I'd had my first meeting after delivering the screenplay to Polanski, as he did with *The Pianist,* he said, 'Let's start at the end.' He always likes to start and get the end right and then he works backwards. And he said, 'I want you to try and put in the scene with Fagin in the cell,' the hanging of Fagin. And that was at three or four o'clock in the afternoon.

I went back from his flat to my flat in Paris and I worked till about midnight and condensed what is a very, very long scene in the novel into what you see in the picture. The next morning, Polanski and I met, I read it to him, he said 'Excellent, wonderful' and we never touched it again. And I don't know why I didn't put the scene in originally. Perhaps because I thought it was too severe, and perhaps this whole thing of the 'childrens' movie, was somehow in my mind. But Polanski wanted it in, I put it in and it was a terrific decision. It just works.

Then I had to feed back into the picture that stuff about 'hanging' into the earlier scenes with Fagin. So I could see why Polanski was so keen then upon the cleaning of the boots scene, because that's got Charlie Bates saying 'Gggraaahhh' and making his grotesque hanging gesture. Roman liked all that, and it puts a thematic thing into it. This is why it's such a bonus working at that initial stage with a director you respect and admire.

**After seeing the film, one wonders how anyone could have left so crucial a punctuation out of the story in previous versions.**

Yes, and a friend of mine said, 'God, you changed the end.' No one remembers it from the book either. It's a huge chapter, 'The Jew's Last Night Alive' it's called.

**In the prison cell, when Oliver asks Fagin to get down on his knees to say a prayer, is that meant to be an attempt at a conversion to Christianity?**

Well, that may be your interpretation. He says, 'Let's go down on our knees,' but Jews don't go down on their knees so I didn't read that into it. I just thought that was part of the drama of the scene. The real heart of the scene is the forgiveness, which of course is a Christian element. And I think it's very touching that Oliver has some gratitude towards him. It's not dragging Fagin into a Christian conversion, it's a forgiveness, a reconciliation. And we were determined to be true to the Dickensian characterisation.

And it's a wonderful line of Oliver's, isn't it, 'Oh God forgive this wretched man.' Wonderful, the tears glinting on his cheeks as he goes.

And again Polanski's cleverness, the thing of building the gallows in the background as they're leaving is awfully good. It's described in huge detail in the Dickens: the remarks of the crowd, people who can't wait to see the man hanged, the public execution. And Edward Hardwick as Brownlow, God, he's just marvellous.

*One critic thought your version 'trumps even Dickens himself' whilst some others were less enthusiastic. If you're personally pleased with the results of a film you've spent so long adapting and it gets mixed reviews, does such an ambiguous reception in any way affect your overall sense of a project's worth?*

No, it doesn't. This project was not a success in one sense, in that very few people went to see it. More people saw it in Poland than in the United States. We made a cultural miscalculation with this film. We thought people would still be interested in it, they're not.

*If not now, perhaps future generations will be more enlightened in their discovery of what many deem to be the novel's definitive adaptation.*

Not now, but they may be in ten years' time. Oh, I think it'll be a classic in ten years' time, but we timed it wrongly. And there's nothing you can do about that. We were disappointed with that, yes. But I'm very proud of the job we did. It doesn't affect my satisfaction at what we did, not at all. But it's a disappointment that it didn't make a greater impact.

*Apparently the DVD is flying off the shelves.*

I'm delighted to hear that. You know it was ignored when it came to awards, totally ignored. I thought Ben Kingsley should have been nominated for an Oscar at least. Brilliant performance, and he didn't win anything. No one got anything at all.

*People have got so used to watching adaptations of the classics on television, when* Oliver Twist *is shown, they'll watch and in huge numbers.*

Well, you may be right, and I hope you are. I really hope you are.

# Q&A

*What are the practical advantages of adaptation over the original screenplay for the screenwriter?*

The writing of original screenplays is a perfectly honourable and splendid operation, but there are several factors that come into play. Firstly, the writer will not be in control of that finished product, unlike in the theatre or with a novel where the author has absolute control. In the movies, as everyone knows, it's handed over to producers and directors. That is the first block on writing an original screenplay. The second is the agony of trying to get it made if you do it without a commission. If you do it just because that's the thing you most want to write and in the medium you most want to write it and you have to set it up as well, it's misery. It can take years, by which time the thing may be out of date or the idea may no longer appeal to you, and yet you have to keep faith with it because you've done it.

Adaptations are much easier. You have to acquire the property so someone has to invest in that, and it has an easier run. I know that might sound superficial, but I think it's at the heart of the matter.

There is also another factor. In America, in the United States, writers believe in film as a way of expressing themselves, and here we don't. I think in Europe we believe the theatre is a way of expressing ourselves, the novel is a way of expressing ourselves, even television is a way of expressing ourselves. But movies, for some reason we don't. I think it's because of this thing I mentioned before, the handing over of the movie to someone else and in the end the director's going to be in charge. And there's nothing you can do about that, that's the way the system works.

### How does one decide what audience to write for?

Well, it depends upon what game you're in. If you're in the commercial game, you write the same film that made a lot of money last week. If you regard films as an art form, you have to do what appeals to you, your peer group and your intellectual peers. But you have to be very strict about it because you cannot write every kind of genre. You have to write only what you can write, so it's a very individual question. It's a question for each and every writer to answer. But if you're in a big market – if that's what you want, a popular game – you have to write popular movies. It's a question of taste in the end.

### Your first love is plays for the theatre.

Well, I was brought up in the theatre. I fell in love with the theatre when I was six years old. I loved the theatre then and I still do. I have a feeling though that it's not quite as central to our social and our artistic life as it was perhaps when I began, that the movies are more fashionable and more sought after.

### How and when did screenwriting come to you?

Very early, I was very lucky. My first two television plays were made into films and that's how I got in, as a result of the second one, which was called *Private Potter*. In those days, they used to make 'novelisations' of films. And Pan Books said to some guy, would he do a novelisation of our film. He turned out to be the story editor of Twentieth Century Fox, that was his day job, and they were looking for a writer for *A High Wind in Jamaica*, and that's how I got into the bigger league. It was just good fortune.

**After being approached and agreeing to write your first screenplay, A High Wind in Jamaica, *how did you learn a craft that was so different from playwriting?***

I had a marvellous teacher in the director, Alexander Mackendrick, who I mentioned briefly earlier. He was already on board the film. I always think that the greatest piece of good luck that I ever had was that I wasn't asked to write a screenplay without a director.

He was already employed by Twentieth Century Fox to do the movie. He was an extremely good teacher and later went on to accept the Deanship of the Film School of the newly-established California Institute for the Arts. I think I may be the last screenwriter who actually worked with him. I've been able to pay him lots of tributes over the years and I was able to thank him when I was first nominated for an Oscar for *The Dresser.* I was in California and I got hold of his number to tell him, 'Sandy, I owe everything to you about writing movies.' And he was so touched. He was a terrific director. He did *Sweet Smell of Success*, he did a whole lot of good movies. So I was awfully grateful to him.

I remember the film starts with the sea coming in when the high wind starts and the children have to be sent back to England, and I did descriptions that lasted three pages of the sea coming in. Sandy looked at me and said, 'All you put is the sea coming in, I'll worry about all that' and that was wonderful. I didn't know anything about writing screenplays, nothing. I'd used a book called *Baby Doll* by Tennessee Williams, published by Penguin. It was a screenplay, the most marvellously laid out screenplay. And that's how I learned.

People get very worried about how you lay out a screenplay. That's the easiest part. It's what you put in the scenes that's so difficult. So I was very fortunate in that way.

**When choosing subjects to adapt, what advice do you have on what works best in plays, novels, stories, works of non-fiction, articles, etc.?**

What works best for you. I'm often asked this question and I always say, 'I don't look for subjects, they look for me.' You inform yourself with certain subjects, with certain things that are of interest to you. And things come into that basket, they drop in.

*The Pianist* is very much me – Nazi Germany, music – bang, in it goes. *Taking Sides,* obviously, that came out of me. Anything to do with the theatre, *Being Julia*. It's in my ken and my sphere of interest. Or there's something that's so new to you and you think, 'My God, I'd like to test myself on this. I don't know if I can do it.' So, in a way, I don't choose what I'm going to do.

But I do have to be absolutely certain that the world I'm offered, in the book or the play or whatever it is, is a world I can live in and enrich. You've got to be able to feel that that's your world. And sometimes one is blinded by the fame of the original novelist, and it isn't exactly one's world. I've found that. Then you have to be strong about those things.

I'm very fortunate now to be offered a lot, so I get a choice. But when I was starting out, when I wasn't offered a lot, I knew when I could do something and when I couldn't do it. And although sometimes one so needed money, with children growing up and mortgages and God knows what, one did things one shouldn't have done. And on the whole, they were luckily never made because they were so bad.

**Did you know that at the time? 'I'm not right for this'?**

Oh absolutely, of course I knew it. And I was desperately unhappy; I actually couldn't sleep at night. I had to do a film once about Leon Trotsky who was the most hateful man. And I was simply stuck; I was in a state of total despair writing it. But I needed the delivery money desperately, and so of course I took it. But it was never made, thank God. It was pretty terrible.

**When you were a struggling writer approached to write something you didn't think would work or else wasn't right for you, did you mention it or take the money and run?**

No, I never took the money and ran, but I took the money and did what best I could and limped.

There is no shame in having to earn a living. Where's the shame in having to feed your children or pay the rent or the mortgage? So of course you have that when you're young. I did, I had it a lot. And not so very long ago. I was very broke. I had to put my house on the market. If not through the kindness of a bank manager who doubled my overdraft on no security at all, I would have been dead. We would have had to take our children out of school but the Bursar there said, 'Oh, don't do that. We're a rich school. We'll be alright.' And we got through it. But there were threatened foreclosures on the house and all that. Dreadful times.

You've got to make a living, you've got to get by. But no one asked you to be a writer so you can't blame society for not making a living. If it's something you want to do, that's part of it.

**How would you advise today's young screenwriter to deal with being offered something that may not be right for them?**

Well, they've got to know it's their world, that they can successfully write it because what they're inclined to do is to take anything. I understand that; God, I understand it. You're going to be desperate to make a living. And something comes your way; of course you're going to jump at it.

But even so, you have to be fortunate. Because it can only do you harm if, in the end, you can't do it. That's the terrible thing. It will harm you. Perhaps it will harm you inside, as the Trotsky film did me, or it will harm your reputation if you do it badly, if they get rid of you and say, 'He was useless.'

**In your collection of short stories about a screen writer, One. Interior. Day., your central character is caught in just such a situation and describes working on a story whose content is 'fruitless, hopeless and sterile' as akin to being 'touched by a cursed hand, and risking infection of his own spirit with deadly microbes'.**

Well, all I can say is that it did happen to me and I was ill as a result of working on something I should not have worked on – the Trotsky film. But I needed the money. And I found it appalling. Trotsky was a disgraceful, monstrous, destructive human being, and it just infected me. I was quite ill. I mean psychologically, I was laid low. That's why I say you've got to take your time and consider exactly what's being offered very carefully.

*Invariably, someone reading this book may think, 'That's all right for him, a successful writer, I have to write what I'm told, what's going to sell.'*

It's not a luxury for me to write what I write. If I can't get it produced, then it doesn't get put on. But I've been lucky in getting things produced.

Now that people come and interview me – and that's only because of the Oscar, not because of me, don't forget that – I'm often asked to look back over my career and I think, well, I've been quite lucky or clever even with the films I've done. There are one or two that I would like not to have done but, as I said, I was bringing up a family so that's another matter.

But generally, I did things like broadcasting and television and other things rather than do movies that I wasn't right for. I can't write just anything, I can only write what I can write. If they offered me *Lethal Weapon 12*, I couldn't do it. That's why I love some of these things the Americans do. *The Bourne Identity* I think is a wonderful film. I know I could never do it, not in a million years, so I admire it for that.

So perhaps it's nothing to do with me, it's just my instincts that say 'I can't do that sort of thing' and so don't do it. And I was fortunate in that. Plays are entirely different. You can do what comes to you. There's no question of not being right for that.

*How a subject inspires the writer is the key – for someone who writes* The Bourne Identity, *someone else will be imagining* Amadeus.

You see a play or a film and think. 'God, I wish I'd had that idea.' But that's what's so beautiful about it. Tom Stoppard, whom I admire greatly, sees in Zurich 1917 his brilliant play, *Travesties*, with James Joyce and Dada and all these people.

Even if it had come past me, I wouldn't have written it in the same way because I'm not informed with those things.

### When did you take the big leap and go from being something else to being a professional writer?

I was an actor until 1959 when I married. And I was very out of work. We had a little flat in Barnes, and I was about to take work as a builder on the Hammersmith Flyover road extension. And my father-in-law, who ran an office machinery company, gave me a typewriter that November for my birthday. I had nothing to do so in three weeks I wrote a novel about South Africa. I didn't know what I was doing. All I know was that my wife was out shopping and when I finished the novel I couldn't catch my breath. I really hyperventilated. Genuinely, I'm not over-dramatising in retrospect.

And when my wife came back from shopping, she said, 'What's the matter?' I said, 'I finished a novel.' It was all typed, without double spacing. And a friend came to dinner called Llewellyn Rees who'd been Wolfit's manager, and Llewellyn said, 'What have you been doing?' I said, 'I've written a novel, Llewellyn.' He said, 'Oh, I know a publisher.' I said, 'Don't be silly, everybody writes a novel.' He said, 'Let me show it to him.' So I gave him this single spaced thing which my wife and I bound like we'd seen plays bound. She did it very well, she's very good at all that.

A few weeks later, Jonathan Cape asked if I would come in and see them, and they bought the novel. They hadn't published a novel about South Africa since *Cry, The Beloved Country*, so I thought I was going to win the Nobel Prize, you know. And the Americans bought it, and the Swedes, and it went into translation. I thought I was on my way. Of course, I had a rude awakening because the next book is much more difficult, the next step in your life. The first thing is easy, the second thing is much more difficult. When it goes with such ease, you think it's going to be like that always, and it ain't.

But I knew that I was on to something in myself. I can't explain it, I just knew it. And then I sat down and wrote *The Barber of Stamford Hill*, a television play that was performed. And I was put under contract to ATV for two plays a year for a thousand pounds a year. The first time I ever made a living as a writer. And for a long time I felt fraudulent calling myself a 'writer' because my ambition had been to be an actor. That's how that change took place. I've never questioned it much but that's precisely what happened.

And my son was born, my novel was published and my first television play was performed all within the space of about three or four months of 1960. So my life changed dramatically and I started to make a living. And *High Wind* came shortly after that. And the four thousand pounds I made bought me a Mini Minor, two suits from Brioni, two pairs of shoes from Bally Swiss. And I bought my wife some clothes, and we ran up a big overdraft, and we never looked back.

### Did your career take off as a screenwriter after A High Wind in Jamaica?

No, it didn't work like that. That would have been in the early to middle sixties. I forget when it dried up, but eventually it did. And I found some work in Italy which paid. I used to go to Rome every other week first class. It was very glamorous. My wife would come out and join me; it was great fun.

I was learning about films and I worked with some very good people – Mario Monicelli, Valerio Zurlini, Suso Cecchi d'Amico. But I was very lowly, all I was doing was taking literal translations of Italian screenplays and turning them into some form of readable English. But it was a way of learning the screenplay. I learned a lot about that. They do very flowery screenplays in Italy; they're not like ours which are all rather sparse. I learned about that, and it was also a tremendous help to my making a living.

But I was impatient, as some of your younger writers might be. I wanted to write plays for the theatre, but the British theatre was so locked into the whole Anti-Establishment movement that John Osborne had initiated with *Look Back in Anger* that unless plays were, what they called in those days, committed, they couldn't get on. So I knew that I should not go into the theatre; some inner self-preservation told me that. So I wrote novels. And my novels were wonderfully received and read by my family and friends. I don't think I made a penny out of them. But I loved writing them, and I learned to write. And it didn't really change for me until the end of the seventies when I was already in my mid-forties when I wrote *The Ordeal of Gilbert Pinfold*. I adapted the Evelyn Waugh novel for the theatre. That was the first big success I had. It was wonderfully received. And then I wrote *The Dresser.*

So the time when I was going to Italy was a period both of pleasure – in going to Italy and finding out about Italy because it's a wonderful place, a magical place – and also of being dissatisfied with what I was writing, so it was twofold. It was also a rather difficult period as my family were young and growing up.

**The extraordinary thing in all that is the somewhat random choice of a typewriter as a birthday present from your father-in-law with no prior knowledge of the potential such a tool would unlock in you.**

That's because he made them. He was a director of Block and Anderson, duplicating machines and that sort of thing.

*What if he'd given you a set of golf clubs instead?*

I would have become a professional golfer, I know, but it is very odd.

*Can you say something about visual vs. dialogue, theatrical vs. cinematic?*

As I've already mentioned, in the theatre the place where you sit is called the auditorium, that's a place where you listen. Auditorium means a place where you listen. In the cinema, you sit in a place where you watch this huge image. Theatre is a medium of language, the cinema is not, though it can be. I think we're too harsh on the cinema, in a sense.

We are so strict about the short concentration span now and the images flashing before you, I think it's gone much too far. And on the whole, if you look at *Oliver Twist*, you see we don't go in for that contemporary pacing which is so often already out of date, even while filming is taking place.

If you look at older films, if you look at *Casablanca* or at any of those so-called classics, they have long dialogue scenes. We don't have that anymore. And, in a sense, you can't do it anymore because the concentration span is much shorter. Nevertheless, I think that movies can deal with serious subjects in dialogue provided the visual impact, from time to time, is intriguing, is magnetic.

*Would you describe yourself as a 'visual' writer?*

No, not at all. I've got a very bad visual sense in a certain way. I think it's rather clichéd, my visual imagination. Nevertheless, I know what you should see next. I'm not sure I'd know the aesthetic of that. But I know that if you have a quiet scene with a man and woman going to bed or something, the next scene should have a snap to it, visually. I know that. But that's a technical link that I have. But if you said, 'Where would be the most beautiful place to set this,' I wouldn't be able to answer that. I can't think in those terms. I have to know what the scene is about more than where it should be set. That's the playwright in me rather than the screenwriter.

### How faithful should adaptations be?

They should always be faithful to the heart of what is being adapted. That is to say, if *Oliver Twist* is about Oliver Twist, you should be faithful to *Oliver Twist*. I don't think one should change genders for the sake of modern tastes. I don't think one should invent relationships that would not have existed historically at that point or in that kind of novel, which people do all the time in adaptations. I think you have to be ruthless about what you're going to cut in order to get it down to the two-hour period because most things you're given to adapt are very long.

In terms of a novel or a non-fiction work that is to be adapted, you have to be faithful to the heart of it, and you have to protect it. As the screenwriter, one of his duties is to protect that art so that when the director says, 'I think Hamlet should be a woman,' you say 'No, I'm going to walk out on this if that goes through.' Fortunately, I never had that kind of severe disagreement with a director. Nevertheless, you have to be quite wary about what they're wanting to do if it's for the wrong reasons.

It's very interesting, on *Love in the Time of Cholera*, the heroine is very severe. She's a wonderful woman, but severe. She doesn't give an inch: she's tough on her children, tough on her husband, tough on her lover, etc., etc. And there was a move to soften her, and we had a very long discussion about that. Not an argument, a proper discussion. And I won in the end by not doing it in the way that was suggested – I avoided the notion of a flashback in which she would have remembered her lover but which I thought would have been sentimental. Nevertheless, it was right in one sense, she wasn't rounded enough in my screenplay. She just needed a little attention, like a little sandpaper, taking off the edge. And I found a way to do that. But I felt, during the long discussion that we had, that I was, in a way, protecting Gabriel Garcia Marquez, the original author, because his intentions were not to make her soft and sentimental. So that sort of thing, I think it's a duty to defend that.

**But something like Baz Luhrmann's version of Romeo + Juliet, the updating and modernising was completely true to the heart of that story.**

Yes, and I think he did a wonderful job on that. You know, all Shakespeare was in modern dress when it was first done. They didn't pay any attention to historical detail at all. For the Roman plays, they wore a sheet over their shoulders and said it was a toga. They were all modern dress so there's no disgrace in doing *Romeo and Juliet* in punk or whatever. No, he did that very well, I think.

**How does the screenwriter decide how to tell his version of the story?**

With adaptations, when you read the novel or the source material, a point of view will appear. Now, the most important thing in the writing of a novel is the point of view. That's to say, is it an 'I' novel where the narrator is the hero and tells you the story, or is it 'God's' point of view, or is it several points of view like *Rashomon*, where one incident is viewed very differently by a number of people? So the novel will be the clue to the point of view.

I don't think the screenwriter should impose himself in that sense on the novel unless it's an absolutely essential way of telling the story. I wrote the screenplay for a book called *The Diving Bell and the Butterfly* about a man who's had a savage stroke and has got what's called 'Locked-In Syndrome'. He's totally useless physically, but his brain is as bright and as intelligent and as active as when he was well. And it's told in the first person in the book. What I did, I decided the camera should be him in bed when he's got the 'Locked-In Syndrome', but when he remembers himself and his past and thinks of things he would like to do in the future, you can see the real man. So when you see him in his crippled state, you only actually see him when he passes a mirror or in the reflection of a window or the terrible look people have when they look at him. It's a true story and a wonderful title: the diving bell is what he's locked into and the butterfly is his imagination.

So, the point of view is not imposed, but it's expressed as a result of the book that you're working on. And I don't think one should impose oneself as an adaptor.

I would love to write another novel. And I've been trying and fiddling with one recently. It's not very good at the moment but it may come back at me somehow. It's finding the right point of view.

Graham Greene once said to me, 'The most important thing in any novel is the point of view.' Well, it's not in a film. Most films are told from 'God's' point of view, 'God's' eye view of the story. You don't have many 'I' stories in films though there are a few. *The Diving Bell and the Butterfly* is an 'I' film: 'I saw', 'I am', etc. And it's interesting that *The Quiet American* is told in the first person of the Michael Caine character. It's one of the great first-person books ever written because he's not the centre of the story. He affects the ending, morally, but he's not the centre. The Quiet American is the centre. So when you come to do a film of it, of course, you have to ignore the first person. And I think the film copes rather well with that. It doesn't bother you that it's no longer an 'I' story.

**What is the process of deciding how is the story told, whether in the first person perhaps with flashbacks or third person?**

That all depends upon the book you're doing. There is no general rule about that.

It's possible to tell a film in the first person but you have to have a voice-over. It's the only way you say that it is first person and you have the camera as the central character. But there are very few subjects that would lend themselves to that. So the usual point of view in the movies is always God. It's God-like, it's a third person. It's someone observing, which is what a camera is in the end. A camera hasn't got a point of view except for which way you point it.

You can change the point of view of who sees the scene of course, but that's a different matter.

**Do you ever use voice-over as narrative?**

Yes I do, a lot. But it has to be rooted. You have to know why the story's being told by the voice-over. And it's very interesting [that] when I started on *Love in the Time of Cholera*, which is a very long, complex novel with complex time changes, I knew I needed a voice-over. And at one point, after about a month or writing, I thought, 'I'll have to stop this, I can't solve this problem.' And then I realised if I stopped, I'd have to give back the money so I immediately went on. And I invented. It's just a couple of lines in the book: he goes up to a lighthouse and talks to the lighthouse keeper.

Well, I used the lighthouse keeper as the reality of why he's telling the story. He talks to the lighthouse keeper, and that solved it. The screenplay was finished about a month or so after that.

I think you can use a voice-over, but it can't be 'God' telling the story. If it's a character, there has to be a reason why he's telling it. That's essential.

**When that happens to you now, when suddenly the solution to a problem falls into place, does that give you the same sort of thrill as when you first started writing?**

Oh, absolutely. Yes, there's no jaded feeling about writing, not to me at any rate. I love writing, and solving solutions of that kind are thrilling.

**How does the screenwriter cope with supplying the required 'happy ending' for a film, even where there is none in the source material?**

The happy ending, the 'up' ending, is a very, very interesting problem. Films on the whole, if they want to be popular films, cannot deal with tragic subjects tragically.

Aristotle believed that catharsis, which is a theatrical device and can be taken to mean purification as by a purgative, was the inevitable result of witnessing tragedy in the theatre. He claimed that it was one of the ways by which human beings can be purged of stress and inner conflict. The cinema repeatedly fails to allow catharsis to take place because of the desire for the 'up' ending and the feel good factor and [this], more often than not, leads to a particular vice of some Hollywood filmmakers that results in manipulation, sentimentality and therefore in gross falsification.

Intensifying the emotion of characters, making the victims too noble or the villains too inhuman, the use of lush music to accompany scenes, even dare I say it, the introduction of a young girl in a red dress as a motif to intensify loss, are to my sensibilities best described as schmaltz and should be resisted.

That is the reason why films so seldom present a genuine tragic experience. It's ridiculous but I'm sure they're right: you should come out feeling good about yourself, good about the movie, and I understand that. But, God, it puts terrible restrictions on you.

The 'happy ending' is a hell of a problem. It is a problem to me and I don't know how to advise anyone else how to deal with it other than to say, when you go into writing a movie, it's going to be part of the problem. And you hope to God that the subject matter has a way of having an 'up' ending that's not sentimental, that's not a lot of people laughing – you know, the laughing ending that we all know from television. Everybody's so happy, after a terrible tragedy, or somebody says, 'Tomorrow's another day!' I'm not being disparaging. It's a bloody hard problem to solve.

**There are some subjects that appear to defy such a possibility such as Schindler's List. How do you get the happy ending on that sort of film?**

Well, we were very fortunate in *The Pianist*. First, because the German saves him in the end and, second, because I came up with the spectacular idea of having him play the Chopin Piano Concerto at the end. It's the only time I've ever seen the audience sit and watch the credits, because we ran the credits over the music. It's a glorious piece of music and is, in itself, uplifting. Chopin is one of the few composers who ever lived who can actually pierce your soul. So, we were fortunate with that.

But it's very difficult. In *Oliver Twist*, for example, we just had him in the coach, and Mr Brownlow puts his arm around him, and you have the music take you out. But that's part of the game. It's a shame really because film is a popular medium, it's not an esoteric medium. It's a big, popular medium and you have to accommodate that.

### How daring can one be in fighting convention?

Oh, all the time. But you'll get caught out if you do it for the sake of defying convention. If it comes out of the material you're doing, then you've got to do it. But the moment you say, 'wouldn't it be great if…' whatever, you're defying convention because you think it would be smart and 'Look, Mummy, I'm a screenwriter and I'm making interesting movies,' you'll get caught out. You may make one or two very successful films and then, 'Good night, sweet prince.'

### What is the place of the 'free' adaptation?

I don't know what that means. I'm not trying to be cute, but what does it mean? That you get hold of a book, you pay a lot of money for the rights and then you ignore it entirely, is that what it means? It's not my game so I don't know what it means.

And it's certainly not the game played by any of the directors I've worked with. This sounds very condescending and I don't mean it to be but it might be a young person's game or people on the make. They might take an old classic and think, 'We could do this as…' whatever. Not like Baz Luhrmann did it because Baz is good. What I mean is *Twelfth Night* set at the White House, that sort of thing. Wanting to be more important than the subject you're adapting.

Taking a classic and totally changing it seems to me ridiculous. I think the adaptor is the servant of the source material. I really do believe that, otherwise there's no point in adapting it.

**Hitchcock's version of The Thirty-Nine Steps *bears little resemblance in many places to the actual book.***

Ah, in that particular case, it's actually better than the book, I have to say. *The Thirty-Nine Steps* is a very, very good film. I read the book recently, just out of interest. It was on my shelf, I didn't know I had it. I looked at it, and it's not very good. It creaks like mad. The film is so much better. The book doesn't have the wonderful scene with the girl in the hotel. No, that film is excellent.

***That's an interesting quandary. If you were working with Polanski and he said, 'I've got this book,* The Thirty-Nine Steps*, but although this creaks and that creaks, there's a really good story in here.***

Yes, I would go with that. And that must happen all the time. It hasn't happened to me much but, you know, I don't do popular things. If I looked at my biography, I'd think, 'God, I don't know how I've made a living.' I don't do big, major movie things on the whole. I just don't do them. So the necessity to escape from the source material and improve it has not come my way very much. So I'm not very expert in that area.

But I can see it would be marvellous, and some people have a wonderful gift with that sort of thing. Mostly Americans, I have to say. They're really good at that. Making a thriller out of something that isn't really a good thriller. They know how to put the screws on. Like *The Bourne Identity*. But that's beyond me.

### What are the limitations on adaptations, if any?

For me personally? I seem to be asked to do very, very difficult things, or they seem to me very difficult. *Love in the Time of Cholera* was very difficult. *The Diving Bell and the Butterfly* was very difficult. I don't know why, but that's just what comes my way. And they're not big, popular subjects. They're not going to have Brad Pitt in them.

One fascinating thing about that – I was at a dinner with several people and David Attenborough, the naturalist, was there, and he talked about the birth of a butterfly. Well, I was just beginning the script for *The Diving Bell and the Butterfly* so I took him aside and I said, 'David, tell me, just exactly how does a butterfly come about?' And he described it and the kind of camera that you use and everything. So you see the butterfly come out and then float free, it's a terrific sequence. And I just described it as he told me really. I know him quite well, but I'd never have thought to phone him in a million years, and he just happened to talk about precisely that. You get those pieces of luck, you know. Divine intervention.

### What's interesting with the Hollywood studios is that when they want difficult or very literary adaptations, they don't go to Americans, they come to you or Tom Stoppard because they assume you're both actually British, which neither of you are.

No, we're not. But they take it that we're cultured or intellectually gifted. But this, of course, is rubbish. American screenwriters are absolutely wonderful writers, I think. Wonderful. Not all of them of course, but a great many of them. And I think it's a kind of snobbery on the part of those Hollywood producers who come to us.

I know with *Love In The Time Of Cholera*, the Gabriel Garcia Marquez book, they went through hundreds of writers. They didn't offer it to anybody before me, but they had long lists. But they were happier with a European writer.

**Having dealt with subjects involving the war, music, etc., it must have been quite a stimulating change.**

It was. When you asked why I took things, that was one of the reasons. I'd never done anything like that. It's a love story. It's set in Latin America and I thought, 'God, yes, I'd love to do that.' The odd thing was that within a week of accepting that, two other things came my way which were also Latin American, sort of magical Mexican things, and I was very pleased I'd accepted *Love in the Time of Cholera*. It was lovely, it was so refreshing for me. A world I knew nothing about, so I had to explore that and understand that. It was lovely.

**Can you compare the thinking involved in adapting a well-known classic such as Shakespeare as against adapting the lesser known or obscure works? Is there a different approach?**

Yes there is. Dickens is a much better example, if you'll forgive me saying so, than Shakespeare, which I've not done. With a Dickens, everybody knows it, that's the problem. Or you may be wrong and think that everyone knows it because it's so well known. And you say, 'How can we make it special?' Polanski and I probably had that conversation. He said, 'We'll just do it properly,' in the perhaps arrogant belief that nobody else has done it properly, I suppose.

With an obscure book, you have a little more freedom. To explore and invent, if you need to. It would be tricky with a Dickens novel like *Oliver Twist* to introduce a character that doesn't exist in the book but who might be able to push the story in another direction. I think that would be very, very difficult to do. But you could do that in the lesser known work.

### Adaptations, almost by definition, involve changes to the source material, such as re-organising the sequence of storytelling.

Oh, you do that all the time. You have to do that. Say it's a novel. (I seem to keep giving examples from Graham Greene, however...) I had a curious and short friendship with Graham Greene and we discussed the novel a lot because I was a novelist then and wanted to write more novels. Greene said to me, 'Anybody can write scenes in a novel.' Anybody can write a good scene – husband and wife parting, lovers re-meeting, whatever. 'The difficulty in a novel is the connecting passages.' Ten years later, yesterday, tomorrow, whatever – those connecting passages to the big, key scenes are the difficulty.

So it is in films. Anybody can write a scene in a film; it's how the story is linked that is crucial in a movie. And so, although there is a resemblance between the novel and the film in general, you sometimes have to check on the novelist – if you're adapting a novel – that he's told it in the order that makes for a good dramatic story because a novelist is often not interested in the drama. He's often interested in a much wider sweep of events. So yes, you have to change them.

Early on in my career, I was very fortunate to be taught the postcard system by the director, Alexander Mackendrick. You take a pile of postcards and you put: 'Exterior. London. Day. – Shot of the city.' Next postcard: 'Interior. John's Office. Night. – John is at his typewriter working.' And you do the whole film in postcards. You put them on a board and you say, 'No, maybe it would be better if you start with John and then see London' or 'Perhaps you do need an exterior there. Perhaps you do need to see him running down the street. You can't just pick him up in the house. You have to see how he gets there.' Whatever it may be. Now, of course, you can do all that on *Final Draft*, the computer programme we all have. That's got a postcard system. And you can fiddle and change and it's much easier to do the postcards on a computer so that you structure a story in terms of scenes.

So I was fortunate to learn that very early, a pile of postcards. I might only do a sequence with it now. I won't do the whole film that way. But you have to structure the story and that's one of the ways of doing it. You can even do the novel in postcards to see how the film should be. I sometimes did the novel on green postcards and white for the movie. These are all just simple technical aids to organise your material, which is very, very important in movies.

*Again, talking about changes to the source material, what are your thoughts about the adaptor imposing a different climax?*

Imposing. I'm worried about that word. I think if you find a different climax, it has to arise out of the material itself. To be imposed sounds as if you're disturbing what is already there.

*Have you ever come across the idea of changing the plot to sub-plot?*

(*Laughter*) No. That I don't think is a good idea.

*When you're writing a screenplay, do you ever think of budgetary constraints or do you just go where your mind takes you?*

No, they'll tell you that afterwards. But, of course, in the sense of your question, you have to be aware that you can't just write anything. You can't have a chase with four thousand extras. But you only know about budgetary constraints after you've finished. They say, 'Ronnie, 'You can't have this scene. We've got to cut this down.' And sometimes that is a practicality that you have to obey.

*With such considerations, do you edit yourself?*

Well, if they told me that, I would change it. I actually love budgetary constraints. I always think it improves the movie. I think the idea that you can have a limitless budget is a nonsense. You're dealing in the real world. There's no point.

*What sort of problems does chronology present to the adaptor?*

There is a problem about chronology, that's time passing. Time passing is one of the most difficult things to overcome whenever I write a screenplay. How do you tell them it's a year later without a caption? How do you tell them time has passed? It's very hard.

The other day I was watching *A Man for All Seasons* and I noticed there's a shot through a little window of Thomas More's cell in the Tower of London, and the season's change. That's quite clichéd. We did it in *The Pianist*. You suddenly see autumn leaves being blown down an alleyway or something and that tells you time has passed. Chronology is always a problem, especially over a very long period.

I remember being very bogged down in *The Browning Version* because I didn't know how to go from the end of a daylight sequence, a picnic on the hillside overlooking the cricket at his school in the daytime, to the next scene at night, with the leading character, played by Albert Finney, getting ready to go out. I knew that you couldn't have a shot of the house with lights on or any kind of exterior. You wanted to go straight into the scene and I didn't know how. I was stuck for two or three days, and I phoned Ridley Scott and said, 'Look, I've got a problem here' and I explained it to him. He said, 'Well just start with his wife tying his bow tie.' And I thought, God, it would have taken me a month to work that out. When I tell it now, I think how stupid I was because it's such an obvious solution, and it works marvellously. But that's the difference, Ridley thinks visually.

In *Love in the Time of Cholera* I have a fifty-two year period to encounter, so you have to have two sets of actors because they start off at seventeen and they end up seventy. And, you know, the man can grow a moustache and the woman can have her hair swept up rather than in ringlets or whatever it is. But it's a constant problem, the chronology in a film, and it has to be solved. And it should be solved with a certain degree of smartness, elegance.

**And the trick is always avoiding captions if possible.**

Yes, or voice-overs, you know – 'I didn't see him for forty-two years.' You have to be very careful of all that.

**What are your thoughts on adding character detail (traits, quirks, etc.) that don't necessarily exist in the source material? Do you resist that?**

Ah yes, this is a Hollywood thing – that the man's always poking his ear or he has a tick. It depends. If it's essential to his character, I would put it in. But I would never impose that. I'd rather leave that to the actor. If the actor felt that there was some characteristic that was needed, that would be fine.

Hollywood feels that that is a character thing, it's not. It's a behaviourist thing. And I don't think one should put behaviour into a character. That should come out of the character, if you see what I mean.

## What's your approach to choosing a style for your story?

When it comes to style, it has to come out of the heart of the book. It's not to be imposed. I think bad directors impose their own style, and it's just a way of showing off. They shoot through chair legs or tree branches and say it's style. It's not style, style is expressing the heart of the book.

## How precisely would you define a scene?

Well, I define a scene by the word 'drama'. I think the actual meaning of 'drama' is 'something done'. Something has to happen in a scene. Even if they're saying, 'Did you sleep well last night?', there's got to be a reason for asking that. And there has to be tension of one kind or another in every scene in every movie. And every play too.

It's to do with something happening. It can be very trivial, but there's got to be something happening. You can't just have a scene where people have a leisurely conversation about the weather unless it actually matters to the movie. Unless they need good weather for the job they're going to do or whatever. So that's how I would approach it. And I always know when one's written a flat scene because nothing happens in it.

### Are there any rules for the number of scenes?

No, there can't be. The number of scenes depends upon what the story requires.

### How do you know if you need a particular scene?

Well this is difficult because, in the old days, there were what were called 'obligatory scenes'. I'll give you a very good example: in Graham Greene's novel, *The Heart of the Matter*, the one set in West Africa, Scobie, the policeman, sees survivors being taken off a ship on to the quayside, some on stretchers and some helped by sailors. They've been wounded in a torpedo attack. And one of the figures that passes him is a beautiful woman on a stretcher. And they look at each other, in the book, and the next thing they're in bed together. They're having an affair.

Now J. B. Priestley said to me, 'I don't like that. You've got to have the obligatory scene. How did he get her into bed?' Well, you don't have to have the 'obligatory scene', the fact is he got her into bed. And you have to trust that that's true. That she would want that and that he would want that. So, there's an old-fashioned view that there are things called 'obligatory scenes' but I don't believe there are.

And you can tell the story very boldly sometimes by saying, 'Oh God, shouldn't he see her again?' You say, 'No, you don't need that.' Just go to them doing whatever they're doing. So I think you have to use your own judgement in avoiding the 'obligatory scenes' sometimes. Or you may be wrong to avoid it. But there's no rule about it, I'm afraid. It's a question of your taste and judgement.

*It's almost an era choice, it comes as a pleasant shock to the quicker audience who have already made the mental bridge and anticipated such a possibility.*

Exactly.

*How do you know when a scene is finished?*

This is very difficult for the screenwriter. I like to write to a climax in a scene, some kind of dramatic climax. And when it's edited, you find they've taken that out and it's gone to the next scene. And you think, 'It's much better their way.'

You cannot do it on the page, you can only do it when it's been filmed. I don't know why. I've talked to lots of people about this. Many writers have this problem. When do you come out of a scene? What's the 'out' in a scene? Well, I now ignore that because I've never got it right. Never. So I write to the climax of a scene and, if in the editing it doesn't work, they'll take it out. So I trust the editing process, which I do think is where the film is actually made.

*What would you say to writers who would disagree with that.*

I'd say they're wrong because the visual image and the screenplay are two different things. Once it's realised on film, something happens and you've got to acknowledge that. You just simply have to.

*When there is normally so much which could be included in an adaptation, how do you know when you've reached the end point? Is time the best constraint, limiting the screenplay's pages to the standard length of a feature film?*

I can understand this question very well and I don't think it is as simplistic as it may appear. As I've already mentioned, I'm very fortunate to have an instinct about time. I have a sort of in-built clock. I know when I'm going a bit long here. You can't do that the first time through. But when you've done your own first draft – not the one you deliver – and it comes out at a hundred and forty pages, you know you're too long so you've got to go through it meticulously and unpick it and see what you don't need.

It's not something you can judge in advance, it's only something you can judge in retrospect. But don't worry about it. Getting it down on paper is the most difficult thing, and then you can fiddle with it. That's the essential thing. But I can see the concern. It's an insecure world and that's a question of insecurity about length. But that's not the important thing. The important thing is to tell the story properly, you can cut it afterwards.

*A screenplay's length seems to be a universal question for novice writers. I've seen scripts of 250 pages that the writer imagines could possibly be a final draft.*

It is extraordinary, that. But it's just that my upbringing, my training in the theatre, showed that a play is two hours, two and a quarter hours. So you learn that.

**How does the adaptor choose the start and end of the film that may vary greatly from the source material's beginning and ending?**

I think that's something that arises out of the material. These questions seem to imply that you can make these decisions before you write and I don't think you can. You can only make these decisions as a result of writing. That's my method. You just take your life in your hands and write the bloody thing and see what problems are thrown up by that process.

**The adaptation process may require cherry-picking characters as well as condensing, combining or losing characters, sub-plots, themes, etc. Of necessity, the information provided by three characters may be given to one in the film.**

Yes, you can do that. We did that in *Oliver Twist*. I should also say something else about *Oliver Twist*, a very interesting thing Polanski said to me. There's a famous line in *Oliver Twist* of Mr Bumble's, 'If the law supposes that, the law is a ass,' which is not in our film.

It's inclusion depends on Mr Bumble marrying the woman who runs the workhouse right at the beginning. And when we were talking about what we would cut, I said, 'You know we're going to cut a very, very famous line?' Polanski said, 'You cannot put in ten scenes for one famous line.' And that's a very good piece of advice. You just can't do it.

**And how many writers have spent ages trying to do just that?**

David Lean did it. He has that whole sub-plot in his film which is meaningless, I think. Just for the one-liner. I think even the musical does it. Because they're scared of people saying,

'How could they miss out such a famous line?' Nobody took any notice of our leaving it out.

**Can you say something about the writer's influence on the director's decisions: casting, etc.?**

None. (*Laughter*) And the writer shouldn't really expect any. Not in the movies, he shouldn't.

**You mentioned using postcards. Do you use any of the other conventional tools: character arc, three act structure, etc.?**

I do use the three act structure: Act One, Act Two and Act Three. It's just a very good way of seeing where you are. And if anybody's very worried about time, you know, 'How long is a script?', it's very good to say something around thirty-five minutes an act.

When I was discussing screenwriting with Tom Stoppard at a public conversation recently, there was a question from the audience asking Tom for his 'methodology' for plotting and creating the story. And after he had ascertained the questioner's definition of 'methodology', which included possible elaborate character biographies and character pictures pinned on the wall and plotline cards and so forth, Tom paused and said, 'I feel I do all of those things without needing to do them in fact.' (*Laughter*)

**Is it legitimate to use other source material?**

Yes, you can do that, but I can't see the need for it. Perhaps I can see it in an historical piece. I can see it more in *Taking Sides,* for example. There may be stuff that other people have done about the Nazi period or the mention of a simultaneous event. Yes, you can do that. There are no rules. This is the most terrible thing to realise.

**How does one approach things that fall outside of today's Political Correctness as exemplified by a title like Agatha Christie's Ten Little Niggers?**

That title is not germane to the story.

**But if in such a story, they talked about 'niggers'?**

Then I would have 'niggers'. I would say 'niggers' if it's true to the period. And I've had that recently. But you'd loose this battle if you did. If you said, 'I think they should say "nigger"', you can be sure that that would be changed by the producers or the distributors. It's not the writer's prerogative. This is where the writer is not in control in the movies.

**But you, as a writer, would be true to the period.**

I would. If I could be, I certainly would be. But they'd say, 'Can you change this!' I'd say, 'No, I can't.' and it would be changed. You can be sure it will. They'll dub it and say 'black' or whatever. You can't win that battle, but I think you should try. You should fight Political Correctness.

And the whole thing about smoking. We had letters. As *Oliver Twist* was being filmed, Roman and I had a letter from an American academic saying, 'I hope there will be no smoking in your film.' A long, long letter. Well the boys smoked pipes, we took no notice of that. So you can get away with that, but sometimes it's unlikely. You just have to take your chances really.

***In adapting anything from another medium with its own length, how does one decide the new time parameter?***

Well, I've never adapted a short story but I think that must have terrible difficulties about time. Where do you expand it? Why do you expand it? Why do you want to make it two hours when it's only twenty minutes? Those are very difficult things to answer in the abstract. You'd have to be very specific about it. That's why they made 'portmanteau' pictures in the forties and fifties. You know, Somerset Maugham's *Trio* and *Quartet*. They were three and four stories because none of the stories expanded.

***Two brilliant Stephen King short stories worked very well, The Shawshank Redemption and The Green Mile.***

Yes, obviously it can be done. I haven't read them, but I can see there would be difficulties.

***Have you ever been approached to adapt an epic film?***

No, but epics can present particular difficulties. There was a wonderful one called *Sodom and Gomorrah* with a wonderful opening: a woman running along a beach and she was chased by a patrol on horseback trying to catch up with her. And when they got near and the camera went in very, very close, the leading captain of the group leant down and said, 'Beware the Sodomite patrols.' (*Laughter*). It was terrific. My wife and I saw it at the Hammersmith Odeon and the audience went berserk. There was also another wonderful line when Stewart Granger, playing Lot, told the queen to follow him out of the city that was going to be destroyed, and she said, 'I will not go with you, Lot.' (*Laughter*) So I have a great deal of sympathy for the difficulties that arise from that genre. You know, 'This Christianity, can anybody join?'

### Have you ever adapted TV to cinema?

Yes, I've already mentioned that I've done two of my own plays. That's how I first started. *The Barber of Stamford Hill* was my first television play, and we made it in black and white into an hour long film, maybe a little longer, with John Bennett and Megs Jenkins. And *Private Potter* with Tom Courtney, which is my second television play. Yes, I've done that. That was from television to film. I think we spoiled *Private Potter* by 'opening it out'. We didn't know enough then.

### Did you use the same cast?

From *Private Potter*, Tom was there, and Leo McKern. Yes, I think we did use a lot of the same cast, but not all, I'm sure, because they weren't all free at the same time.

### I think this question was aimed more at the Star Trek sort of adaptation.

Ah, I've not done that. I don't get asked to do that. I write in a very specialised area and it's not the popular area. And people should be made aware of that. (*Laughter*) It's just a different world.

### Have you ever adapted fantasy such as X-Men?

No, I can't do that. It's not because I don't, it's because I have no gift for it. I've not got that kind of imagination.

### Have you ever adapted docudrama?

I've done a lot of docudrama. *Mandella* was docudrama.

*Can you say something about adapting a true life story?*

That can be very tricky. For one thing, it's very, very difficult because you have to have legal clearance. We had a lot of trouble when I did *Mandella* because Mrs Mandella objected to them being seen in bed together. I had a scene where they lay side by side in bed, and though they had three children, she found it very offensive that they were in bed together. We didn't change it, but you come up against these problems.

I was asked quite recently to do something about a true event that took place a few years ago in the United States. I was asked to adapt a story using actual court transcripts, the actual location and the actual people involved. And when I was in America for the preliminary discussions, the studio asked me what characters I would use and I said, 'As far as I know, I'll use such-and-such characters.' And they said, 'We'll get clearance.' And so they go to them and they give them, I forget what it's called, a 'True Life Contract' or something. And the people give permission for themselves to be used.

*Even so, presumably the lawyers play a big part.*

Lawyers. This was a meeting with lawyers. Then they'll go through it like mad. But I don't bear any of that in mind while I'm writing because it would then be terribly inhibiting. And I'd much rather be told afterwards, 'You cannot say that' or 'You can't suddenly make him bear his bum in public because he didn't do that' or whatever it might be.

*If you're writing a play or screenplay with a location unfamiliar to you, do you go there?*

I would love to go there, but the opportunity doesn't arise. Firstly, I would have to finance it myself, which I wouldn't mind doing now. I couldn't have done it in my early days, I couldn't have afforded it. But, in the end, it's time consuming.

Normally, the place is not important enough to telling the story. It will be, presumably, when we make the movie, but to get it going, I don't think it's necessary. With *Love in the Time of Cholera*, I hadn't been to Colombia, I trusted Garcia Marquez on his description of where he was born and set his novel. It's perfectly brilliantly done. So no, I don't. And I'm not good on location. I get bored with directors looking through lenses.

But let me say something that comes under the heading of good advice from personal experience. It's to do with this actual event that I was recently asked to adapt. After being in America for a week of conversations, I came back and started work on it, started the research. And after about three months work, I knew I had made a terrible, terrible mistake. Firstly, I have no insight into small town American mentality; secondly, I don't know the American institutional system that applied in this case, things that we take for granted because we know the system here so well; and thirdly, I found the characters, the actual people, extremely limited. And so I decided with much regret to break it off and return the money. I wired the money back. Of course my agents weren't pleased, but I'm the one who has to do the writing and I simply couldn't. And the real reason was that I have no insight into the American small towns. That's jolly difficult to do if you don't know the 'smell of it', and you can't just get that in a research document. In this instance, you had to go there, live there, because the system which was so crucial to that story is so completely different from ours. So I withdrew.

And I can tell you that it was because I didn't obey something which I've talked to you about before – a writer should always know what he can write. And I should have known that in the beginning, and I was careless because I was so courted and wooed. You get caught up in it. It's the bullshit side of our business and I was caught in it. And I deeply regret it and I had a really anguished time over it. Really. And now it's over, but that's a lesson well worth articulating.

**Once a project has been offered, how useful is your agent's input in discussing it? Have you ever used them as a sounding board?**

No, never. I personally don't and wouldn't. In certain cases with films, I would now – not before, because I didn't have the position – I would ask Ben Smith or Judy Daish what they thought, only in terms of, 'Do you think this is a film I should go with?' I might take their advice on whether it's something I should do. But not on the content. Never. I'd never discuss that with anybody except the people involved.

**When considering adapting for the screen, what are the rights issues: getting a release, taking an option or public domain material?**

Well, as you will have gathered from the *Being Julia* story, I'm not in the 'rights obtaining' business. I find I have no patience. To be a producer, you have to have enormous patience, and you have to have several projects on the go. Otherwise you'd go mad. You can't have just one at a time like a writer has.

**So, for the writer who wants to adapt, who's just starting out, having neither professional nor financial backing, he'd have to write something on spec and hope for the best.**

Yes, or he'd have to find someone who shares that interest and will go ahead and try to get the rights. Or else find something in the public domain, of course. That's the best. Public domain's cheapest.

**How do you keep the faith and not get cynical when coping as an intelligent, mature writer in an industry obsessed by youth and their ideas?**

Well, I've been through that. I'm now in my early seventies and I've never been busier in my life. And it's true that I've had an extraordinary last few years and that, I believe, is unusual. I've had a lovely time. But in order to keep faith – I'm going to sound very, very pretentious now – it depends [on] how you regard yourself.

I've always regarded myself as a writer, as a playwright, as an artist. And, for the most part, I've brought that attitude to bear when writing movies. But if you're not that, and you just think it's a scriptwriting operation – the word 'scriptwriting' as opposed to screenplay writing has a different connotation, as if you're just preparing a technical document – then it's difficult to keep faith. It's very difficult.

But I've always been fortunate in being able to express what I've wanted to express through my plays or my novels. So in that sense, I've had a privileged position. But so have Tom Stoppard and Harold Pinter and David Hare. The main English screenwriters of what I would call the 'serious' kind have had another way of expressing themselves outside of the movies. Which comes back to the very first thing we said, which was, 'Do you want to write a play where you're in control or a movie where you're going to hand it over to the director?'

**Have you done an adaptation where the author of the original has not liked the film? And how do you feel about that?**

I've had ones where the widows liked it. I don't know if I've done a living author. Oh yes, I've done Roald Dahl in television, but he was very happy about those. I think he just loved being adapted; he didn't mind what they were like.

**If brought in to do a further draft of someone else's screenplay based on a book, etc., do you start from scratch or work to improve the draft as presented?**

I've only done this once recently. A very famous director came to me with a screenplay which was already set up with two major stars, so I was rather impressed with that, as one would be. And he gave me the screenplay, which was not to my taste, but I liked the director very much, and they then made me an offer I couldn't refuse. The director phoned me and was very sweet, and when people beg you to do things it's very flattering. So I re-wrote it completely. Completely, except for the big, set sequences which were really the director's sequences.

It was a very interesting experience for me and for the director concerned because we come from different ends of filmmaking. He has a vision of the film, I have a vision of the screenplay. And those are very different. And structure: I was very strict about how you tell the story, he was rather uninterested in that. I don't know if I made him more interested but it wasn't part of his concern, he was interested in character.

But I won't do that again. I find it not a productive process at all and at my time of life there's not enough time for that.

### What's your routine for writing: regular hours, at home or do you go away, etc.?

I'll tell you exactly what I do. This has been my routine for nearly fifty years. It was easy when my children were going to school because we had a very strict routine; you had to get them up and get them to school.

Roughly speaking, I rise at 7:15 or 7:30am. I need two hours before I'm in tune. It takes me a long time, a lot of coffee. I make my own breakfast because my wife doesn't eat breakfast. We've been married a long time, you know, so that's our deal. And I have to have a shower and a shave. I can't go to work in a dressing gown, don't ask me why but that's what I have to do. I then sit down and I might do a crossword. I've already done *The Times* crossword with my wife, we do that every morning. I then might do another one or play a few games on the computer. And then I start and I work through till about 12:30pm or 12:45pm.

I then go through and have lunch if I'm at home or out if I have to go for a meeting. Then I come home, and I always have a sleep every afternoon. I read for half an hour, I sleep for an hour. I'm sure this is very boring for people. This is the most boring life imaginable, but I love it. I try to go to bed about 1:30pm so I'm awake at 3:00pm. I have a cup of tea and a chocolate biscuit – it's very important the chocolate biscuit – and then I go back to my work and look at what I've written during the morning. And sometimes you get an urge to go on and sometimes you don't. But I do correct. I correct constantly, re-write and re-write.

And I was given a marvellous piece of advice, again by Graham Greene: 'Always stop when it's going well.' So that you know that you've got something exciting to do. It's been a wonderful piece of advice. Very difficult to obey because sometimes you're in a scene and you think, 'God, this is going well.' Good, leave it there. Leave it there and come back to it tomorrow morning. And that's been my life for nearly fifty years and I love it.

### You don't go anywhere specific to write?

No, I can write anywhere. It's a great, great, good fortune. And now with the laptop, it's just spectacular. I just take that and I'm there. I go to my place in Paris or to my place in Sussex. Mostly I love writing in Paris because nobody bothers me. I don't get invited out to lunches or get tempted to talk to nice people like you. It doesn't happen in Paris.

### Do you set yourself a daily goal of what you hope to accomplish? Five pages a day, three hundred words, that sort of thing?

I don't really. Sometimes you do as much as ten pages a day, and the next day you might do one. I don't set myself those goals but I can see that it would be quite helpful to. It would be quite nice to set a goal and achieve it. But the problem is, if you don't achieve it, you get terribly depressed.

### What's your advice to a writer who is stuck with a problem and it's looming the next day?

I think the advice given me by Graham Greene was the best, stop when it's going well. But to work through a writing block, a temporary writing block, of, 'Where does this scene go? How do I get on with this scene?', I think must be dreadful.

I used to do things – I'd have a bath. I always found a bath released my thoughts, or I'd go for a walk. But now I can't walk because of my arthritic ankle so that's been denied me, but a bath is still possible. But I don't find I need it very much.

I'm very, very fortunate, I've never had a writer's block. I've never had that thing of, 'Oh, I can't write any more'. But people get it all the time.

**One can think of many writers who enjoyed great success very young and may not have lived up to their early promise. You found real success late in life. Do you think this is an advantage?**

I didn't write *The Dresser* till I was forty-six. I agree with you. Too much, too soon is a disaster. I said that to some young writers I gave a talk to. A woman in the audience said, 'It's getting late for me, I'm not a girl any more.' She was in her late thirties or early forties. I said, 'If it's going to happen for you, the timing is totally irrelevant. It'll happen when it happens. It can happen when you're eighty.'

You cannot say, 'God, I should have made it by the time I was thirty.' Made what? They never tell you what 'it' is. Has he made it? Made what? 'Have you written a good work?' is all that matters to a writer. Whether the world appreciates it or not is something that you have no control over. If you're true to yourself and what you can write, and the world crosses your path, terrific.

**In your screenplays, is there a specific 'Ronald Harwood voice' in style, content, etc?**

No, certainly not in my screenplays. In my plays there is, but not in my screenplays. There is a style of writing in my screenplays that is particular to me. I don't use technical language, I am very careful about the prose and I try to make it as readable as possible. When I read other people's screenplays, I see how little they bother with that. But I take immense care about those things and I hope I'm not the only one who does.

### Do you do a lot of research for screenplays?

Oh, absolutely. I'm immersed in research at the moment for something. But even if you're fortunate enough to be given a researcher on a film – another piece of advice to writers – always do your own research because your eye is different from a researcher's eye. Your eye will pick up things that will make a dramatic scene which a researcher may not even think about.

So yes, I do research. Research is the loveliest part. You're just absorbing the subject matter.

### What about Oliver Twist or The Statement, did you do much research for those?

Quite a bit for *The Statement* because I had to know a lot about the background to the French Resistance and the French police and the Militia that existed during the war, which is somewhat described in the novel by Brian Moore, but not enough. I had to know more.

In *Oliver Twist*, Polanski would bombard me with stuff that was not of interest to me. Stuff on how London looked in Dickens' time. I looked at them but it didn't actually affect me. I want to know what the story is and that's my main concern.

### Before success put you in such demand, did you always get enthusiastic and excited about the films you worked on and deeply disappointed if they weren't made, or were you more pragmatic and businesslike in your approach for the sake of sanity?

No, I was disappointed, I was very disappointed. If I'd worked three, four, five, six months on a script – you know, there's always a hopeful moment. 'It looks as if it's going to be done. Oh, I think they're going to do my film' – and when it's not, the depression is immense. But I then got out of it by writing something else.

I think I misused the films in my early days to subsidise my playwriting or my novel writing, and I don't think that did me much good. And I only came to realise how important the films were in their own right when I realised that film was really the art of the twentieth century. And I came to that conclusion when I realised I had to give of myself to everything I did in movies. And I didn't always do that as a younger writer.

*After all the efforts of the director and writer to deliver their successful vision, can you say something about the unforeseen further possible difficulties that can be thrown up within the Hollywood system?*

Well, Tom Stoppard put it down to there being so much at stake. He says that very congenial fellow artists, in the end, will do anything to a final cut rather than loose twelve members of an audience in Nebraska. They're terrified of excluding. If, in their rational moments, they know it's nonsense, in their irrational moments they really think, 'If I don't take out this four syllable word, the film will fail.' Or worse, 'If I do take the difficult word out, the film will succeed.' It becomes completely crazy. People go mad in that last furlong before they have to show their film to anybody.

And in America, I've not known it here, they give cards to preview audiences, and they're given a list of questions: 'How much did you enjoy that? Who did you like best? What did you think was wrong?' And they collect them up afterwards and they're taken very, very seriously. And it's so demoralising. 'Ron, they don't like the kid.' (*Laughter*) It's terrible.

The director Mike Nichols heard that after the first private screening of *The Graduate*. The big cheese from the studio said, 'Well of course, the problem is the boy.' (*Laughter*)

**What would you say your strengths and weaknesses are as an adaptor?**

My weakness is being too faithful to the original material. And that I'm not daring enough for the material. And my strength is that I am faithful to the original material. That's true and that's a pretty good answer. It is absolutely true. I am too faithful sometimes and, therefore, not daring enough, not inventive enough. It hasn't so far screwed me up but I can see that it could be a problem.

**As most of your screenplays have been for Hollywood companies, have you ever considered moving to America?**

Never. Now this is the best advice I give anybody: don't go to Hollywood and live there if you're British or foreign in any way because you will cut yourself off from your life's blood. The language you hear, the accents you hear, the world you draw on is where you are. And to go there is to be taken into a mad house. I know a lot of people who did go there and had a very bad time as a result.

**After first becoming established as a writer of screenplays, did you seek out filmmakers to work with or do they all come to you?**

No. (*Laughter*) Well, I can't say they came running or anything. No, they came to me. But it's a very small circle that I dealt with.

**Did your agents, Jeff Berg and Ben Smith at ICM, suggest things like, 'You should be working with so-and-so, I'll get you together'?**

Well, they do that now, but that's very recent. I get calls saying so-and-so is coming through London. He'd love to meet you and I think you should have lunch with him. But I've told them I don't like that sort of thing. They're bullshit meetings. So, on the whole now, they don't do it. It's time wasting too. I can have a lunch at home. I don't have to have a lunch with a director or a producer.

But in the early days, people didn't come to me, people I wished had, like John Schlesinger whom I knew very well socially. We'd been actors together but he never came near me. I would have loved to have been asked by John to write a movie, but I wasn't his kind of writer. And I knew that, secretly. I knew that Freddie Raphael was more his kind of writer. So you just bide your time really.

**Have you a favourite screenplay you've written that's never been made?**

I wrote one about General Wingate. It looked as if it was going to be made but wasn't. I think I did a very, very good job of it. And another one about the assassination of the Arch-Duke Franz Ferdinand from Sarejevo. I'm not sure that's as good. I haven't looked at it again, but I have a feeling it may not be as good.

**Were these commissioned?**

Yes, Wingate was for Norma Hayman and she adored it, but we didn't get very far with that. The other one was for an Austrian producer who came to me. He wanted to make an English language version.

*But you've never done that thing that the young writer does, writing the great work on spec?*

No, I've never done that, not in movies. But I do that in plays all the time. Every play. I've never been commissioned to write a play. Ever.

*Have you written a play that's never been produced?*

No, I haven't.

*Is there anything you'd have liked to have adapted, either done by others or never done?*

Yes, there are things. I would have loved to have done the Evelyn Waugh trilogy of *Sword of Honour* for television, which is a long three-part book. I took it to the BBC, but they gave it to somebody else and I was deeply hurt. I don't know why they did that, and it was not very successful. As Gore Vidal said, 'When a friend of mine gets a good review, a little bit of me dies.' Well, I must say, I felt that about that. But I would have loved to have done that.

And then there are things that you see like *Capote*, which I would have loved to have done. But no, I couldn't have done it as well as they did it. So, you know, it's no good going through life like that.

*You have achieved everything writers dream of – great success and wealth and standing.*

Oh God, don't say that. It'll all be taken away from me tomorrow.

**_Rather than retiring to a more sedate schedule, why do you continue to work at such a punishing rate?_**

Because I've got enormous energy and I can't do anything about that. I can't play sport any more because of my ankle. I used to play tennis twice a week. I was a good tennis player. I used to play with a pro mid-week and not work on that day, then sleep and have a bath. Oh, it was lovely.

But that's been denied me. And I can't go for country walks any more. So I've got nothing else to do but write, and I've got an enormous amount of energy which, thank God, doesn't seem to have diminished with my great age. And I remember saying to Priestley when I was working with him on _Good Companions_ in 1976, 'Are you going to retire, Jack?' And he said, 'Writers don't retire,' rather brutally, rather fiercely. And there's no thought of that in me, of stopping. I just love working, it's what I do.

**_Did you find that break of going out and having a fierce tennis match helpful?_**

Yes, that was lovely. I got rid of a lot of physical energy which I now can't get rid of and it's very hard on me. That's why I'm going to see some doctors, to see if they can reconstruct my ankle. It was always my ambition to drop dead on a tennis court, you see, but it's been denied.

# Appendix A

# *The Dresser*

A direct comparison of the original stage play
and the adapted screenplay

## Opening In

*That's why I call it 'Opening In'. You have to go into the play or book
and see what's already there that you can express visually. And with
The Dresser, I thought really that one should see some 'Opening In'
because film gave us an opportunity to explore in a way that even
the theatre can't. 'Close-up' is the art of the movie. You can see
emotion and feel it and have one or two scenes outside. And so
that's what we did. Since it's a touring company, you might as well
see them tour.*

### Original Play Script (a)

SIR'S *dressing room and corridor. Light on* NORMAN, *who wears a lost, almost forlorn expression. Light grows to reveal a mud-stained overcoat and crumpled Hamburg lying on the floor. Footsteps.* NORMAN *becomes alert. He rises.* HER LADYSHIP *enters. She stands just inside the doorway*

HER LADYSHIP: He does nothing but cry.

NORMAN: Are they keeping him in?

HER LADYSHIP: They wouldn't let me stay. The doctor said I seemed to make matters worse.

NORMAN: I shouldn't have taken him to the hospital. I don't know what came over me. I should have brought him back here where he belongs.

HER LADYSHIP: Why is his coat on the floor? And his hat–?

NORMAN: Drying out. They're wet through, sodden, if you don't mind my saying so. So was he. Drenched. Sweat and drizzle–

HER LADYSHIP: How did he come to be in such a state, Norman? When you telephoned, I thought at first he'd been hurt in the air raid–

NORMAN: No–

HER LADYSHIP: Or had an accident–

NORMAN: No, not an accident–

HER LADYSHIP: No, I know because they said there was no sign of physical injury–

NORMAN: Your ladyship–

HER LADYSHIP: He's in a state of collapse–

NORMAN: I know–

HER LADYSHIP: How did he get like that?

NORMAN: Your ladyship–

HER LADYSHIP: What happened to him?

NORMAN: Sit down. Please. Please, sit down.
   (*She does so*)
   We have to remain calm, not to say clear-headed.

HER LADYSHIP: The doctor said it must have been coming on for weeks.

NORMAN: If not longer.

HER LADYSHIP: I didn't see him this morning. He left the digs before I woke. Where was he all day? Where did you find him?

## Screenplay (a)

EXT. MARKET SQUARE & ENVIRONS – EVENING

NORMAN, wearing hat, coat and scarf, wandering along a row of stalls and barrows. The 'All-Clear' is sounding and then dies away. Distant sounds of ambulances and fire engines continue. Smoke from the bombing hangs in the air. Not many people about after the raid. NORMAN stops at a stall –

NORMAN

Excuse me, do you have any Brown and Polson's cornflour? I'm at the Alhambra this week, and we use it instead of face powder. Now, I could arrange two complimentaries for any performance if you just happen to have one tiny packet –

(smiles enchantingly)

STALL-KEEPER

Face powder. You'll be lucky. Miss.

NORMAN gives him a withering look, moves on, but there is a sudden shout from somewhere. NORMAN turns sharply, and is horrified by what he sees –

CUT TO

NORMAN AND HIS POV: a little way off, surrounded by a small knot of people, stands SIR near a candle-maker's stall. A tall tallow candle gutters, playing havoc with the shadows. SIR is taking off his overcoat –

SIR

God help the man who stops me!

He throws the coat to the ground. NORMAN starts to run towards him as SIR takes off his hat, throws it down and viciously stamps on it.

CUT TO

CLOSER SHOT SIR: as NORMAN reaches the knot of people who surround him. SIR lifts both hands heavenwards –

SIR

How much further do you want me to go?

**Original Play Script (b)**

NORMAN: What happened was this, your ladyship: after the last 'All-clear' sounded I went into Market Square as dusk was coming on, a peculiar light, ever so yellowish, smoke and dust rising from the bomb craters, running shadows, full of the unexpected. I had hoped to find a packet or two of Brown and Polson's cornflour since our supplies are rather low and the stuff's scarce and you never know. So I was asking at this stall and that was when I heard his voice.

HER LADYSHIP: Whose voice?

NORMAN: Sir's, of course. I turned and saw him by the candle-maker who was shutting up shop for the night. He was lit by one tall tallow candle which was guttering and he looked like that painting of him as Lear, all greens and dark blues seen through this peculiar light. He was taking off his overcoat, in this weather. "God help the man who stops me," he shouted, and threw the coat to the ground just like Lear in the storm scene. Look at it. I don't know if I'll ever get it clean. And he was so proud of it, do you remember, or perhaps it was before your time? The first Canadian tour, Toronto, Raglan sleeves, fur collar, and now look at it.

HER LADYSHIP: What happened after he took off his coat?

NORMAN: Started on the hat, Dunn's, Piccadilly, only a year ago, down on the coat it went and he jumped on it, stamped on his hat, viciously stamped on his hat. You can see. He lifted both hands as he does to convey sterility into Goneril's womb and called out, "How much further do you want me to go?" His fingers were all of a fidget, undoing his jacket, loosening his collar and tie, tearing at the buttons of his shirt.

HER LADYSHIP: Were there many people about?

NORMAN: A small crowd. That's why I ran to him. I didn't want him to stand there looking ridiculous with people all round, sniggering.

HER LADYSHIP: Did he see you? Did he know who you were?

NORMAN: I didn't wait to find out. I just took his hand and said, "Good evening, Sir, shouldn't we be getting to the theatre?" in my best nanny-voice, the one I use when he's being wayward. He paid no attention. He was shivering. His whole body seemed to be trembling, and such a trembling.

HER LADYSHIP: You shouldn't have let the public see him like that.

## Screenplay (b)

He starts to undo his jacket, loosen his collar and tie, his shirt buttons. Some sniggering and laughter from the onlookers. NORMAN quickly pushes his way through to him, takes him by the hand –

NORMAN

(as to a child)

Good evening, sir, shouldn't we be getting to the theatre?

SIR is shivering and deeply distressed. NORMAN tries to pull him away when a WOMAN, wearing bombazine, her hair in curlers, comes forward, collecting up his clothes, including his hat and coat –

BOMBAZINE WOMAN

Come on, love, you'll catch your death. Put your clothes on like a good boy –

SIR turns baleful eyes on her–

SIR

Thank you, my dear, but Norman usually looks after me. I'd be lost without Norman –

NORMAN

I'm Norman! I'm his dresser.

The BOMBAZINE WOMAN hands over the bundle of clothes to NORMAN.

BOMBAZINE WOMAN

(to Norman)

Take care of him, pet.

She grasps SIR'S hand and kisses it.

BOMBAZINE WOMAN

(to Sir)

I were first took to see you when I were but a lass. I'm sorry you're poorly. You were lovely in 'The Corsican Brothers'.

## Original Play Script (c)

NORMAN: It's easy to be wise after the event, if you don't mind my saying so, your ladyship, but I tried to spirit him away, not easy with a man of his proportions, only just then, a woman approached, quite old, wearing bombazine under a tweed coat but perfectly respectable. She'd picked up his clothes and wanted to help him dress. I just stood there, amazed, utterly amazed. He said to the woman, "Thank you my dear, but Norman usually looks after me. I'd be lost without Norman," so I thought to myself this is your cue, ducky, and said, "I'm Norman, I'm his dresser." The woman – she had her hair in curlers – took his hand and kissed it, saying, "You were lovely in *The Corsican Brothers*." He looked at her a long while, smiled sweetly, you know the way he does when he's wanting to charm, and said, "Thank you, my dear, but you must excuse me. I have to make an exit," and ran off.

HER LADYSHIP: He said, I have to make an exit?

NORMAN: Well, of course, I went after him, fearing the worst. I didn't know he could run so fast. I just followed a trail of discarded clothing, jacket, waistcoat, and thought we can't have Sir doing a striptease round the town. But then I found him. Leaning up against a lamp-post. Weeping.

HER LADYSHIP: Where?

NORMAN: Outside the Kardomah. Without a word, hardly knowing what I was doing, I led him to the hospital. The Sister didn't recognise him, although later she said she'd seen him as Othello last night. A doctor was summoned, short, bald, bespectacled, and I was excluded by the drawing of screens.

HER LADYSHIP: And then you telephoned me.

NORMAN: No. I waited. I lurked, as Edmund says, and heard the doctor whisper, "This man is exhausted. This man is in a state of collapse." Then the Sister came out and said I must fetch you at once. That's when I telephoned. And that's how it happened.
(*Pause, 'All-clear' sounds.*)

HER LADYSHIP: He did nothing but cry.

NORMAN: Yes, you said.

HER LADYSHIP: I left him lying on top of the bed, still in his clothes, crying, no, weeping, as though he had lost control, had no choice, wept and wept, floodgates. What are we to do? In just over an hour there'll be an audience in this theatre hoping to see him as King Lear. What am I to do?

## Screenplay (c)

SIR

(smiling)

Thank you, my dear, but you must excuse me. I have to make an exit.

And he suddenly runs off. NORMAN, holding the bundle of clothes, chases after him –

NORMAN

Sir! Sir!

And as he goes out of shot


EXT. ALLEY-WAY – EVENING

NORMAN chasing after SIR, having to pause to pick up SIR'S discarded clothing, tie, jacket, collar. SIR disappears round a corner. NORMAN retrieves SIR'S waistcoat, and


EXT. STREET – EVENING

SIR is leaning up against a lamp-post, weeping. NORMAN enters shot, stands and stares at him helplessly. Gently, he takes SIR'S hand and leads him off, his eyes barely leaving SIR'S face. PASSERS-BY pause to look at them, and


INT. HOSPITAL SIDE WARD – EVENING

NORMAN, carrying SIR'S hat and coat, steps cautiously into the corridor and peers round the door of the side ward to see screens round a bed. He hears the murmur of the DOCTOR'S and SISTER'S voices, and


EXT. STREET – EVENING

HER LADYSHIP and NORMAN walk towards the theatre.

HER LADYSHIP

What are we to do, Norman? There'll be an audience in the theatre tonight hoping to see him as King Lear. What am I to do?

NORMAN

Don't upset yourself for a start.

### Original Play Script (d)

NORMAN: Don't upset yourself for a start –

HER LADYSHIP: I've never had to make this sort of decision before. Any sort of decision before. As soon as I came out of the hospital I telephoned Madge and asked her to meet me here as soon as possible. She'll know what to do.

NORMAN: Oh yes, Madge will know what to do. She won't upset herself, that's for certain. Madge will be ever so sensible. Of course, Stage Managers have to be. I had a friend once, had been a vicar before falling from the pulpit and landing on the stage. Ever so good as an Ugly Sister. To the manner born. His wife didn't upset easily. Just as well, I suppose, all things considered. Madge reminds me of her. Cold, businesslike, boring.

(*Pause.*)

HER LADYSHIP: The doctor took me into a little room littered with enamel dishes full of blood-stained bandages. He apologised. They'd been busy after the air-raid. The smell made me faint. He asked me about his behaviour in recent days. Had I noticed anything untoward? I smiled. Involuntarily. Untoward. Such an odd word to use.

NORMAN: What did you say, if you don't mind my asking?

HER LADYSHIP: I lied. I said he'd been perfectly normal. I didn't want to appear neglectful. I should have been more vigilant. Only last night I woke –

(*Footsteps.* IRENE *enters the corridor.*)

Is that Madge?

NORMAN: No. Irene.

(IRENE *exits.*)

You were saying. Last night you woke.

HER LADYSHIP: He was looking down at me. He was naked. It was bitter cold and he was shivering. He said, "Thank you for watching over me. But don't worry too much. Just go on looking after me. I have the feeling I may do something violent."

NORMAN: Talk about untoward. I'm glad you didn't tell the doctor that, they'd have locked him up for good.

HER LADYSHIP: This morning, our landlady reported something untoward. After breakfast, while I was still asleep, he listened to the news, she said, and wept. Afterwards, he sat at the dining table writing, or trying to write, but all he did was to crumple up sheet after sheet of paper. When I came down I smoothed them out to see what he'd written. My Life. My Life. The rest of the page was empty.

## Screenplay (d)

HER LADYSHIP

I've never had to make this sort of decision before. Any sort of decision before. I'm glad I telephoned Madge. She'll know what to do.

NORMAN

Oh yes, Madge will know what to do. Madge will be ever so sensible. Of course, Stage Managers have to be.

EXT. NEAR THE STAGE DOOR – EVENING

HER LADYSHIP

I should have made him rest. The doctor said he'd come to the end of his rope and found it frayed.

NORMAN

Doctors. Just imagine trying to explain to a doctor what Sir's been through. 'Well, you see, Doctor, he's been trying to recruit actors for his Shakespearean company but all the able-bodied and best ones are in uniform, and the theatres are bombed to bits as soon as you book them, not to mention the trouble this week with Mr Davenport-Scott.' Doctors. He'd have had his hypodermic rampant before you could say 'As You Like It'.

HER LADYSHIP

What's the latest on Mr Davenport-Scott?

NORMAN

If you don't mind, I'd rather not discuss Mr Davenport-Scott with a lady. I'll tell Madge all about it when she comes in.

INT. SIDE WARD – EVENING

DOCTOR filling a syringe. CAMERA PULLS BACK to reveal SIR lying on the bed, SISTER one side of him, a NURSE the other.

DOCTOR

Now, this won't hurt. It's just to make you sleep. You want to sleep don't you?

## Original Play Script (e)

NORMAN: He said to me his autobiography would be his only memorial. "Have you written much," I asked? "Not a word," he said. And last night, after Othello, he asked me, "What do we play tomorrow, Norman?" I told him *King Lear* and he said, "Then I shall wake with the storm clouds in my head."

HER LADYSHIP: I should have made him rest. The doctor said he'd come to the end of his rope and found it frayed.

NORMAN: So would anyone if they'd had to put up with what he's had to put up with. You should've told the doctor all about the troubles –

HER LADYSHIP: No. Civilians never understand.

NORMAN: That's true. Especially doctors. They never understand anything. I could kick myself for taking him to the hospital.

HER LADYSHIP: It was the right thing to do.

NORMAN: I hope so. Doctors. Just imagine trying to explain to a doctor what Sir's been through. "Well, you see, doctor, he's been trying to recruit actors for his Shakespearean company but all the able-bodied and best ones are in uniform, and the theatres are bombed to bits as soon as you book them, not to mention the trouble this week with Mr Davenport-Scott." Doctors. He'd have had his hypodermic rampant before you could say 'As You Like It'. That's all they know. Hypodermics. If a doctor had been through half of what Sir's been through, his rope wouldn't be frayed, it'd be threadbare.

HER LADYSHIP: What's the latest on Mr Davenport-Scott?

NORMAN: If you don't mind, I'd rather not discuss Mr Davenport-Scott with a lady. I'll tell Madge all about it when she comes in. Suffice to say he will not be making an appearance this evening. Of course, I told Sir. I said, "Don't, I beg you, don't let your business manager double as The Fool in *King Lear*." Now he's lost both in one fell blitzkrieg if you'll pardon the expression.

(*Pause.*)

HER LADYSHIP: Madge is right. There's no alternative. We'll have to cancel.

NORMAN: Oh no, your ladyship, cancellation's ever so drastic.

HER LADYSHIP: He's ill. There's no crime in being ill, it's not high treason, not a capital offence, not desertion in the face of the enemy. He's not himself. He can't work. Will the world stop turning? Will the Nazis overrun England? One Lear more or less in the world won't make any difference.

## Screenplay (e)

He approaches SIR who suddenly becomes aware of what is happening. With a wild gesture he pushes the DOCTOR away.

SIR

Sleep. Sleep? 'Glamis hath murder'd sleep, and therefore Cawdor shall sleep no more; Macbeth shall sleep no more.'

The NURSE and SISTER try to hold him down. He fights like a wild animal, and

INT. SIR'S DRESSING ROOM – EVENING

Knock on the door and MADGE enters.

MADGE

Any further developments?

HER LADYSHIP shakes her head.

MADGE

We had better see the manager. Perhaps you ought to come with me.

NORMAN

Oh, your ladyship, please, let's not rush things –

MADGE opens the door, about to leave –

MADGE
(to Her Ladyship)

There's no alternative. I'll be in my room.

MADGE goes.

HER LADYSHIP

Madge is right. He's in hospital. We can't play King Lear without the King. We have to make a decision.

She goes. NORMAN follows –

## Original Play Script (f)

NORMAN: Sir always believes it will.

HER LADYSHIP: Who really cares whether he acts or not?

NORMAN: There's bound to be someone.

> (*Pause*.)

HER LADYSHIP: I never imagined it would end like this. I've always thought he was indestructible. All the years we've been together. Seems like a lifetime.

NORMAN: Even longer he and I. This'll be the first time we've ever cancelled. I want to go to the hospital –

HER LADYSHIP: No, Norman –

NORMAN: I want to sit with him and be with him and try to give him comfort. I can usually make him smile. Perhaps when he sees me –

HER LADYSHIP: They wouldn't even let me stay.

> (NORMAN *fights tears. Pause*.)

NORMAN: Sixteen years. I wish I could remember the name of the girl who got me into all this. Motherly type she was, small parts, play as cast. I can see her face clearly. I can see her standing there, Platform 2 at Crewe. A Sunday. I was on Platform 4. "Norman" she called. We'd been together in *Outward Bound*, the Number Three tour, helped with wardrobe I did, understudied Scrubby, the steward. That's all aboard a ship, you know. Lovely first act. "We're all dead, aren't we?" And I say, "Yes, Sir, we're all dead. Quite dead." And he says, "How long have you been – you been – oh you know?" "Me, Sir? Oh, I was lost young." And he says, "Where – where are we sailing for?" And I say, "Heaven, Sir. And hell, too. It's the same place, you see." Lovely. Anyway. "Norman!" she called. What was her name? She'd joined Sir, oh, very hoity-toity, I thought, tiaras and blank verse while I was in panto understudying the Ugly Sisters. Both of them. "Are you fixed?" she shouted at the top of her voice. Well. To cut a short story shorter, Sir wanted help in the wardrobe and someone to assist generally, but mainly with the storm in *Lear*. I've told you this before, haven't I? Put me on the timpani, he did. On the first night, after the storm, while he was waiting to go on for 'No, you cannot touch me for coining', he called me over. My knees were jelly. "Were you on the timpani tonight?" "Yes, sir," I said, fearing the worst. "Thank you," he said. "You're an artist." I didn't sleep a wink. Next day he asked if I'd be his dresser.

> (*Pause*.)

## Screenplay (f)

NORMAN

Forgive me, your ladyship, it's not a decision you
have to make, it's the right decision –

As he leaves the room –

INT. STAIRS AND LANDING – NIGHT

MADGE leads, HER LADYSHIP follows. NORMAN stops them on the landing.

NORMAN

Please, your ladyship. I had a friend, before one's
face was lined as the saying goes, in a very low
state he was, a pain to be with. Someone close to
him, his mother, I believe, though it was never
proved, understandably upset, made a decision. A
little rest, she said, among those similarly
off-centre, in Colwyn Bay, never a good date, not
in February, wrapped in a grey rug, gazing at a
grey sea. Talk about bleak. Mother-dear made a
decision but it was the wrong decision. My friend
never acted again.

MADGE

We have to face the facts.

NORMAN

I've never done that in my life, your ladyship, and I
don't see why I should start now. I –

BERYL, dressed as a page in 'Lear' comes down the stairs, slinks by them in
embarrassment. When she has passed –

NORMAN

I just like things to be lovely. No pain, that's my
motto.

MADGE

But things aren't lovely, Norman.

She goes. HER LADYSHIP follows. NORMAN trots after them –

## Original Play Script (g)

HER LADYSHIP: My father was exactly the same. Always exaggerated his illnesses. That's why I thought it was not very serious. I thought –

NORMAN: Madge. You can always tell. She walks as if the band were playing Onward Christian Soldiers.

(MADGE *knocks on dressing room door and goes in*.)

MADGE: Any further developments?

(HER LADYSHIP *shakes her head*.)

We had better see the manager. Perhaps you ought to come with me.

NORMAN: Oh, your ladyship, please, let's take our time, let's not rush things –

MADGE: (*to* HER LADYSHIP) There's no alternative.

HER LADYSHIP: Madge is right, he's in hospital. We can't play *King Lear* without the King. No one will pay to see the crucifixion of the two thieves. We have to make a decision.

NORMAN: Forgive me, your ladyship, it's not a decision you have to make, it's the right decision. I had a friend, before one's face was lined, as the saying goes, in a very low state he was, ever so fragile, a pain to be with. You weren't safe from him on top of a bus. If he happened to sit beside you, he'd tell you the ABC of unhappiness between request stops. Someone close to him, his mother, I believe, though it was never proved, understandably upset, made a decision. A little rest, she said, among those similarly off-centre, in Colwyn Bay, never a good date, not in February, wrapped in a grey rug, gazing at a grey sea. Talk about bleak. Mother-dear made a decision but it was the wrong decision. My friend never acted again.

MADGE: (*to* HER LADYSHIP) We have to face the facts.

NORMAN: I've never done that in my life, your ladyship, and I don't see why I should start now. I just like things to be lovely. No pain, that's my motto.

MADGE: But things aren't lovely, Norman.

NORMAN: They aren't if you face facts. Face the facts, it's facing the company I worry about. Poor lambs. What'll happen to them? And the customers? There was a queue at the box office this afternoon, if four elderly spinsters constitute a queue. Pity to give them their money back, they've likely had enough disappointment in life as it is. It's no good Sir talking about responsibility and service and struggle and survival and then you go and cancel the performance.

## Screenplay (g)

INT. UPPER FLOOR – NIGHT

Passage on top floor of theatre. Rooms one side. Doors to flies the other. MADGE goes to her door, unlocks it, turns on the light. HER LADYSHIP stands near the door, NORMAN in pursuit.

NORMAN

No, things aren't lovely if you face facts. It's facing the company I worry about. Poor lambs. What'll happen to them? It's no good Sir talking about struggle and survival and you go and cancel the performance.

MADGE

It's a disease.

HER LADYSHIP

What is?

MADGE

Hopefulness. I think we should discuss this in private.

She goes into her room. With a regretful look at NORMAN, HER LADYSHIP follows. Alone, NORMAN is overcome with tears.

CHARLES, the Stage Door Keeper, calls out.

CHARLES

Norman. Your ladyship.

NORMAN

Your ladyship.

INT. STAGE DOOR KEEPER'S OFFICE – NIGHT

The huddled figure of SIR, seated on a low stool, his hands holding his head. CAMERA PULLS BACK as HER LADYSHIP and NORMAN enter shot. CHARLES hangs uncertainly in the background.

## Original Play Script (h)

MADGE: (*to* HER LADYSHIP) It's a disease.

HER LADYSHIP: What is?

MADGE: Hopefulness. I think we should discuss this in private. I'll be in my room.

   (*She goes.* HER LADYSHIP *is about to follow.*)

NORMAN: Yes, well, perhaps it is a disease, but I've caught something much worse from Sir.

HER LADYSHIP: What?

NORMAN: A bad dose of Holy Grail.

   (*He laughs, but the laughter turns to tears.* HER LADYSHIP *goes to him.*)

HER LADYSHIP: Years ago, in my father's company. The unmentionable Scots tragedy. A new Macduff. Couldn't remember the lines. My father should've sacked him at the end of the first rehearsal. But no, my father said, "He'll know it, he'll know it." He never did.

NORMAN: Oh well, that was the Scots tragedy. Everyone knows that's the unluckiest play in the world. That's the one superstition I believe in absolutely. That play would turn a good fairy wicked.

HER LADYSHIP: In the fight scene. The man couldn't remember the fight. He thrust when he shouldn't have and sliced my father's face across. The right cheek seized up in a lopsided grin. The only part left to my father was Caliban.

NORMAN: It's not the same thing –

HER LADYSHIP: I 'll be in Madge's room if I'm wanted.

NORMAN: Don't decide yet, your ladyship, let me go to the hospital, let me see how he is, you never know –

HER LADYSHIP: I do know. I realise now I've witnessed a slow running-down. I've heard the hiss of air escaping. We'll call the company together at the half. I'll tell them –

   (NORMAN *is suddenly alert.*)

   – that tonight's performance is cancelled, that the engagement is to be ended –

   (*Heavy footsteps. Both look at each other. Footsteps nearer.* SIR *enters in a dishevelled state. Long pause.*)

NORMAN: Good evening, Sir.

SIR: Good evening, Norman. Good evening, Pussy.

## Screenplay (h)

CHARLES

I asked him, joking like, if he'd been in a fight. He said nowt. I thought he wanted his key, but he just sat down there –

NORMAN and HER LADYSHIP try to get SIR to stand –

HER LADYSHIP

(to Norman)

Telephone the hospital.

SIR

Do not telephone the hospital. Get me to my room. To my room. I must don my robes.

HER LADYSHIP looks helplessly at NORMAN who is filled with the excitement of crisis –

HER LADYSHIP

(a whisper; to Norman)

What are we to do?

NORMAN

Charles, you help Her Ladyship. I won't be a tick –

He goes.  CHARLES helps HER LADYSHIP get SIR to his feet, and

INT. BOTTOMLEY'S OFFICE (BEHIND BOX OFFICE) – NIGHT

A small, shabby room. MADGE is seated one side of the desk listening to BOTTOMLEY who is on the telephone –

BOTTOMLEY

Well, I don't know exactly, Mr Mowbray. It'll mean giving back an awful lot of money. We're full tonight and Wednesday for 'Lear'. 'Richard III' is looking healthy, 'The Merchant of Venice' cosy, but 'As You Like It', cool. No, he doesn't have an understudy —

NORMAN enters excitedly. MADGE looks up.

NORMAN

Hold hard, Mr Bottomley, Richard is himself again!

# Appendix B

# *Taking Sides*

A direct comparison of the original stage play
and the adapted screenplay

## Direct Adaptation

*I think I did two drafts. But it wasn't difficult, it was never agonised. I think the modern trend which is so influenced by commercials, that everything has to be in short, sharp, brief images, is so pervasive and overwhelming now that I was very pleased that we were able to keep long dialogue scenes, longer than usual at any rate. I think that just made a different kind of film and a film to which people have to listen as well as look at.*

## Original Play Script (a)

(FURTWÄNGLER *hesitates, loses confidence, turns and marches off.* RODE *shrugs apologetically and also goes.*)

ARNOLD: (*Incensed, almost losing control*) Jesus God, that prick, that arrogant prick, who the fuck does he think he is? Who the fuck? Who the fuck?

(*He paces.* EMMI *watches him, alarmed.*)

DAVID: Major.

(ARNOLD *doesn't seem to hear.*)

Major.

(ARNOLD *stops pacing;* DAVID *again summons the courage.*)

ARNOLD: (*Suddenly calm*) Okay, I owe you one.

DAVID: When you question him, could I ask you to treat him with more respect?

ARNOLD: With more what? More what?

DAVID: Respect –

ARNOLD: That's what I thought you said. Respect? Are you kidding?

DAVID: He may just be the greatest conductor of this century and that merits respect.

ARNOLD: Yeah, yeah, great conductor, great artist, that's what everybody keeps telling me, and you know what I say to that?

DAVID: I can guess what you say to that. Major –

ARNOLD: You know what I say he is?

DAVID: Yes, I think I can guess that, too –

ARNOLD: David, I just don't understand a thing about you. You're a Jew. Are you a Jew?

DAVID: Yes, I'm a Jew, I'm also a human being –

ARNOLD: A human being, oh, good, I'm relieved, I thought you were going to say you were a music lover. This man, this great artist has made anti-Semitic remarks like you wouldn't believe/ I got letters –

DAVID: (*Interrupting*) Major, Major.

(ARNOLD *is still.*)

Show me a non-Jew who hasn't made anti-Semitic remarks and I'll show you the gates of paradise.

ARNOLD: What is it with you? Where are your feelings, David? Where's your hatred, your disgust? Where's your fucking

## Screenplay (a)

FURTWÄNGLER goes out.

> STEVE
>
> Jesus God, who the hell does he think he is? Who
> the hell does he think he is?

DAVID and EMMI gaze at him as he tries to regain control.


INT. WAITING ROOM – DAY

The door to the landing is open and RODE is there pretending to sweep. He looks in to see FURTWÄNGLER sitting, holding his handkerchief over his nose and mouth.

> RODE
>
> Would you perhaps like to have a glass of water,
> Herr Professor?

FURTWÄNGLER doesn't seem to hear. RODE hesitates, then continues to sweep.


INT. STEVE'S OFFICE – DAY

DAVID and EMMI look at him, puzzled.

She goes to the door, opens it, nods. RODE quickly disappears. FURTWÄNGLER looks at EMMI.

> FURTWÄNGLER
>
> What is this man doing here?

EMMI doesn't answer. All eyes on the door. FURTWÄNGLER enters.

> STEVE
>
> Dr Furtwängler! Come in, come in, sit down.

FURTWÄNGLER, deeply suspicious, goes for the uncomfortable chair.

> No, no, take this one, it's more comfortable.

He holds the other chair for FURTWÄNGLER, who sits.

> If it's too hot, open your tie.
>
> FURTWÄNGLER
>
> (interrupting)
>
> I wish to say something.
>
> STEVE
>
> Go ahead, be my guest.

## Original Play Script (b)

outrage, David? Think of your parents and then think of him conducting 'Happy Birthday, dear Adolf'. I mean, for Chrissake, whose side are you on?

(*Brief pause.*)

So what's this about the Swede in Nürnberg?

DAVID: It doesn't matter now. It's probably irrelevant.

(*Brief pause.*)

ARNOLD: Okay, Emmi. Go get him. Oh, and Emmi. Don't announce him. Just let him come in.

(*She goes. Uneasy silence while they wait.* EMMI *opens the door for* FURTWÄNGLER *who re-enters, angry and resentful.*)
Wilhelm! Nice to see you. How are you? Been keeping well? Not too hot for you? Come in, come in, sit down.
(FURTWÄNGLER, *deeply suspicious, goes for the witness chair.*)
No, no, take this one, it's more comfortable –
(ARNOLD *places the visitor's chair and holds it for* FURTWÄNGLER *who sits.*)
Isn't this heat something else? You want to loosen your tie, take off your jacket? Just relax, because the good news is that this is the last time you'll have to see me.
(FURTWÄNGLER *eyes him suspiciously.*)
But the bad news is that I still have to test the case against you, see if it'll stand up, and if it does, then I hand over to the civil authorities, to your own people, a guy called Alex Vogel, you ever heard of him?

FURTWÄNGLER: Yes, I've heard of him.

ARNOLD: And what have you heard?

FURTWÄNGLER: That he's a Moscow hack, a communist.

ARNOLD: That's the one. Not a nice man. We are not on first name terms. So, today, thank your lucky stars, you've only got me to deal with.
(*Silence;* ARNOLD *waits; nothing from* FURTWÄNGLER.)
Now, let's take it nice and easy. Okay?
(*Still nothing from* FURTWÄNGLER.)
I don't want to go over all the old stuff because I have one or two new things that have come up –

FURTWÄNGLER: (*Interrupting*) I wish to say something.

ARNOLD: Go ahead, be my guest.

FURTWÄNGLER: (*Takes out a piece of paper*) When I last saw you, I was unprepared, I did not know what to expect. In the past weeks, I have been thinking more carefully and making some notes.
(*Glances at notes; more to* DAVID.)

## Screenplay (b)

FURTWÄNGLER takes from his pocket a piece of paper with notes. He blows his nose. The room is warming up. It will become like an airless court room, a pressure-cooker.

FURTWÄNGLER

When I last saw you, I was unprepared. I did not know what to expect. In these past weeks, I have been thinking more carefully and making some notes.

(Glances at the notes.)

You have to understand who I am and what I am. I am a musician and I believe in music. I am an artist and I believe in art. Art in general, and music, in particular, has for me mystical powers which nurture man's spiritual needs. I must confess, however, to being extremely naive. I insisted for many years on the absolute separation of art and politics. My entire life was devoted to music because, and this is very important, because I thought that I could, through music, do something practical.

STEVE

And what was that?

FURTWÄNGLER

Maintain liberty, humanity and justice.

STEVE

Gee, that's a thing of beauty, honest to God, a real thing of beauty. I'm going to try to remember that. Liberty, humanity and justice. Beautiful. But you used the word 'naive'. Are you now saying you think you were wrong? That art and politics can't be separated?

FURTWÄNGLER

I believe art and politics should be separate, but that they weren't kept separate I learned to my cost.

STEVE

And when did you first learn that – when you sent the telegram? Was that the surrender signal, the waving of the white flag?

FURTWÄNGLER

What telegram?

STEVE

'Happy birthday, dear Adolf, love Wilhelm.' Or words to that effect. That sounds to me like you were dropping on your knees and saying, 'Okay, Adolf, you win. You're the number one man. Have a swell party.'

## Original Play Script (c)

You have to understand who I am and what I am. I am a musician and I believe in music. I am an artist and I believe in art. You could say that art is my religion. Art in general, and music, of course, in particular, has for me mystical powers which nurture man's spiritual needs. I must confess, however, to being extremely naive. I insisted for many years, until quite recently in fact, on the absolute separation of art and politics. I truly had no interest in politics, I hardly read newspapers, my entire life was devoted to music because, and this is very important, I believed that I could, through music, create something practical.

ARNOLD: And what was that?

FURTWÄNGLER: The maintenance of liberty, humanity and justice.

ARNOLD: Gee, Wilhelm, that's a thing of beauty, honest to God, a thing of beauty. I'm going to try to remember that. How's it go? Liberty, humanity and justice. Beautiful. But you used the word 'naive'. Are you now saying you think you were wrong? That art and politics can't be separated?

FURTWÄNGLER: I believe they must be kept separate, but that they weren't kept separate I learned to my cost.

ARNOLD: And when did you first learn that? When you sent the telegram? Was that the surrender signal, the waving of the white flag?

FURTWÄNGLER: What telegram?

ARNOLD: 'Happy Birthday, dear Adolf, love Wilhelm.' Or words to that effect. That sounds to me like you were dropping on your knees and saying, 'Okay, Adolf, you win. You're top dog in everything, so let's be pals. Have a swell party.' Is that when you decided you couldn't keep art and politics separate, when you sent the telegram?

FURTWÄNGLER: I have no idea what you're talking about.

ARNOLD: I'm talking about the birthday greetings to your old pal, Adolf.

FURTWÄNGLER: I never sent him birthday greetings or any other kind of greetings.

ARNOLD: Think carefully, Wilhelm –

FURTWÄNGLER: I don't have to think carefully. This is utterly ridiculous. I never sent him a telegram.

(DAVID, *who has been consulting the file* ARNOLD *gave him, raises a discreet finger.*)

ARNOLD: Yes, David?

DAVID: (*Apparently innocently*) Why not show Dr Furtwängler the evidence? It may refresh his memory.

## Screenplay (c)

FURTWÄNGLER

I have no idea what you're talking about.

STEVE

The birthday greetings you sent to your old pal, Adolf Hitler.

FURTWÄNGLER

I never sent him any birthday greetings or any other kind of greetings.

STEVE

Think carefully, Wilhelm – maybe not in your own name, but as Privy Councillor or Vice-President.

FURTWÄNGLER

I don't have to think carefully. This is utterly ridiculous.

DAVID and EMMI exchange the briefest of looks. DAVID raises his hand.

STEVE

Yes, David?

DAVID

Why not show Dr Furtwängler the evidence. It may refresh his memory?

FURTWÄNGLER

You won't find it because no such telegram exists.

STEVE

Well, I tried, you got to admit I tried. I thought I might just trap you there, Wilhelm, but David here was too quick for me. Smart move, David, smart move. No, I don't have the telegram, but I know it exists. And I want you to know, Wilhelm, we're going to keep looking for it because I believe you sent it.

FURTWÄNGLER

Then you are wrong.

STEVE

Art and politics, yeah, art and politics. Let's look at that. You and the Berlin Philharmonic toured the Third Reich, played in countries the Nazis had conquered. Are you saying that conducting in occupied territories from 1939 on wasn't a commercial for Adolf and all he stood for?

## Original Play Script (d)

(ARNOLD *shoots* DAVID *a sharp, furious look.*)

I can't seem to find it here, Emmi, perhaps you have the telegram in your files –

EMMI: No, I have never seen such a telegram –

DAVID: Major, if you tell me where the telegram is –

FURTWÄNGLER: You won't find it because no such telegram exists.

(*Ominous silence. Then,* ARNOLD *forces a boisterous laugh.*)

ARNOLD: Well, I tried, you got to admit, I tried. I thought I might just trap you there, Wilhelm, but David here was a little too quick for me. Smart move, David. Smart move. No, I don't have the telegram, but I know it exists. And I just want to tell you, Wilhelm, we're going to keep looking for it because I happen to believe you sent it.

FURTWÄNGLER: Then you are wrong.

(ARNOLD *is not pleased.*)

ARNOLD: Art and politics, yeah, art and politics. Are you saying that touring abroad, conducting the Berlin Philharmonic Orchestra in foreign lands from 1933 on wasn't a commercial for Adolf and all he stood for?

FURTWÄNGLER: We never, never officially represented the regime when we played abroad. We always played as a private ensemble. As I think I already told you, I was a freelance conductor –

ARNOLD: You know something? You should've written our policies for us because you got more exclusion clauses than Double Indemnity. Don't give me fine print again, I'm an expert when it comes to fine print. What d'you imagine people thought? The Berlin Philharmonic's taken over by Josef's Propaganda Ministry but Wilhelm's a freelance, so music and politics are now entirely separate? Is that what you believed ordinary people thought?

FURTWÄNGLER: I have no idea what ordinary people thought –

ARNOLD: No –

FURTWÄNGLER: – because I had only one intention, from 1933 onwards. Whatever I did, and this is also the real reason I did not leave my country, I had only one intention and that was to prove that art means more than politics.

ARNOLD: Did that include Herbert von Karajan?

FURTWÄNGLER: (*Flustered*) What – what – I don't know what you mean –

ARNOLD: Tell me about von der Müll.

FURTWÄNGLER: (*Taken off guard*) Von der Müll?

## Screenplay (d)

FURTWÄNGLER

We never, never officially represented the regime when we played abroad. We always performed as a private ensemble. As I think I already told you, I was a freelance conductor –

STEVE

You know something? You should've written our insurance policies for us because you got more exclusion clauses than Double Indemnity. What do you imagine people thought? The Berlin Philharmonic's taken over by Doctor Gŏbbels and his Propaganda Ministry but Wilhelm is a freelance, so art and politics are now entirely separate? Is that what you believed ordinary people thought?

FURTWÄNGLER

I have no idea what ordinary people thought –

STEVE

No –

FURTWÄNGLER

No, because I had only one intention. My only intention whatever I did was to show that music means more than politics.

STEVE

Tell me about von der Null.

FURTWÄNGLER
(taken off-guard)

Von der Null?

STEVE

Yes, von der Null –

FURTWÄNGLER

Von der Null –

STEVE

How long's this going to go on, Wilhelm? I say von der Null, you say von der Null, I say von der Null, you say von der Null, we could go on all day. You know who von der Null is, don't you? Edwin von der Null, music critic –

FURTWÄNGLER

Yes, I know who he is –

## Original Play Script (e)

ARNOLD: Yes, von der Null –

FURTWÄNGLER: Von der Null –

ARNOLD: How long's this going to go on, Wilhelm? I say von der Null, you say von der Null, I say von der Null, you say von der Null, we could go on all day. You know who von der Null is, don't you? Edwin von der Null, music critic –

FURTWÄNGLER: Yes, I know who he is –

ARNOLD: Isn't it true that because he gave you bad reviews and praised this young guy, von Karajan, called him a goddam miracle, said he was better than you, you had von der Null conscripted into the army and nobody's heard from him since?

FURTWÄNGLER: That's an outrageous lie!

ARNOLD: You sure you didn't call one of your close buddies and say, 'God in heaven, did you see what that guy von der Null wrote about me? I want him out the way.' And the same with that other critic, Steinhauer. He had the nerve to accuse me, the greatest conductor on earth, of not playing enough modern music. Send him to Stalingrad. Isn't that what you did? You don't like criticism, do you? You certainly didn't like them saying there was another conductor who was better than you –

(FURTWÄNGLER *rises angrily*.)

FURTWÄNGLER: *(Exploding; pacing)* Please stop playing these games with me. You seem to take pleasure in teasing and baiting and hectoring me. Have some regard for my intelligence. We are dealing here with matters concerning my entire existence, my career, my life. Why you should introduce the name of – of another conductor is beyond my understanding.

ARNOLD: I'll tell you why. You remember we talked about you playing for Adolf's birthday? And you told me that Josef got to your doctors first, that you were tricked, outflanked?

FURTWÄNGLER: Yes, and that's what happened –

ARNOLD: I have a different story to tell. I don't believe you were tricked. Not in the way you describe. I believe something else happened. I've looked at the Hinkel Archive, made a few enquiries, I've seen records of phone calls, and putting it all together, this is what I think happened. I think Josef said, 'Wilhelm, if you won't conduct for Adolf's birthday, we'll get the Miracle Kid, the guy that critic von der Null thinks is the greatest conductor in the world, the guy you call K. He's not just willing to conduct for Adolf, he's offered to sing 'Happy Birthday' as a solo.'

## Screenplay (e)

STEVE

Isn't it true that because he gave you bad reviews and praised this young guy, von Karajan, called him a goddamn miracle, said he was a better conductor than you, then you had von der Nüll conscripted into the army and no one's heard from him since?

FURTWÄNGLER

That's an outrageous lie!

STEVE

You sure you didn't call one of your close buddies and say, 'God in heaven, did you see what that guy von der Nüll wrote about me? The greatest conductor on earth. I want him out the way. He had the nerve to accuse me. I am not playing enough modern music. Send him to Stalingrad.' Isn't that what you did? You don't like criticism, do you, Wilhelm? You surely didn't like them saying there was another conductor who was better than you – Are you saying the name von der Nüll was never mentioned in your talks with Gőbbels?

FURTWÄNGLER
(uncomfortable)

Well. Once he said he'd read what this man wrote about me.

STEVE

And what did he say?

FURTWÄNGLER

He said, 'Don't mind him. His job is to criticise, your job is to conduct.'

STEVE

And what happened to Von der Nüll?

FURTWÄNGLER

I have no idea.

STEVE

You've really no idea? I'll tell you what happened. He died in Stalingrad.

FURTWÄNGLER

I'm sorry.

**Original Play Script (f)**

(*Silence*)

Come on now, Wilhelm, admit it. K worried you, didn't he? He always worried you. In 1942, he's thirty-four years old, you're already fifty-six. He's the Young Pretender, the comet, yeah, the miracle. He's tilting at your throne. Your position's in danger. And Josef and Hermann keep saying to you, 'If you don't do it, little K will.' Never mind art and politics and symbols and airy-fairy bullshit about liberty, humanity and justice. You were tricked all right, because they got you where you were most vulnerable. Youth was knocking on the door, and I don't care how great you are, how noble, how fantastic with your little white stick, because it's the oldest story in the book. The ageing Romeo jealous of the young buck, the Heavyweight Champion of the World frightened of the Young Contender. And the great maestro terrified of the new boy on the podium. Wasn't that how they got you, Wilhelm, time after time? Admit it. The real reason you didn't leave the country when you knew you should have was that you were frightened. You were frightened that, once you were out of the way, you'd be supplanted by the Miracle Kid, the Party's boy twice over, flashy, talented little K.

FURTWÄNGLER: This is absolute nonsense –

DAVID: (*Overlapping*) Major, wait a moment, where is this leading? This isn't establishing –

ARNOLD: (*Turning on him, cutting him off*) Not now, David, I haven't finished with him. As a matter of fact, I've hardly begun. I'm only just developing my theme. Isn't that what you call it in classical music, developing a theme? Okay, Wilhelm, so they played on your insecurity. That's human, understandable, nothing to be ashamed of. After all, it's pretty well agreed that little K's got what it takes, and nearly everyone in the Party loved him. Jesus, he's a member twice over, he's one of theirs. But, take note of what I said. I said nearly everyone in the Party because there's one exception. One guy doesn't like little K as much as he likes you, there's one guy who thinks little K is not fit to brush your coat tails, and that guy just happens to be – yeah, the number one man, your old pal, Adolf. He thinks you're the greatest and when he says, I want Wilhelm for my birthday party, boy, they better go get Wilhelm. So, Josef calls and threatens you with little K. And you said to hell with the Ninth in Vienna, I'll give it to Adolf as a birthday present in Berlin. That's the trick they played, they got you by the balls and

## Screenplay (f)

STEVE

Now, that young conductor, what's his name?
(playing with FURTWÄNGLER)
That miracle kid, you know who I mean. Von
Karajan! But you called him something else.
C'mon. What did you call von Karajan?

Silence.

Say it.

Silence.

I'll say it, then. 'Little K.' Is that right? You couldn't
even bear to say his name –

FURTWÄNGLER rises angrily and starts to pace.

FURTWÄNGLER

Please stop playing these games with me. Why
you should bring up the name of another
conductor is beyond my understanding.

STEVE

I'll tell you why. You remember we talked about
you playing for Hitler's birthday? And you told me
that Gðbbels got to your doctors first, that you
were tricked?

FURTWÄNGLER

Yes, that's what happened –

He sits heavily, wipes his brow. He is sweating now.

STEVE

I have a different story to tell. I don't think you
were tricked. Not in the way you describe. I believe
something else happened. I've seen the Hinkel
Archive, I've seen records of phone calls, and
putting it all together, this is what I think
happened. I think Gðbbels said, 'Wilhelm, if you
won't conduct for Adolf's birthday, we'll get the
Miracle Kid, the guy that critic, von der Null, thinks
is the greatest conductor in the world. He's not
just willing to conduct for Adolf, he's offered to
sing 'Happy Birthday' as a solo.'

Silence.

Come on, admit it. K worried you, didn't he? He
always worried you. In 1942, he's thirty-four years
old, you're already fifty-six. And Gðbbels and
Gðring keep saying to you, 'If you don't do it, little
K will.' Never mind art and politics and symbols
and airy-fairy bullshit about liberty, humanity and
justice because I don't care how
great you are. It's the oldest story in the book.
(a wry look at David)
The ageing Romeo jealous of the young buck. The
real reason you didn't leave the country when you

**Original Play Script (g)**

they squeezed. Hard.

DAVID: Major, I simply can't see how this line of questioning –

ARNOLD: (*Turning on him*) David, what is this? What are you all of a sudden. Counsel for the Defense? What you want me to say? Objection overruled? Objection sustained? My line of questioning is establishing motive. Counsellor, plain, ordinary human motive. Why did he stay? Why did he play for them? Why was he the flag carrier for the regime? Why was he their servant? Not art or culture or music and its mystical power, but good old-fashioned insecurity, fear and jealousy. And that was only part of his reason for staying –

FURTWÄNGLER: (*Suddenly interrupting, blurting out*) Of course there was a conspiracy against me, a campaign –

(*He stops. Silence. DAVID is about to say something but ARNOLD points a finger at him to stop him speaking.*)

They controlled the press. Every word that was written, every word that was published. When I resigned from the Philharmonic, when I refused to take part in a film they made about the orchestra, oh, countless things of that kind, refusing to co-operate in one way or another, they were determined to keep me in my place. You mentioned the critic, Edwin von der Null. His praise of – of – that man may have been genuine, I have no idea. But his remarks were encouraged and guided, and then seized on. They wanted another 'star', as they called it, to take my place. They had their own concert agency under a man called Rudolf Vedder, a human being beneath contempt. He was determined to foist K on the public. I'm not going to recount the difficulties I had with that man but if I tell you that his chief ally in this was Ludolf von Alvensleben, personal adjutant to Heinrich Himmler, and when that particular individual did not get his way he threatened only one sanction: death. They controlled every aspect of our lives. They manipulated, bullied and imposed their monstrous will. When they finally understood that I would do everything in my power to prevent art from being directed and supervised, they determined to undermine me. They regarded any action of dissent, however small, as a criticism of the state, tantamount to high treason.

ARNOLD: And you didn't have von der Null conscripted because of that review he wrote?

## Screenplay (g)

knew you should have was that you were frightened that, once you were out of the way, you'd be supplanted by the Miracle Kid, the Party's boy twice over, flashy, talented little K.

FURTWÄNGLER

This is absolute nonsense –

STEVE

Well, I'm just beginning to develop my theme. Isn't that what you call it in classical music, developing your theme? Okay, so they played on your insecurity. That's human, understandable. But, there is one guy who doesn't like little K as much as he likes you – yeah, the number one man your old pal, Adolf. He thinks you're the greatest, and when he says, I want Wilhelm for my birthday, boy, they better go out get Wilhelm. So, Josef calls and threatens you with little K. And you said to hell with the Ninth in Vienna, I'll give it to Adolf as a birthday present in Berlin. That's the trick they played, they got you by the balls and they squeezed. Hard. Why did you stay? Why did you play for them? Why were you the flag-carrier for their regime? Jealousy –

FURTWÄNGLER
(interrupting)

Of course there was a conspiracy against me, a campaign – even abroad.

Brief silence; all eyes on him.

STEVE

You see, Wilhelm, I'm talking about ordinary, everyday reasons. Which is why I want to discuss your private life. How many illegitimate children do you have?

DAVID

Major, I don't see how this line of questioning could –

STEVE

David, what are you, Counsel for the Defence now?

(to FURTWÄNGLER)

Did you hear the question?

FURTWÄNGLER
(barely audible)

I have illegitimate children.

STEVE

What?

## Original Play Script (h)

FURTWÄNGLER: (*Blazing*) I've told you, it's absolute nonsense. How could I have managed such a thing? He was in their power, not mine. It's a total lie. And I have never in my life tried or even wanted to silence my critics, never. I believe serious criticism to be an essential part of cultural life.

(*Turning to* DAVID; *becoming excited.*)

And the reason you have detected a certain distaste I have for K is not because I was jealous or insecure but because I have serious criticism to make of him. In my opinion, he is an intellectual conductor. He does not experience the piece afresh each time. He conducts only what he knows and wants, in other words the nuances, which is why the nuances are all exaggerated. The slow tempi are too slow, the fast ones too fast. The whole effect is somewhat hysterical – (*He falls silent.*)

ARNOLD: Wilhelm, I'm trying to understand you, I really am, believe me. You see, when you talk about cultural life, I'm lost. Because I am, to put it at its best, totally uncultured. So when I look at you, I don't see the great artist, the greatest conductor alive, I see a man, an ordinary guy, like a million other ordinary guys. And I ask myself, what keeps him in a situation which he says he did everything in his power to resist, except get the hell out of it? What keeps him here, I ask myself? Not being a cultured guy, I don't buy all this stuff about music creating liberty, justice and humanity. I look for ordinary reasons, reasons I can understand, reasons my buddies can understand. So, if I said to my buddies, imagine you love your wife – well, maybe I'm stretching reality here – no, stay with me – I say to them, imagine you love your wife and they tell you you're being sent overseas. But they exempt some young guy who it's possible could take your wife's fancy. What would you do? Like a man they'd say, Steve, we'd do everything we could to stay put. See, Wilhelm, I'm talking about ordinary, everyday motives. Which is why I want to discuss your private life.

DAVID: Oh, come along. Major, this can't be right –

ARNOLD: (*Quietly*) Objection overruled. Counsellor. I'm establishing motive.

(*To* FURTWÄNGLER.)

How many illegitimate children do you have?

DAVID: Major, this is outrageous, what has this to do with anything at all?

ARNOLD: You'll see. Wilhelm, did you hear the question?

## Screenplay (h)

> FURTWÄNGLER
>
> I said I have illegitimate children. I don't know how many –
>
> STEVE
>
> You like the women, don't you, Wilhelm?

No response.

> Isn't it true that before every concert you got a woman in your dressing room and gave her the old conductor's baton, isn't that true –?
>
> DAVID
> (indicating EMMI)
>
> Major, this is deeply offensive and repugnant –
>
> STEVE
>
> You bet –
>
> DAVID
>
> – and totally irrelevant.
>
> STEVE
> (continuing to FURTWÄNGLER)
>
> Not so, Counsellor. That secretary of yours, she wasn't just your secretary, she procured women for you, didn't she? As many and as often as you wanted –
>
> FURTWÄNGLER
>
> Stop this, please, stop this now –
>
> STEVE
>
> No, I'm not going to stop it. Hitler himself offered you a beautiful house and a personal bomb shelter –
>
> FURTWÄNGLER
>
> I absolutely refused the house and the bomb shelter.
>
> STEVE
>
> But you see what I'm getting at? You get a gorgeous house, you're highly paid. What are you gonna do, stay or leave? One voice comes back at me: stay!
>
> DAVID
>
> Major, that's not a good argument. If Dr Furtwängler did indeed enjoy all these – these privileges, he enjoyed them because of who he is and what he is. That's true of any leading artist in any country in the world.

## Original Play Script (i)

FURTWÄNGLER: (*Barely audible*) I have illegitimate children –

ARNOLD: What?

FURTWÄNGLER: I said I have illegitimate children. I don t know how many.

ARNOLD: No, I bet you don't. Four, five, six?

> (*No response.*)

> You like the ladies, don't you, Wilhelm?

> (*No response.*)

> Isn't it true that before every concert you got a woman in your dressing room and gave her the old conductor's baton, isn't that true?

DAVID: Major, this is deeply offensive and repugnant –

ARNOLD: You bet –

DAVID: – and totally irrelevant.

ARNOLD: Not so, Counsellor. The women threw themselves at you, didn't they, Wilhelm? That secretary of yours, Berta Geissmar, who's now working for *Sir* Thomas Beecham, she wasn't only your secretary, she was your procuress, wasn't she? She procured women for you, didn't she, as many and as often as you wanted –

FURTWÄNGLER: Stop this, please, stop this –

ARNOLD: No, I'm not going to stop it, because if I said to my buddies, you're living in a whorehouse where you get the whores free, you going to leave? See, Wilhelm, I think you stayed because you were in paradise here. Adolf himself offered you a beautiful house and a special bomb shelter –

FURTWÄNGLER: I absolutely refused the house and the bomb shelter –

ARNOLD: But you see what I'm getting at? You didn't leave because you felt an affinity with your people, or because you wanted to preserve the traditions of which, I think you said, you were a guardian, or because you believed that art and music and culture were above politics. See, if I said to my buddies, you're top dog in your profession, favourite of the number one man in the country, you get all the women you lust after, you're highly paid, you get a gorgeous house and a personal, private bomb shelter if you want it, what you going to do, leave or stay? One voice comes back at me: *stay*!

DAVID: That's not a good argument. Major. If Dr Furtwängler did indeed enjoy all these – these privileges, he enjoyed them because of who he is and what he is –

ARNOLD: Now we're back to the great artist –

## Screenplay (i)

STEVE

But it still doesn't make them saints. They still have to get up and piss in the middle of the night, don't they? They can still be vindictive and envious and mean just like you and me. Well, just like me. Can't they?

No response. To FURTWÄNGLER:

Okay, Wilhelm, go home now. Go home and think about these past twelve years.

FURTWÄNGLER

I don't understand what you mean.

STEVE

No, that's your problem, Wilhelm. You understand nothing. We'll call you. Go!

FURTWÄNGLER leaves.

DAVID

Major.

STEVE goes to his desk and, as DAVID rises uncertainly:

STEVE

What?

DAVID

Your manner –

STEVE

My manner? Why don't you go downstairs, get a cup of coffee and calm down? What's the matter, Emmi? What's going on with you? What's wrong?

EMMI

I'm sorry but I have to leave. I'll find other work. You'll have to get someone else, that's all.

STEVE

What is this, Emmi?

EMMI

I can't do this. It's not right.

## Original Play Script (j)

DAVID: Right. His position would have guaranteed him anything he wanted wherever he chose to live and work. That's true of any leading artist in any country in the world. They're rare specimens, Major, and that sets them apart –

ARNOLD: Okay, but it doesn't make them saints. They still have to get up and piss in the middle of the night, don't they? And they can be envious and vindictive and mean just like you and me. Well, just like me. Can't they?

(*No response.*)

See, Wilhelm, everybody says what a great benefactor you were to the Jews, but what about that Italian conductor –

FURTWÄNGLER: I don't understand what you're talking about, but if you're now referring to Arturo Toscanini, he is not a Jew, of course, but he is greatly loved by you Americans –

ARNOLD: No, I was thinking of another Italian –

FURTWÄNGLER: (*Not hearing* ARNOLD; *again addressing* DAVID, *rather over-excitedly*) – and to my taste, he is too disciplined, his tempi are too strict. If he were a greater artist, if he had deeper insights, a livelier imagination, greater warmth and devotion to the work, he would not have become so disciplined. This is why his success is disastrous. Inspiration and understanding in art are more important than discipline and autocratic behaviour –

ARNOLD: (*Interrupting*) But otherwise you like the guy. (*He chuckles.*) I'm beginning to get the picture. You're not crazy about any of your rivals, are you? I guess it was the same with this other Italian, the one I was thinking of, de Sabata –

FURTWÄNGLER: De Sabata?

ARNOLD: Vittorio de Sabata. I have a letter here, written in 1939, which states: (*Reading.*) 'What should I do when Dr Furtwängler said to me that it was a piece of impudence for that Jew de Sabata to conduct Brahms. Since the day when de Sabata performed *Tristan* in Bayreuth, Furtwängler speaks only of 'Jew Sabata'.'

FURTWÄNGLER: Who wrote that letter?

ARNOLD: I'm not at liberty to tell you that. But it's a genuine letter David, you have a copy in the file, it's a genuine letter.

FURTWÄNGLER: There's only one thing I can say. I have never said anything that goes counter to my convictions and simply cannot have said anything that did. Of course there were instances when I was speaking to specific Party members. I had to use their language, one had to say Heil Hitler, for example, but quite apart from these instances, I did not make any compromises by saying things other than I believed. And I have always been

### Screenplay (j)

> STEVE
> 
> What's not right?
> 
> EMMI
> 
> I have been questioned by the Gestapo just like that. Just like you questioned him.
> 
> STEVE
> 
> Emmi, stop! I want to show you something. Let me show you something and then if you want to leave, you can leave, please, please. His friends, they did this. And he gave them birthday concerts.
> 
> EMMI
> 
> But he had no idea, a lot of people had no idea. I only realised what was really going on when I got arrested.
> 
> STEVE
> 
> If he had no idea, why did the Jews need saving? This is my question, Emmi, to all Germans: Why did the Jews need saving in this country? Why, if people had no idea?
> 
> EMMI
> 
> I would like to go now, please.

But STEVE turns on the projector and the Bergen-Belsen film flickers into life.

INT. US OFFICERS' CLUB – NIGHT

Band playing. Couples dancing. DAVID and STEVE at the bar, each with a drink in front of them, lost in their own thoughts. Then:

STEVE signs to the barkeeper to fill their glasses but DAVID puts a hand over his glass. Then:

> DAVID
> 
> Can I ask you a favour, Major?
> 
> STEVE
> 
> Yeah –
> 
> DAVID
> 
> When you question him again, could you treat him with more respect?
> 
> STEVE
> 
> With more what? More what?

## Original Play Script (k)

frank in my attitude towards the Jews –

ARNOLD: I believe that. But just answer the question, don't give me explanations –

FURTWÄNGLER: But I have to explain. An attitude must exist in one to make such an outburst possible. And this is what I deny. I know that even in the greatest anger I couldn't have said such a thing. De Sabata was my friend, one of my few close friends. I invited him to conduct my orchestra. We discussed his programme, we discussed everything –

ARNOLD: Okay, so, here's another letter, July 4, 1933, written by you to the Minister of Culture, Bernhard Rust. It's about this modern composer, a Jew, Arnold Schönberg, who was about to be suspended. There's a copy of this one, too, in your file, David. This is what you wrote, Wilhelm. (*Reading.*) 'Arnold Schönberg is considered by the Jewish International as the most significant musician of the present. It must be recommended that he not be made a martyr.' What do you say to that?

FURTWÄNGLER: I say exactly what I said before. You have to use their language –

DAVID: And you didn't finish the letter. Major. (*Reading.*) 'And if he is suspended now – and I would not indeed consider this right – the question of indemnity should be treated with generosity.' He's pleading for the man, not condemning him –

ARNOLD: Then what about these things he said? 'Jewish pen-pushers should be removed from the Jewish press', 'Jewish musicians lack a genuine affinity with our music', and 'Jewish musicians are good businessmen with few scruples, lacking roots.' You deny you said these things?

FURTWÄNGLER: But it depends on the circumstances, to whom one was speaking, these attitudes simply don't exist in me, I used their language, of course I did, everyone did.

DAVID: Major, you have to balance those things – if indeed he said them – against his assistance to his Jewish colleagues. Listen to this. Major, from the transcript of the proceedings at Nürnberg–

ARNOLD: (*Enjoying this*) Okay, Counsellor, here we go, it's your day in court. But be careful. There's nothing I enjoy more than a guy putting his own neck in the noose.

DAVID: A Swedish businessman, Birger Dahlerus, testified in cross-examination that he had several meetings with Hermann Göring. 'I first saw Göring', Dahlerus testified, 'embroiled in a stormy interview with Wilhelm Furtwängler,

## Screenplay (k)

> DAVID
>
> Major, he may just be the greatest conductor of this century and that merits respect.
>
> STEVE
> (flaring, hissing)
>
> David, I don't understand a thing about you. You're a Jew. Are you a Jew?
>
> DAVID
>
> Yes, I'm a Jew. But I like to think first I'm a human being.
>
> STEVE
>
> A human being, oh, good, I'm relieved, I thought you were going to say you were a music lover. This man, this great artist, has made anti-Semitic remarks like you wouldn't believe. I got letters.
>
> DAVID
>
> Major, show me someone who hasn't made an anti-Semitic remark and I'll show you the gates of paradise.
>
> STEVE
> (over-reacting and overlapping)
>
> What is it with you, David? Where are your feelings? Where's your hatred, your disgust? Where's your fucking outrage, David?

He starts to go, then comes back to them.

> Think of your parents, David, and then think of him conducting 'Happy Birthday, dear Adolf'. I mean, for Chrissake, whose side are you on? Grow up! Just grow the fuck up!

The customers stare at him as he stalks out. The band plays.

CUT TO

INT. STRAUBE APARTMENT – EVENING
DAVID and EMMI, sitting.

> DAVID
>
> I want you to come back to the office. May I come in? If you are there you can influence what happens. What good can you do by leaving. If you go, you are giving up and how can you help Furtwängler or me? Don't think about leaving. Stay.

**Original Play Script (I)**

the famous conductor of the Berlin Philharmonic, who was vainly seeking permission to keep his Jewish concert master.'

FURTWÄNGLER: Yes, I remember well, I was pleading for Szymon Goldberg, a wonderful musician and a wonderful man, the youngest concert master the orchestra ever had. Thank God he escaped, and I pray that he is safe now –

ARNOLD: Why is it, Wilhelm, that everything you say touches me so deeply?

DAVID: (*Flaring*) Emmi, read some of those letters to Mrs Sachs. Pick any two, read them –

(EMMI, *uncertain, looks at* ARNOLD, *who, indifferent, gestures for her to do as she's been told. She selects a letter at random.*)

EMMI: (*Reading*) From Heinrich Wollheim. 'I am half Jewish and a former member of the Berlin State Opera Orchestra. I lived near the Swiss border and so was easily able to help friends and colleagues to escape. When the Gestapo finally caught up with me, I was sent to the concentration camp at Dachau. My wife contacted Dr Furtwängler who interceded on my behalf with Himmler and Göbbels and arranged for me to be his copyist. I believe Himmler said to him, "Well, Privy Councillor, we know you like to help criminals." I remained in Dachau but received better treatment than most of the other inmates. If Dr Furtwängler had not stood by me so steadfastly during my imprisonment, I certainly would not have come out of it with my life. I certainly would have been consigned to a "commando" unit, which would not have done my health any good.'

DAVID: Go on, Emmi, read another.

EMMI: I can't decipher this signature, but – (*Reading.*) 'Please remember that helping Jews was a capital offence. People were being publicly hanged on mere suspicion of such activities but Dr Furtwängler helped anyone who asked him. I personally testify to having seen literally hundreds of people lined up outside his dressing room after concerts to ask for his help. He never turned anyone away. He gave me money because I was unable to feed myself or my family and then he helped me to escape to Sweden. He helped countless people in similar ways.'

DAVID: Doesn't sound like much of an anti-Semite to me, Major. These were acts of enormous courage –

ARNOLD: (*Smiling*) You don't listen to what I say, David. How many times have I got to tell you I was in insurance? You think I can't smell a phoney policy when it's shoved under my nose? Sure, he helped Jews but that was just insurance, his cover, because the whole time he was maestro of all he

# Screenplay (I)

INT. STEVE'S OFFICE – DAY
Hot. Windows closed. FURTWÄNGLER seated. DAVID and EMMI present. STEVE looks up from his notes.

> STEVE
>
> Everybody says what a great benefactor you were to the Jews. But –
>
> (Holds up a sheaf of papers.)
>
> – I have things here you said and wrote. Listen to this: 'The Jew composer Schönberg is admired by the Jewish International.' And what about this: 'Jewish musicians lack a genuine affinity with our music.' 'Jewish musicians are good businessmen with few scruples, lacking roots.' You deny you said these things?

> FURTWÄNGLER
>
> Those attitudes do not exist in me.

> STEVE
>
> I believe that. But just answer the question, don't give me explanations –

> FURTWÄNGLER
>
> Speaking to Party members I used their language, of course I did, everyone did –

> DAVID
> (with some irony)
>
> Major, sorry to interrupt, but maybe we have to – maybe we have to balance those things against his assistance to Jewish colleagues.

STEVE tenses.

> This is a transcript of the proceedings at Nuremberg. A Swedish businessman, Birger Dahlerus, testified in cross-examination that he had several meetings with Hermann Göring. 'I first saw Göring,' Dahlerus testified, 'embroiled in a stormy interview with Wilhelm Furtwängler, the famous conductor of the Berlin Philharmonic, who was vainly seeking permission to keep his Jewish concert master.'

Holds up his package of letters and dumps them on EMMI'S desk.

> Emmi, pick one of these, any one, read it out loud.

EMMI is uncertain. STEVE shrugs indifferently.
She picks an envelope and takes out the letter.

> EMMI
> (reading)
>
> 'Please remember that Dr Furtwängler risked his life to help anyone who asked him. I personally testify to having seen literally hundreds of people

## Original Play Script (m)

surveyed. (*Turning on* FURTWÄNGLER.) See, Wilhelm, I think you're cunning, devious, dealing off the bottom of the pack. You were their boy, their creature. That's the case against you, old pal. You were like an advertising slogan for them. This is what we produce, the greatest conductor in the world. And you went along with it. You may not have been a member of the Party because the truth is, Wilhelm, you didn't need to be.

(*Suddenly, to* EMMI.)

Emmi, put that record on –

(EMMI *puts on the record of the Adagio from Bruckner's Seventh Symphony.*)

ARNOLD: You know what that is?

FURTWÄNGLER: Of course I know what that is –

ARNOLD: Okay, so what is it?

FURTWÄNGLER: Bruckner's Seventh. The Adagio.

ARNOLD: Who's conducting?

FURTWÄNGLER: I am.

ARNOLD: You know the last time it was played on these air waves?

FURTWÄNGLER: How should I know such a thing?

ARNOLD: Well then, I'll tell you. The last time this music was played on these air waves was after they announced that your pal Adolf had blown his brains out. Listen to it.

(*They listen.*)

Did they pick little K's recording? Did they pick some other band leader? No, they picked you and why? Because you and nobody else represented them so beautifully. When the Devil died they wanted his band leader to play the funeral march. You were *everything* to them.

(*The music plays.*)

FURTWÄNGLER: (*Near to breakdown but struggling for control*) I have always tried – I have tried to analyse myself closely. You are right. Major, I am no better than anybody else. But I must always say what my instincts are. In staying here, I believed – I thought – I walked a tightrope between exile and the gallows. You seem to be blaming me for not having allowed myself to be hanged.

(DAVID *takes the record off.*)

I tried to defend the intellectual life of my people against an evil ideology. I did not directly oppose the Party because, I told myself, this was not my job. I would have benefitted no one by active resistance. But I never hid my opinions.

## Screenplay (m)

lined up outside his dressing room after concerts to ask for his help. He never turned anyone away. After he heard me play – I am a violinist – he gave me money because I was unable to feed myself or my family and then he helped me to escape to Sweden. He helped countless people in similar ways.'

DAVID

And this, only one of these letters, Major. I have lots of them.

STEVE

(smiling)

How many times have I got to tell you I was in insurance? You think I can't smell a phoney policy when it's shoved under my nose? Sure, he helped Jews, but that was just insurance, his cover, because all the while he was maestro of all he surveyed,

(turning on Furtwängler)

See, Wilhelm, I think you're their boy, their creature. You were like an advertising slogan for them: this is what we produce, the greatest conductor in the world. And you went along with it. The truth of the matter is, Wilhelm, you didn't need to be a member of the Party. I made a mistake when I asked you for your Party number. I should've asked you for your non-Party number. Just like some other well-known artists.

(suddenly, to Emmi)

Emmi, put that record on –

EMMI puts on the record of the Adagio from Bruckner's Seventh Symphony. After a moment:

Do you know what that is?

FURTWÄNGLER

Of course I know what that is –

STEVE

Okay, so what is it?

FURTWÄNGLER

Bruckner's Seventh. The Adagio.

STEVE

Who's conducting?

FURTWÄNGLER

I am.

## Original Play Script (n)

As an artist I was determined that music, at least, would remain untouched, untainted. If I had taken any active part in politics I couldn't have remained here. Please understand me correctly: an artist cannot be entirely apolitical. He must have some political convictions because he is, after all, a human being. As a citizen, it is an artist's duty to express these convictions. But as a musician, I am more than a citizen. I am a citizen of this country in that eternal sense to which the genius of great music testifies. I know that a single performance of a great masterpiece was a stronger and more vital negation of the spirit of Buchenwald and Auschwitz than words. Human beings are free wherever Wagner and Beethoven are played. Music transported them to regions where the torturers and murderers could do them no harm.

(ARNOLD *reacts as if a volcano is about to erupt inside him. A great, uncontrollable surge of anger wells up in him, causing him to pace alarmingly. He grabs the baton from his desk, stands trembling before* FURTWÄNGLER, *and snaps it in half. He pushes his face close to* FURTWÄNGLER *who recoils, terrified.* DAVID *half stands, ready to intervene physically. During this* EMMI *puts her fingers in her ears.*)

ARNOLD: (*His rage erupting with quiet, terrifying menace*) Have you ever smelled burning flesh? I smelt it four miles away. Four miles away, I smelt it. I smell it now, I smell it at night because I can't sleep any more with the stench of it in my nostrils. I'll smell it for the rest of my life. Have you seen the crematoria and the gas ovens? Have you seen the mounds of rotting corpses being shovelled into gigantic craters by the men and women who murdered them? I saw these things with my own eyes. And I've seen it every night since, night after night, and I wake screaming seeing it. I know I won't sleep undisturbed ever again. You talk to me about culture and art and music? You putting that in the scales, Wilhelm? You setting culture and art and music against the millions put to death by your pals? The pals you could call to save a couple of Jews when thousands, millions of them, were being annihilated? Is that what you're putting on the scales? Yes, I blame you for not getting hanged, I blame you for your cowardice. You strutted and swaggered, king-pin in a shithouse. You talk to me of walking a tightrope between exile and the gallows, and I say to you, lies –

FURTWÄNGLER: (*Breaking down*) I love my country, I believe in art, what was I to do?

# Screenplay (n)

                        STEVE
You know the last time it was played on these air
waves?
                        FURTWÄNGLER
How can I know such a thing –?
                        STEVE
I'll tell you, then. The last time this music was played
on these air waves was after they announced that
your pal Hitler had shot himself. Listen to it.

They listen.

Did they pick little K's recording? Did they pick
some other conductor? No, they picked you, and
why? Because you represented them so
beautifully. When the Devil died, they wanted his
bandleader to conduct the funeral march. You
were everything to them.

The music plays.

                        FURTWÄNGLER
                    (near to breakdown but
                     struggling for control)
I have always tried to analyse myself carefully and
closely. In staying here, I believed I walked a
tightrope between exile and the gallows. You
seem to be blaming me for not having allowed
myself to be hanged.

DAVID takes the record off.

I didn't directly oppose the Party because I told
myself, that was not my job. If I had taken any
active part in politics I could not have remained
here. But as a musician, I am more than a citizen. I
am a citizen of this country in that eternal sense to
which the genius of great music testifies. I know
that a single performance of a great masterpiece
was a stronger and more vital negation of the
spirit of Buchenwald and Auschwitz than words.

An uncontrollable surge of anger wells up in STEVE, causing him to pace alarmingly. He
grabs the baton from his desk, stands trembling before FURTWÄNGLER, and snaps it in
half. He pushes his face close to FURTWÄNGLER, who recoils, terrified. DAVID
half-stands, ready to intervene physically. During this EMMI puts her fingers in her ears.

                        STEVE
                    (quiet, terrifying)
Have you ever smelled burning flesh? I smelt it
four miles away. Four miles away, I smelt it. Have
you ever seen the gas chambers,

**Original Play Script (o)**

ARNOLD: Act courageously. Just think of real courage, think of what men like Emmi's father did, risking their lives, not their careers –

(*He sees* EMMI *has her fingers in her ears, yells at her.*)

For Chrissake, Emmi, take your goddam fingers out of your ears –

(*She does so, tense, strained.*)

I'm talking about your father, I'm talking about real courage, I'm talking about him risking his fucking life –

(*She screams, the chilling sound of one who can take no more.* RODE *comes to the door and looks in. All stare at her, shocked.*)

EMMI: My father only joined the plot when he realised we could not win the war.

(*She cries quietly.*)

ARNOLD: Get out, Helmuth, you revolt me.

(RODE *goes.*)

FURTWÄNGLER: (*Desperate*) Major, what kind of a world do you want? What kind of world are you going to make? Don't you honestly understand the power of art to communicate beauty and pain and triumph? Even if you can't admit it, don't you believe that music especially transcends language and national barriers and speaks directly to the human spirit? If you honestly believe the only reality is the material world, you will have nothing left but feculence more foul-smelling than that which pervades your nights – (*Near to breakdown.*) This isn't just, this isn't fair. How was I to know what they were capable of? No one knew. No one knew they were gangsters, atrocious, depraved. (*He breaks down, buries his face in his hands.*) Oh God, I don't want to stay in this country. Yes, yes, it would have been better if I'd left in 1934, it would have been better if I'd left – (*Suddenly retching.*) I'm going to be sick –

(*He stands, a hand to his mouth.* EMMI *goes to him.*)

ARNOLD: (*Yelling*) Helmuth!

(RODE *comes to the door.*)

Show your friend to the toilet and then tell him to get the hell out of here.

(RODE *and* EMMI *help* FURTWÄNGLER.)

Emmi, Helmuth can manage –

(EMMI *ignores him and exits with* RODE *and* FURTWÄNGLER. ARNOLD *stares into space as if bereft.* DAVID *seems drained.*)

DAVID: We'll never understand. Only tyrannies understand the power of art. I wonder how I would have behaved in his position? I'm not certain I'd have 'acted courageously'. And what about you, Major? I have a feeling we might

## Screenplay (o)

the crematoria? Have you seen the mounds of rotting corpses? You talk to me about culture, art and music? You putting that in the scales, Wilhelm? You setting culture, art and music against the millions put to death by your pals? They had orchestras in the camps. They played Beethoven, Wagner. The hangmen were playing chamber music at home with their families. I don't understand the Germans' relationship with music. What do you need music for? Your pals you could call to save a few Jews when millions of them were being annihilated? Yes, I blame you for not getting hanged, I blame you for your cowardice. You strutted and swaggered, you fucking piece of shit, king-pin in a shithouse. You talk to me about walking a tightrope   between exile and the gallows, and I say to you, lies –

FURTWÄNGLER
(breaking down)
I love my country, I believe in music, what was I to do?

STEVE
Look around you. See the country you served. Look at people who had real courage, who took risks, who risked their lives. Like Emmi's father.

He sees EMMI has her fingers in her ears, yells at her.

Emmi, take your fingers out of your ears –

She does so.

I'm talking about your father.

She screams. Stillness. All eyes on her.

EMMI
My father only joined the plot when he realised that we could not win the war.

She cries quietly.

FURTWÄNGLER
(desperate)
What kind of a world do you want, Major? What kind of world are you going to make? Do you honestly believe that the only reality is the material world, so you will be left nothing, nothing but feculence ... more foul-smelling than that which pervades your nights –

(near to breakdown)
How was I to understand, how was I to know what they were capable of? No one knew. No one knew.

He breaks down, buries his face in his hands, weeps.

## Original Play Script (p)

just have followed orders.

ARNOLD: I'm only a claims assessor. Who cares about me? But everyone kept telling me your man was something special. And you know what? He's not special at all.

DAVID: You know what I say he is, Major?

ARNOLD: No, what do you say he is, David?

DAVID: I say he's like a fallen priest –

ARNOLD: And what would you know about priests, Lieutenant Vile?

DAVID: (*A smile*) Only what I read in books.

ARNOLD: Yeah, and what did you read?

DAVID: That they can be inadequate human beings. They can lie, they can fornicate, they can drink, they can deceive. But they can still put God into the mouths of the faithful. If you believe in that sort of thing.

ARNOLD: You know what I say *you* are, David?

DAVID: I know what you say I am, Major.

ARNOLD: Yeah, but you're worse. You're a liberal piece of shit. You don't know right from wrong.

> (EMMI *returns, slightly dazed, holding a visitor's card.* ARNOLD *goes to his desk, lifts the telephone and dials.*)

ARNOLD: (*Into the telephone*) Give me Alex Vogel. Major Arnold.

> (DAVID *turns to the records near Emmi's desk, starts to sort through until he finds what he's looking for.*)

EMMI: (*To* DAVID; *quietly*) He thanked me and gave me his visiting card. He asked me to have dinner with him.

> (DAVID *half smiles, then removes the Bruckner and puts another record on the turntable.*)

ARNOLD: (*Into the telephone*) Vogel? Major Arnold. I don't know if we've got a case that'll stand up, but we can sure as hell give him a hard time –

> (*At full volume the sound of the subdued opening of Beethoven's Ninth Symphony.*)

ARNOLD: (*To* DAVID) Hey, turn that off, can't you see I'm on the phone? (*Into the telephone.*) Yeah, yeah, but it makes no – never mind, we got a tame journalist who'll write what we'll tell him. (*Listens.*) Yeah, a guy called Delbert Clark. *New York Times* –

> (*The great chords sound.*)

## Screenplay (p)

> I don't want to stay in this country. Yes, I should have
> left in 1934, it would have been better if I'd left –

He is suddenly overtaken by nausea and faintness, stands, a hand to his mouth.
EMMI goes to him.

STEVE

> Get him out of here –

EMMI helps FURTWÄNGLER out. STEVE strides to the window, opens it, puts his
head out into the fresh air.

INT. WAITING ROOM – DAY
EMMI helps FURTWÄNGLER to a chair. She watches him solicitously. He breathes
deeply.

FURTWÄNGLER

> Thank you, Fraulein. You have been most kind.

> (He rises.)

He smiles at her. She is embarrassed.

INT. STEVE'S OFFICE – DAY
STEVE is trying to get a number on the telephone. DAVID is packing up his papers.
DAVID turns to the records, starts to sort through until he finds what he's looking
for. He removes the Bruckner and puts another record on the turntable.

STEVE<br>(into the telephone)

> Major Arnold. Get me General Wallace. General?
> Major Arnold, about Furtwängler. I don't know if
> we've got a case that'll stand up, but sure as hell
> we can give him a hard time –

At full volume the sound of the subdued opening of Beethoven's Ninth Symphony.

STEVE<br>(to David)

> Hey, turn that down, would you? Can't you see
> I'm on the phone?

> (into the telephone)

> Never mind, we got a journalist who'll do
> whatever we tell him.

But DAVID ignores him, sits, implacable, listening.

INT. STEVE'S BUILDING – DAY
FURTWÄNGLER walks slowly down the stairs, a broken man struggling to regain
his composure. EMMI watches him.

**Original Play Script (q)**

ARNOLD: Jesus Christ, what the hell are you doing? Turn that goddam thing down –

(*But* DAVID *ignores him, sits, implacable, listening.* RODE *opens the door a crack, stands listening with a sickly smile.*

FURTWÄNGLER *stumbles into the bomb rubble, as if a broken man struggling to regain his composure.*)

ARNOLD: Turn if off!

(ARNOLD *rises carrying the telephone, goes to the door of the back room but the flex won't reach. He stands in the doorway, talking and listening, his back to the others who sit, expressionless, listening.*

*In the rubble,* FURTWÄNGLER *hears the music but he cannot identify its source. His left hand trembles but it is only his way of sensing the tempo.*

*After a while the music and the lights begin to fade to Blackout.*)

## Screenplay (q)

INT. STEVE'S OFFICE – DAY
The music at full blast. DAVID, at an open window, keeps his back to STEVE, still on the telephone.

STEVE

> Turn it off!

EXT. STEVE'S BUILDING – DAY

FURTWÄNGLER, on the stairs, stops, hearing the music echoing through the building.
FURTWÄNGLER'S left hand begins to tremble, but it is only his way of sensing the tempo.
FURTWÄNGLER slowly continues down the stairs.

STEVE'S VOICE

> We handed Wilhelm Furtwängler over to the civil authorities and he was charged with serving the Nazi regime, with uttering anti-Semitic slurs, performing at an official Nazi Party function and with being a Prussian Privy Councillor. Dr Furtwängler was acquitted. I didn't nail him. But I sure winged him. And I know I did the right thing. Furtwängler resumed his career but he was never allowed to conduct in the United States. He died in 1954. Little K succeeded him as head of the Berlin Philharmonic.

INT. CONCERT HALL (ARCHIVE)
FURTWÄNGLER conducting. GÖBBELS and other high-ranking Nazis in the audience. When the music finishes, FURTWÄNGLER turns and bows. GÖBBELS rises and shakes hands with him. FURTWÄNGLER takes his handkerchief and wipes his hands. The film replays this gesture several times – FURTWÄNGLER wiping his hands.

Fade out.

# Appendix C

# *Oliver Twist*

A direct comparison of the original novel
and the adapted screenplay

## Invention

*I thought it important for Fagin to make this contact with Oliver. In the novel, his advice is simply described in the narrative so I had to make up Fagin's 'the greatest sin is ingratitude' speech. I turned what was described in the third person into dialogue. That's my line, 'They hang you for anything, these days.' And in a later scene, everybody thinks it's a Dickens' line, 'They're as close as Cain and Able,' but that was my line too.*

## Novel (a)

Chapter XIV

COMPRISING FURTHER PARTICULARS OF OLIVER'S STAY AT
Mr BROWNLOW'S, WITH THE REMARKABLE PREDICTION WHICH ONE
Mr GRIMWIG UTTERED CONCERNING HIM,
WHEN HE WENT OUT ON AN ERRAND

As fate would have it, Mrs Bedwin chanced to bring in, at this moment, a small parcel of books, which Mr Brownlow had that morning purchased of the identical book-stall keeper, who has already figured in this history; having laid them on the table, she prepared to leave the room.

'Stop the boy, Mrs Bedwin!' said Mr Brownlow; 'there is something to go back.'

'He has gone, sir,' replied Mrs Bedwin.

'Call after him,' said Mr Brownlow; 'it's particular. He is a poor man, and they are not paid for. There are some books to be taken back, too.'

The street-door was opened. Oliver ran one way; and the girl ran another; and Mrs Bedwin stood on the step and screamed for the boy; but there was no boy in sight. Oliver and the girl returned, in a breathless state, to report that there were no tidings of him.

'Dear me, I am very sorry for that,' exclaimed Mr Brownlow; 'I particularly wished those books to be returned to-night.'

'Send Oliver with them,' said Mr Grimwig, with an ironical smile; 'he will be sure to deliver them safely, you know.'

'Yes; do let me take them, if you please, sir,' said Oliver. 'I'll run all the way, sir.'

The old gentleman was just going to say that Oliver should not go out on any account; when a most malicious cough from Mr Grimwig determined him that he should; and that, by his prompt discharge of the commission, he should prove to him the injustice of his suspicions: on this head at least: at once.

## Screenplay (a)

EXT. PARK, NEAR BROWNLOW'S HOUSE – DAY

On a park bench behind some bushes but with a view of the house, sit NANCY and BILL with BULL'S EYE at their feet. They're eating, taking bits of food from NANCY'S basket placed between them.

AN ERRAND BOY, carrying a small parcel, runs along, goes through the gates of Mr Brownlow's house, up the steps and rings the bell.

After a moment, the door is opened and he hands over the parcel, turns and goes.


INT. BROWNLOW'S STUDY – DAY

MR BROWNLOW and MR GRIMWIG are playing chess. A knock on the door and OLIVER enters, holding the small package the errand boy delivered.

MR GRIMWIG

Hello, what's that?

MR BROWNLOW

This is young Oliver Twist.

OLIVER bows.

OLIVER

Sir, the bookseller's boy brought a package, do you want me to – ?

MR BROWNLOW

Oh, stop him, Oliver, there are some books to go back –

OLIVER goes.

MR GRIMWIG

Is that the boy who had the fever?

MR BROWNLOW

That's the boy.


EXT. BROWNLOW'S HOUSE, PENTONVILLE – DAY

OLIVER charges to the corner of the road towards the park.

## Novel (b)

'You *shall* go, my dear,' said the old gentleman. 'The books are on a chair by my table. Fetch them down.'

Oliver, delighted to be of use, brought down the books under his arm in a great bustle; and waited, cap in hand, to hear what message he was to take.

'You are to say,' said Mr Brownlow, glancing steadily at Grimwig; 'you are to say that you have brought those books back; and that you have come to pay the four pound ten I owe him. This is a five-pound note, so you will have to bring me back, ten shillings change.'

'I won't be ten minutes, sir,' said Oliver, eagerly. Having buttoned up the bank-note in his jacket pocket, and placed the books carefully under his arm, he made a respectful bow, and left the room. Mrs Bedwin followed him to the street-door, giving him many directions about the nearest way, and the name of the bookseller, and the name of the street: all of which Oliver said he clearly understood. Having superadded many injunctions to be sure and not take cold, the old lady at length permitted him to depart.

'Bless his sweet face!' said the old lady, looking after him. 'I can't bear, somehow, to let him go out of my sight.'

At this moment, Oliver looked gaily round, and nodded before he turned the corner. The old lady smilingly returned his salutation, and, closing the door, went back, to her own room.

'Let me see; he'll be back in twenty minutes, at the longest,' said Mr Brownlow, pulling out his watch, and placing it on the table. 'It will be dark by that time.'

'Oh! you really expect him to come back, do you?' inquired Mr Grimwig.

'Don't you?' asked Mr Brownlow, smiling.

The spirit of contradiction was strong in Mr Grimwig's breast, at the moment; and it was rendered stronger by his friend's confident smile.

## Screenplay (b)

EXT. PARK, NEAR BROWNLOW'S HOUSE – DAY

Concealed behind bushes, BILL and NANCY watching the house.

OLIVER comes towards the park railings, looking for the errand boy.

BILL and NANCY are watching him.

>                          NANCY
>                       (a whisper)
>            That's him –

BILL slowly rises, moves towards OLIVER and is about to make a grab for him when OLIVER turns and goes back towards the house.


INT. BROWNLOW'S STUDY – DAY

MR BROWNLOW and MR GRIMWIG at their game as OLIVER enters.

>                         OLIVER
>            No sign of him, sir.
>                     MR BROWNLOW
>            Dear me, I'm very sorry for that. I particularly
>            wished these books to be returned tonight.

He takes up three books from the table beside him.

A mischievous look in MR GRIMWIG'S eye.

>                     MR GRIMWIG
>            Send Oliver with them. He'll be sure to deliver
>            them safely.
>                         OLIVER
>            Yes, do let me take them, if you please, sir. I'll run
>            all the way.

MR BROWNLOW hesitates. MR GRIMWIG, amused, watches him.

MR BROWNLOW becomes defiant for MR GRIMWIG'S benefit.

>                     MR BROWNLOW
>            You shall go, my dear.

He gives OLIVER the books.

## Novel (c)

'No,' he said, smiting the table with his fist, 'I do not. The boy has a new suit of clothes on his back, a set of valuable books under his arm, and a five-pound note in his pocket. He'll join his old friends the thieves, and laugh at you. If ever that boy returns to this house, sir, I'll eat my head.'

With these words he drew his chair closer to the table; and there the two friends sat, in silent expectation, with the watch between them.

It is worthy of remark, as illustrating the importance we attach to our own judgments, and the pride with which we put forth our most rash and hasty conclusions, that, although Mr Grimwig was not by any means a bad-hearted man, and though he would have been unfeignedly sorry to see his respected friend duped and deceived, he really did most earnestly and strongly hope at that moment, that Oliver Twist might not come back.

It grew so dark, that the figures on the dial-plate were scarcely discernible; but there the two old gentlemen continued to sit, in silence, with the watch between them.

## Screenplay (c)

MR BROWNLOW (cont'd)

Ask Mrs Bedwin to tell you the way. (ostentatiously)
And give the bookseller this, the money I owe him –

He hands over a five pound note to OLIVER.

OLIVER

(on his way)

I won't be long, sir.

He runs out of the room.

MR BROWNLOW

How long do you think it'll take him?

He takes out his pocket watch and places it on the table.

MR GRIMWIG

Oh, you really expect him to come back, do you?

BROWNLOW looks out of the window.


EXT. BROWNLOW'S HOUSE – POV FROM WINDOW – DAY

MRS BEDWIN is telling OLIVER the directions to the bookshop. He is impatient to be on his way.

MR BROWNLOW'S VOICE

You don't.

MR GRIMWIG'S VOICE

With a five pound note in his pocket? No, I do not.

OLIVER runs off.


INT. BROWNLOW'S STUDY – DAY

MR BROWNLOW looking out of the window, MR GRIMWIG watching him.

MR GRIMWIG

If ever that boy returns to this house, I'll eat my
own head, sir. And yours.

MR BROWNLOW is made anxious and looks at his watch.

## Novel (d)

Chapter XVIII

HOW OLIVER PASSED HIS TIME, IN THE IMPROVING
SOCIETY OF HIS REPUTABLE FRIENDS

About noon next day, when the Dodger and Master Bates had gone out to pursue their customary avocations, Mr Fagin took the opportunity of reading Oliver a long lecture on the crying sin of ingratitude; of which he clearly demonstrated he had been guilty, to no ordinary extent, in wilfully absenting himself from the society of his anxious friends; and, still more, in endeavouring to escape from them after so much trouble and expense had been incurred in his recovery. Mr Fagin laid great stress on the fact of his having taken Oliver in, and cherished him, when, without his timely aid, he might have perished with hunger; and he related the dismal and affecting history of a young lad whom, in his philanthropy, he had succoured under parallel circumstances, but who, proving unworthy of his confidence and evincing a desire to communicate with the police, had unfortunately come to be hanged at the Old Bailey one morning. Mr Fagin did not seek to conceal his share in the catastrophe, but lamented with tears in his eyes that the wrong-headed and treacherous behaviour of the young person in question, had rendered it necessary that he should become the victim of certain evidence for the crown: which, if it were not precisely true, was indispensably necessary for the safety of him (Mr Fagin) and a few select friends. Mr Fagin concluded by drawing a rather disagreeable picture of the discomforts of hanging; and, with great friendliness and politeness of manner, expressed his anxious hopes that he might never be obliged to submit Oliver Twist to that unpleasant operation.

Little Oliver's blood ran cold, as he listened to the Jew's words, and imperfectly comprehended the dark threats conveyed in them. That it was possible even for justice itself to confound the innocent with the guilty when they were in accidental companionship, he knew already; and that deeply-laid plans for the destruction of inconveniently knowing or over-communicative persons, had been really devised and carried out by the Jew on more occasions than one, he thought by no means unlikely, when he recollected the general nature of the altercations between that gentleman and Mr Sikes: which seemed to bear reference to some foregone conspiracy of the kind. As he glanced timidly up, and met the Jew's searching look, he felt that his pale face and trembling limbs were neither unnoticed

## Screenplay (d)

INT. SMALL ROOM, FAGIN'S PLACE – DAY

OLIVER, wearing the tattered shirt, is gazing out of the small window. In the room, a table, a couple of rough bunk beds, clutter.

On the other side of the door, the key is turned. The door opens and FAGIN stands there, all smiles, bearing a plate of food and a mug which he puts on the table.

                              FAGIN
           A little something for your luncheon, my dear.

OLIVER sits and eats perfunctorily. FAGIN watches, then sits opposite him.

                        FAGIN (cont'd)
           Shall we have a little chat, Oliver, shall us?
                          (no response)
           I expect you'd welcome the sound of a human
           voice again, eh, my dear?
                          (no response)
           You know what I consider the greatest sin in the
           world, my dear? Ingratitude. And that's what you
           are guilty of. Ingratitude. We took you in,
           cherished you, and if we 'adn't you might 'ave
           died of hunger. And how do you repay us? You
           run away, cry out for the police, and cause us
           great anxiety. And expense.
                        (OLIVER eats, not looking
                        at him)
           There was a lad once, just like you. I was a father
           to 'im. He run away, like you, and he indeed went
           to the police. And can you guess how he ended
           up? They hanged him. At the Old Bailey.
                        (OLIVER now looks at him,
                        a little fearful)
           Certain evidence was made available, not all of it
           precisely true, but all of it necessary to provide for
           my own safety and that of my friends. Yes, poor
           boy. Hanged. Terrible thing, hangin', Oliver.
           Dawn. The gallows. The rope. The noose.
                        (he snaps his fingers;
OLIVER gazes at FAGIN)

## Novel (e)

nor unrelished by that wary old gentleman.

The Jew, smiling hideously, patted Oliver on the head, and said, that if he kept himself quiet, and applied himself to business, he saw they would be very good friends yet. Then, taking his hat, and covering himself with an old patched great-coat, he went out, and locked the room-door behind him.

## Screenplay (e)

FAGIN (cont'd)

And you don't always have to be guilty, you see, Oliver. They hang you for anything these days. That's 'cos they're so very fond of hanging.

He smiles, rises, pats OLIVER'S head.

FAGIN (cont'd)

But if you do as you're told, we'll be very good friends yet.

(opens the door)

You must feel free to walk about, now, Oliver. Yes, feel free.

He goes, leaving OLIVER alone and frightened.

## Novel (f)

Chapter L

THE PURSUIT AND ESCAPE

Crackit went to the window, and shaking all over, drew in his head. There was no need to tell them who it was; his pale face was enough. The dog too was on the alert in an instant, and ran whining to the door.

'We must let him in,' he said, taking up the candle.

'Isn't there any help for it?' asked the other man in a hoarse voice.

'None. He MUST come in.'

'Don't leave us in the dark,' said Kags, taking down a candle from the chimney-piece, and lighting it, with such a trembling hand that the knocking was twice repeated before he had finished.

Crackit went down to the door, and returned followed by a man with the lower part of his face buried in a handkerchief, and another tied over his head under his hat. He drew them slowly off. Blanched face, sunken eyes, hollow cheeks, beard of three days' growth, wasted flesh, short thick breath; it was the very ghost of Sikes.

He laid his hand upon a chair which stood in the middle of the room, but shuddering as he was about to drop into it, and seeming to glance over his shoulder, dragged it back close to the wall – as close as it would go – and ground it against it – and sat down.

Not a word had been exchanged. He looked from one to another in silence. If an eye were furtively raised and met his, it was instantly averted. When his hollow voice broke silence, they all three started. They seemed never to have heard its tones before.

'How came that dog here?' he asked.

'Alone. Three hours ago.'

'To-night's paper says that Fagin's took. Is it true, or a lie?'

'True.'

## Screenplay (f)

EXT. TOBY'S HOUSE, JACOB'S ISLAND – DAY

TOBY, carrying a newspaper, hurries along. He sees a couple of PRETTY GIRLS, salutes them and beams.

Then, making sure he's unobserved, he reaches his house, takes a key from his pocket, tries to open the door but it's locked. He knocks loudly.

> TOBY
> Plummy and slam.
> > (a grunt from the other side)
> Dammit, it's me, Barney.

The sound of a wooden bar being raised.


INT. DOWNSTAIRS, TOBY'S HOUSE, JACOB'S ISLAND – DAY

BARNEY admits TOBY.

> BARNEY
> Good borning, Bister Crackit –

TOBY passes him, trots down the passage and up the stairs. BARNEY replaces a heavy wooden bar across the door while.


INT. ATTIC AREA, TOBY'S HOUSE – DAY

OLIVER, FAGIN, CHARLEY and THREE BOYS are sitting around, trying to keep warm. They are all on edge, tense.

THE DODGER, alone in a corner, sits frozen, hugging his knees, staring forlornly into space.

TOBY breezes in, followed by BARNEY.

> TOBY
> Hello, Fagey, hello, lads.

FAGIN stands.

> FAGIN
> What's news, Toby, what's news?
> TOBY
> (full of good cheer)
> I have it here, Fagey, all in the *Daily Chronicle*,
> you're in it, Bill's in it, Oliver's in it –

## Novel (g)

They were silent again.

'Damn you all!' said Sikes, passing his hand across his forehead. 'Have you nothing to say to me?'

There was an uneasy movement among them, but nobody spoke.

## Screenplay (g)

CHARLEY

In the *Chronicle*? You're famous, Fagin –

FAGIN flicks him hard across the head.

FAGIN

(to TOBY)

Read it.

TOBY sits on his old couch, finds the page in the newspaper.

TOBY

(reading with delight)

'More information has reached your correspondent concerning the foul and bestial murder that took place in Spitalfields and which has shocked and appalled the citizens of London. It is believed that the victim, a young woman, now identified only as Nancy, was brutally beaten to death by one William Sykes, a well-known, dangerous villain. The motive is as yet unclear but your correspondent has learned that the murdered woman had informed on her associate and on an infamous fence, Fagin, who is now wanted for the abduction of a young boy, Oliver Twist. Neither Fagin nor Sykes are presently in custody but the police are engaged in searching for them throughout the city and beyond. Sykes, according to the police, is usually accompanied by a fierce shaggy dog.'

(he looks up, beaming)

'Now, how about that, eh?'

Deadly silence.

Then FAGIN begins to moan, rocking to and fro.

# Ronald Harwood's
# **Bibliography**

## SCREENPLAYS

*The Diving Bell and the Butterfly* (2007)
*Love in the Time of Cholera* (2007)
*Oliver Twist* (2005)
*Being Julia* (2004)
*The Statement* (2003)
*The Pianist* (2002)
*Taking Sides* (2001)
*Cry, The Beloved Country* (1995)
*The Browning Version* (1994)
*Cin cin* (1991) (US title: *A Fine Romance*)
*Mandela* (1987) TV
*The Deliberate Death of a Polish Priest* (1986) TV
*The Doctor and the Devils* (1985)
*The Dresser* (1983)
*Evita Peron* (1981) TV
*Operation Daybreak* (1975) (US reissue title: *The Price of Freedom*)
*One Day in the Life of Ivan Denisovich* (1970)
*Eyewitness* (1970) (US title: *Sudden Terror*)
*A High Wind in Jamaica* (1965) (Co-written with others)

## TELEVISION

*Private Potter* (1962) (Co-written with Casper Wrede)
*The Barber of Stamford Hill* (1962)
*Countdown to War*
*Breakthrough at Reykjavik*
*Roald Dahl's Tales of the Unexpected* (12 Episodes)
*The Guests*
*Convalescence*
*The Lads*

## PLAYS

*Country Matters* (1969)
*The Ordeal of Gilbert Pinfold* (from Evelyn Waugh) (1977)
*A Family* (1978)
*The Dresser* (1980)
*After the Lions* (1982)
*Tramway Road* (1984)
*The Deliberate Death of a Polish Priest* (1985)
*Interpreters* (1985)
*J. J. Farr* (1987)
*Ivanov* (from Chekhov) (1989)
*Another Time* (1989)
*Reflected Glory* (1992)
*Poison Pen* (1993)
*Taking Sides* (1995)
*The Handyman* (1996)
*Goodbye Kiss* (1997)
*Equally Divided* (1999)
*Quartet* (1999)
*Mahler's Conversion* (2001)
*See You Next Tuesday* (from Francis Veber) (2003)

## NOVELS

*All the Same Shadows* (1961) (US title: *George Washington September, Sir!*)
*The Guilt Merchants* (1963)
*The Girl in Melanie Klein* (1969)
*Articles of Faith* (1973)
*The Genoa Ferry* (1976)
*One. Interior. Day. Adventures in the Film Trade* (1978)
*César and Augusta* (1978)
*Home* (1993)

## BIOGRAPHY

*Sir Donald Wolfit C.B.E. – his life and work in the unfashionable theatre* (1971)

## MISCELLANEOUS

*All the World's a Stage* (13 part BBC series – written and presented) (1984)
*The Ages of Gielgud: an actor at eighty* (1984)
*Dear Alec: Guinness at 75* (1989)

# Acknowledgements

Emma Hayley at Metromedia Books

Mark Goodall at the University of Bradford

Antony Harwood at Antony Harwood Ltd. (Ronald Harwood's Literary Agent – Books)

Judy Daish at Judy Daish Associates (Ronald Harwood's Literary Agent – Stage Plays)

Jeffrey Berg and Ben Smith at ICM (Ronald Harwood's Literary Agent – Screenplays)

Stephen Page at Faber and Faber Books

Judith Scott at Amber Lane Press

Timothy Burrill

Rainer Mockert

Yves Pasquier

Brooks Riley

Roy Gower at Cineworld

Adrian Sear at Soundtrack Studios, London

Maggie Fergusson and Julia Abel Smith at the Royal Society of Literature

Chris Jones at Living Spirit

Nic Wistreich at Netribution

Lucy Scherer at The Artworks

Sara Mitchell at FinkFilm

Carole Latimer

Bill Godber and all the team at Turnaround Books Limited

John Button and Mike Kirby at Bookcraft Limited
    and
Sir Tom Stoppard

# Useful Addresses

**The Writers' Guild of Great Britain**
15 Britannia Street, London WC1X 9JN
Tel: (020) 7833 0777   Fax: (020) 7833 4777
e-mail: admin@writersguild.org.uk
www.writersguild.org.uk/

**The Writers Guild of America, West**
7000 West Third Street, Los Angeles, CA 90048
Tel: (323) 951-4000   Fax: (323) 782-4800
www.wga.org/

**The Writers Guild of America, East**
555 West 57th Street, Suite 1230, New York, NY 10019
Tel: (212) 767-7800   Fax: (212) 582-1909
www.wgaeast.org/

**The Royal Society of Literature** (c/o Maggie Fergusson)
Strand, London WC2R 1LA
Tel: (020) 7845 4676
e-mail: info@rslit.org

**Final Draft**
www.finaldraft.com/

**The Screenwriter's Store**
802 Capital Tower, 91 Waterloo Road, London SE1 8RT
Tel: +44 (0)845 094 6061   Fax: +44 (0)845 094 3846
e-mail: info@TheSWS.com
www.thescreenwritersstore.net/

**New Producers Alliance**
www.npa.org.uk/

**Amber Lane Press Ltd.** (publisher of *The Dresser* – Stage Play)
Church Street, Charlbury, Oxford OX7 3PR
Tel: +44 (0)1608 810024
e-mail: info@amberlanepress.co.uk
www.amberlanepress.co.uk/

**Faber and Faber Ltd** (publisher of *Taking Sides* – Stage Play and Screenplay and *The Pianist* –Screenplay)
3 Queen Square, London WC1N 3AU
Tel: (020) 7465 0045   Fax: (020) 7465 0034
www.faber.co.uk/

**Penguin Classics** (publisher of *Aspects of the Novel* by E.M. Forster and Oliver Stallybrass)
Penguin Press Marketing, 80 Strand, London WC2R 0RL.
e-mail: penguinclassics@penguin.co.uk
www.penguinclassics.co.uk/

**DVDs of *The Dresser*, *Taking Sides*, *The Pianist* and *Oliver Twist* can be purchased from:**
www.amazon.co.uk
www.borders.co.uk
www.fopp.co.uk
www.hmv.co.uk
www.play.com
www.sendit.com
www.virginmegastores.co.uk
www.whsmith.co.uk

# Index